FEMINISM AND CRIMINOLOGY

for my sisters,
Frances Butterfield and Maxine Cape

FEMINISM
AND
CRIMINOLOGY

Ngaire Naffine

Temple University Press
Philadelphia

Temple University Press, Philadelphia 19122

Copyright © Ngaire Naffine 1996

Published 1996

First published in Great Britain by Polity Press
in association with Blackwell Publishers Ltd.

ISBN 1–56639–507–0 (cloth)
ISBN 1–56639–508–9 (paper)

A CIP catalogue record for this book is available from the Library of Congress.

Typeset in $10^1/_2$ on 12pt Palatino
by Graphicraft Typesetters Ltd., Hong Kong
Printed in Great Britain by TJ Press Ltd, Padstow, Cornwall

This book is printed on acid-free paper.

Contents

—

Acknowledgements

—

I have incurred debts during the writing of this book. My creditors include Peter Goodrich and my friends at Birkbeck College, University of London, who provided good company and intellectual stimulation during my stay at Birkbeck in 1994, when I was writing the book. In particular, I thank my friend Matthew Weait for his thoughtful comments on the introduction. Alison Young, Peter Rush and Richard Collier all provided valuable advice on various versions of the text. Kathy Laster was tireless in her reading of drafts and gave me many detailed and creative comments. Margaret Davies helped as usual, with her clarity and logic. Wai-Quen Chan provided splendid literary assistance. Eric Richards encouraged me all the way, as he always does. I thank Dartmouth Publishing Company for permission to use parts of the introduction to my edited volume, *Gender, Crime and Feminism*. I am also grateful to the *Melbourne University Law Review* for permission to use in Chapter 4 parts of 'Windows on the Legal Mind: Evocations of Rape in Legal Writings' and to the *Modern Law Review* for permission to use in Chapter 4 parts of 'Possession: Erotic Love in the Law of Rape'. Finally I thank Laura Grenfell, Peter Romaniuk and Emma Shaw for their assistance at the final stages.

Introduction

—

It is tempting to begin a book on feminism and criminology with a statement about the neglect of both women and feminism by the discipline. Certainly, a quick scan of the criminology section of any American or British library will turn up many standard student texts in which women and feminism play but a minor role. This exercise will confirm that criminology is still a discipline dominated by men, and that its subject matter is also male-dominated. Criminology, it seems, is mainly about academic men studying criminal men and, at best, it would appear that women represent only a specialism, not the standard fare.

Similarly, feminism as a substantial body of social, political and philosophical thought (indeed the subject of this book), does not feature prominently in conventional criminological writing. When feminism is formally allocated a place in a textbook, it is often to be found within the women's chapter, which is the chapter invariably on women as offenders and as the victims of crime. This is necessarily a constricted use of feminism. Alternatively, feminism is slotted into a chapter entitled 'Gender and Crime', which should deal at least with the implications of masculinity and femininity for the criminality of both sexes, but is often simply another, and misleading, way of designating the now compulsory chapter on women. Thus, feminism is either reduced to, or conflated with, the study of women and crime, implicitly a minor branch of the discipline of criminology. Feminism in its more ambitious and influential mode is not employed in the study of men, which is the central business of criminology. The potential of feminist analyses in criminology at large is, therefore, widely misunderstood and underestimated. The message to the reader is that feminism is about women, while criminology is about men.

A clear illustration of this interesting logic is to be found in the *Oxford Handbook of Criminology*, a weighty volume (1259 pages) intended to present students with a comprehensive account of the current state of the discipline.[1] In the introductory chapter, the editors tell us their thoughts on the organization of the Oxford book.[2] They were aware from the start that the 'dimensions of gender and race' needed careful 'handling', and felt obliged to choose between two approaches. 'Should we insist that gender and race be thoroughly addressed in every chapter? Or should we assign them chapters for specialist coverage?'[3] The editors choose the second option. As a consequence, 'Gender and Crime'[4] is the twenty-first chapter of the book, and there is precious little on gender before this: the preceding thousand pages of the book are remarkably free of any explicit analysis of the implications of gender for the understanding of crime. Then when we get to chapter twenty-one, we discover that this is in fact a chapter about women and crime, not about gender.[5] There is no equivalent chapter on men.

By setting up the intellectual task as they do, the editors of the Oxford book are tacitly asking us to think of criminology as a discipline that is somehow free from the effects of gender when it is in its proper form. Gender is treated as a 'specialist' topic (rather than integral to the analysis of crime), and then we discover that this specialism of gender actually refers to the study of women. In a few easy steps, the editors have established a standard case and an exception or speciality. The standard case is the study of men as non-gendered subjects and the speciality is the study of women as gendered beings. As Jonathon Culler has pointed out, this procedure of comparing a deviant with a standard case is generally assumed to be the appropriate one in any 'serious analysis', whatever the discipline. It is not peculiar to criminology. The method is 'to describe . . . the simple, normal standard case of [whatever the topic], illustrating its "essential" nature, and proceeding from there to discuss other cases that can be defined as complications, derivations, and deteriorations'.[6]

The editors of the Oxford book perform precisely this manoeuvre. 'Gender', which predictably turns out to mean 'women', is treated as a specialism that can come late in the book. The main part of the volume, which is essentially about men (but not as sexed men and therefore not explicitly so), then appears as the natural heartland of criminology, its proper terrain. In criminology, as in other disciplines, it is men, not women, who supply the essential (and therefore unexamined) 'standard case'. Men, themselves, are not compared with others to see what makes them specific and different.

American criminology texts employ a similar logic. In 1991, Stephen E. Brown, Finn-Aage Esbensen and Gilbert Geis published one of the many standard introductory textbooks of criminology tailored for the American student market. C*riminology: Explaining Crime and its Context* is some 730 pages long and divided into three parts: 'foundations of criminology', which introduces the subjects of criminology, criminal justice and crime statistics; 'theories of crime', which traverses the usual range of theories of crime; and 'types of crime'. Women appear in the third section on criminal types. The reason that female crime enters the book this late in the day, well after the general chapters on theoretical criminology, is 'because theories of crime and delinquency until now largely have failed to incorporate gender variables'.[7] And yet, the authors concede, 'Perhaps the most salient characteristic of crime in American society . . . is the extraordinary variation in the rates at which males and females commit most major crimes'.[8]

Although they decry implicitly the practice of setting women to the side (or towards the end) in criminology, because, as they say, sex difference is the most significant feature of crime, Brown and colleagues do just this. Without further apology, they effectively concede on page 495 that the preceding pages of their volume, which purported to be a general treatment of crime and criminology, have really been about men but (somehow) as ungendered subjects. Women appear on page 499 as a special 'type' of offender, whose specificity is their gender, a characteristic which by implication men lack. The topic of feminism is also contained within this women's chapter, neatly labelled and condensed into three pages. Placed thus within the women's chapter, feminism is thoughtfully quarantined from the men's pages (which constitute virtually the entire book). The message is clear: feminism has nothing of interest to say about criminology proper.

A second, more recent example of American textbook writing is the second 1994 edition of C*riminology and Justice* by Lydia Voigt, William E. Thornton, Leo Barrile and Jerome M. Seaman. This book comes in five parts: the usual introduction to the discipline; crime statistics; crime theories; criminal types; and the criminal justice system. Here the subject of 'female criminality' is allotted a few pages in the theory section. It begins with the usual *mea culpa* about the neglect of women: 'Perhaps the most serious indictment of criminological theories is that they are nothing more than specialised theories of male delinquency and criminality'.[9] The authors then concede, in one way or another, that the indictment is fully justified. They say that 'Over the years, attempts have been made to apply some of the popular sociological theories to female offenders', a clear admission that the popular theories have been theories of men.[10] They also reveal that all the social theories of crime hitherto discussed 'have been based on male samples'.[11] But then knowing all this, the authors are unblushing in their conservatism. They adhere to the standard textbook formula: the general and more extensive part of the work is about men (though it is not called the men's part which would be to concede its limited significance), and then the study of some specialist areas includes a short piece on women who are explicitly gendered. And although they include in their women's section a handful of references to feminist work, they do not name it as such. Feminist criminology thus does not even receive the dignity of a label, either within or without the women's chapter.[12]

At this point, it would seem that my introductory statement about the neglect of feminism by criminology would be well justified. It would also seem, by implication, that feminism offers few prospects for criminology. However, to accept this negative appraisal of feminism's achievements would be to ignore a considerable and mature body of writing by feminists on the subject of crime. As this book will reveal, there is a wealth of feminist criminology that is not appearing, to any significant degree in the standard texts on crime.[13] There are feminists who have carried out the more conventional (but necessary) empirical work of documenting sex bias within the criminal justice system. Feminists have questioned the scientific methods deployed by criminologists, as well as their highly orthodox approach to the nature of knowledge. Feminists have engaged with criminological theory, across the range, questioning its ability to provide general explanations of human behaviour. Feminists have provided an abundance of data about crime from the viewpoint of women (to counter the more usual viewpoint of men), and feminists have also helped to develop new epistemologies that question the very sense of writing from the perspective of a woman (or, for that matter, from the perspective of a man).

In short, as this book will make plain, feminist criminology is a healthy, robust and rich oeuvre which poses some of the more difficult and interesting questions about the nature of (criminological) knowledge. A hallmark of feminist criminology, and of feminism generally, is its willingness to put itself about, to engage with its detractors, and to subject itself to precisely the sort of critical scrutiny it has applied to others. The work of feminists consistently displays a sensitivity to its working assumptions and a willingness to subject them to revision. It is, therefore, a matter of concern that the student coming to the criminology textbook literature for the first time is led to believe that feminist criminology is either under-developed or only of minor significance.

Should the student of crime then look to the criminology journals for some indication of feminism's standing within the discipline, the story will be much the same. If we examine the contributions to the leading American and British journals,[14] we discover that feminism is still peripheral to the main concerns of criminology, which, as we will see in the next chapter, remain heavily empirical and often untheoretical. As a rule, the new writing in the discipline continues to display a remarkably consistent disregard for new currents in critical theory.[15] Evidently, the editors of the leading criminology journals of the United States and of Britain do not require their writers to take account of feminist criticism. The vast majority of articles simply proceed to publication as if feminism had never happened.[16]

In 1987, I published a volume on the characterization of women within the main theories of crime, mainly emanating from the United States.[17] There I suggested that the supposedly general or gender-neutral theories of crime worked poorly for women, and that, as a consequence, it was necessary for criminologists to reconsider some of their most basic assumptions about human behaviour. A decade later, it seems that some of the leading figures in American and British criminology[18] have not heeded these comments; nor have they responded to the work of the many other feminists who are now writing about crime. Having been so summarily dismissed, a further temptation for the feminist criminologist is simply to turn one's back on criminology. Despairing of any scholarly connection, one might as well take one's wares elsewhere. One prominent feminist criminologist who took this option some years ago is Carol Smart. Her departure was marked by the comment that criminology needed feminism more than feminism needed criminology.[19] Smart was clearly of the view that other disciplines offered greater possibilities for fruitful intellectual exchange. Indeed, all the major disciplines, even science and law which perhaps have been the most hidebound, now seem to appreciate the worth of the feminist enterprise.

The costs to criminology of its failure to deal with feminist scholarship are perhaps more severe than they would be in any other discipline. The reason is that the most consistent and prominent fact about crime is the sex of the offender. As a rule, crime is something men do, not women, so the denial of the gender question – and the dismissal of feminists who wish to tease it out – seems particularly perverse. Sexual difference runs right through the crime statistics – from large-scale corporate fraud to petty property crime; from major to minor crimes against the person. Crime is also something that men are expected to do, because they are men, and women are expected not to do, because we are women. Crime, men and masculinity have an intimate relationship, so intimate that we often fail to see it, and so intimate that it can seem natural. Though the vast majority of men do not enter the official criminal statistics, those individuals who do become known as criminals are usually men.[20] Each year we know this will be true and rarely is anything made of it, even though for many it is a major concern. It would be astonishing were the crime statistics, official or informal, to reveal otherwise. Criminology would tilt on its axis.

The maleness of crime is true of the United States of America, of Britain, of Australia and indeed of all Western countries. Men are the vast majority of violent and non-violent offenders. They are virtually all of the rapists,[21] they are responsible for the majority of other forms of assault, and they are most of the burglars.[22] They even predominate in that area of crime which is sometimes thought to be the preserve of women: larceny.[23] In view of this remarkable sex bias in crime, it is surprising that gender has not become *the* central preoccupation of the criminologist, rather than an after-thought.

Surely it would be natural to ask the 'man question': what is it about men that makes them offend and what is it about women that makes them law-abiding? Several feminist criminologists have remarked upon this myopia, this failure to make central the obvi-ous. According to Maureen Cain, 'so great has been the gender-blindness of criminological discourse that men as males have never been the objects of the criminological gaze'.[24] Anne Edwards has observed that 'although males are the chosen subjects of study in the overwhelming majority of cases, maleness or masculinity are hardly ever mentioned as a possibly significant variable'.[25] This insensitivity to the significance of the (male) sex of the offender who forms the major object of study is, as we will see, particularly marked in the mainstream American literature still appearing in the pre-eminent American journal, *Criminology*.

Not only have criminologists failed to pursue the 'man question' of crime, but they have also been insensitive to the effects of con-ventional understandings of masculinity and femininity on their own understandings of crime. It is as if they have assumed that they themselves are free of these effects, that their own cultural constitution as men can be treated as an irrelevant accident, and not as an integral part of their view of the world. It is true that the fact that it is men, and not women, who form the bulk of the population of offenders is nearly always remarked upon; it is also true, as Edwards has observed, that criminologists spend most of their time studying men. But then not much is made of this pre-occupation with men. It is a basic given, something which goes almost without saying, rather than a central intellectual concern. Criminology has been developed and presented as a study of men (by men) and their relation to crime, but it is a study that is un-interested in men (as men) and that fails to recognise the conse-quent specificity, limitations and underlying assumptions of the discipline.

A common-sense response to this observation about crimino-logy's concern with men, as the standard case, and the slight atten-tion paid to this fact, might be that there is a good reason for this selective focus in the case of criminology (though perhaps not in the other disciplines). After all, it is men who do most of the offending. Criminology poses its first logical question – why do people engage in crime? – and finds that it is men who form the obvious objects of their study, because men are the main offenders. But, in truth, there is nothing inevitable about this first question.

An equally sensible starting point (and it is certainly not the only other starting point)[26] is to ask what it is about people that makes them law-abiding, a question that should immediately bring women to the fore as the more law-abiding sex. In fact, when this question has been posed, it still has not had this effect. Men have stayed in the centre of the picture, which in itself further strengthens the argument to be developed below that criminology has a basic dif-ficulty seeing women as proper subjects of study and as properly inquiring subjects. The question of why people obey the criminal law could be regarded as a particularly good one because, tradi-tionally (and, to many, controversially), criminologists have been concerned with the problem of stopping crime. An inquiry into the lives of women would surely throw light on this problem.

Moreover, there is no inexorable logic about the direction in which criminology's first question has taken the discipline (and its con-sequent treatment of women and of men). Traditionally, crimino-logy's concern with what makes people offend has entailed a comparison with non-criminal men and the question has then been asked, what makes the criminal group more socially pathological, or more aberrant or even less moral than the non-criminal group.

The non-criminal group has been cast in the more favourable light, and the search has been for the reasons for the pathology of the criminal.

However, on the rare occasions when women have been brought into the picture (within orthodox criminology), it has not been to contrast them favourably with the criminal group or to begin to regard women as central figures of interest (because women are generally more law-abiding, and, we might even say more socially responsible, and the crime that women do commit tends to be less serious and less violent). Instead, women have become the aberrant group, even when compared with an aberrant group. So, when women, as the more law-abiding sex and the lesser criminals, have occasionally been contrasted with criminal men, criminologists have rarely seen fit to ask the sorts of questions they have asked about law-abiding men (such as what makes them more socially healthy, or even more moral, than the criminal group).[27]

As lesser criminals, women have often been regarded as inept or unambitious. As law-abiding citizens they seem to lack the offender's energy and drive. We might say that even the criminal looks good when compared with a woman.[28] The idea that an exploration of the lives of women might provide the discipline with powerful insights into human behaviour has not been considered. Nor has the idea been countenanced that an understanding of women might tell men specifically about men. This would allow women a degree of separateness and subjectivity that has not been accorded them by the discipline.

The neglect of women in much mainstream criminology has, therefore, skewed criminological thinking in a quite particular way. It has stopped criminologists seeing the sex of their subjects, precisely because men have occupied and colonized all of the terrain. This myopia is not exclusively a problem of criminology. To Elizabeth Grosz, the blindness of men to their own maleness is a problem which pervades Western culture. In her view:

> the specificities of the masculine have always been hidden under the generality of the universal, the human. Men have functioned as if they represented masculinity only incidentally or only in moments of passion and sexual encounter, while the rest of the time they are representatives of the human, the generic 'person'. Thus what remains unanalysed, what men can have no distance on, is the mystery, the enigma, the unspoken of the male body.[29]

Put another way, criminology is a disciplinary study of men and by men, but one which has been cast as a study which is not especially interested in men as men, how they differ from women, and why they offend so much more than women. It is certainly not interested in what feminists have to say on these questions. Criminology presents itself to the world as a human science, not a science of men, ignoring the cultural, intellectual and ethical significance of the maleness of the subjects it has chosen to study, and the intellectual and ethical significance of the exclusion of women from the field of inquiry. Indeed, criminologists have been remarkably insensitive to their own powers as meaning-makers, as the makers of a discipline of knowledge. Often they have been quite oblivious of the fact that they have been constituting a body of facts and theory all along, selecting certain objects to include in their studies (and in the same moment defining the meaning of those objects), and selecting others to exclude. Instead, there has been a tendency simply to treat crime and the criminal as brutal facts, as phenomena which are naturally occurring out in the world, demanding the criminologist's attention.

The curious consequence is that conventional criminologists have tended not to consider what characterizes the people they have selected as criminology's proper subjects; that is, they know little about men as *men* and what it is about them that conduces to crime even though they are nearly always studying men. They know even less about women and their relation to offending. In short, we may say that the men of criminology have an enormous blind spot. Though they concentrate their efforts on men, they tend not to ask why it is that they are studying men, and why it is mainly men who engage in crime.[30] Nor do they reflect much upon the fact that they themselves (that is, as criminologists) are mainly men, and that as (mainly white, all educated and so middle-class) men they might see the world in a particular and specific, not neutral and universal, way.[31] They have not considered the fact that their own sex might have something to do with what and why they study, and what they have come to make of it: that the identity of the inquiring subject might influence, even constitute, the meaning of the object of inquiry.[32]

My decision to write this book was animated not only by a concern about criminology's ill-founded disparagement of feminism and its unwillingness to engage with theories that could only have invigorated the discipline. It was also motivated by a desire to discover what had gone wrong with the discipline of criminology that it should remain so reluctant to reflect critically upon its own world view. I wanted to know why criminologists were refusing to examine their own working assumptions, and why, as a consequence, they avoided central questions about crime, such as the 'man question', preferring to set aside (or marginalize) the whole question of gender and crime.

My task, then, was to examine the mindset of the discipline from an explicitly feminist perspective. What were the causes of criminology's intellectual closure? How had criminologists come to believe so firmly in their own neutrality and impartiality that they could so confidently dismiss the objections of those who suggested otherwise, without any further reflection? Why did criminologists think as they did about what counted as good knowledge? These questions pressed me into writing a book about the theories of knowledge which, implicitly, have underpinned criminology, and the criminological practices generated by those epistemologies.

A book about an entire discipline and how it thinks as it does about what counts as good scholarship must, of necessity, be schematic. It cannot provide an exhaustive catalogue of each school of criminology and its main exponents, the sort of taxonomy you would expect to find in a standard criminology text. My intention, instead, is to document some of the major shifts in criminological approaches to knowledge, invoking particular examples of research, only as they become relevant. Because this is a feminist criminology book, the intellectual highlights are also somewhat different from those you would find in the standard work. Although I intend to indicate the major intellectual movements in conventional criminology, my larger concern is to make apparent the epistemological development of feminist thought, indicating where and why orthodox criminology has tended to fall by the wayside.

The first part of the book is a feminist history of criminology, which takes us from the nineteenth century to the present day, and so traverses a considerable intellectual territory. The principle focus, however, is the fairly recent history of criminology because the major paradigm shifts of the discipline occurred from about the 1960s. Before that time, a fairly orthodox scientific approach to the study of crime was taken by criminologists generally. After the sixties, there was a questioning of conventional science or positivism and a period of accelerated change in philosophical outlook.

The book begins with an account of the scientific attitude adopted by some of the first men of criminology. Chapter 1 considers how the early criminologists made it their brief to study the criminal man (not the criminal or conforming woman) as a scientific object in a distanced, dispassionate manner, and how they managed to use scientific arguments to justify their quite particular concerns and practices. From the start, criminological man took pride in his capacity for scientific neutrality. With the entry of feminist scientists into criminology (from about the early seventies), however, serious doubts were raised about the methods of the man of science. Chapter 1 also documents the extensive empirical researches of feminists who examined critically the workings of the criminal justice system, as well as the scientific experiments of their fellow criminologists.

Chapter 2 records criminology's shift in the seventies towards a more appreciative understanding of the offender, one which accorded him the same subjectivity as the researcher. The deliberate endeavour was to narrow the distance between criminologist and criminal by recognising the right of the offender to speak authoritatively about his own condition. Feminist interventions into this appreciative criminology, however, were to reveal the limitations of this new way of thinking about crime, for a similar authority was not accorded to women. Again, it was left to feminists to document the interior worlds of women and then to question the adequacy of the existential stories told by men.

Chapter 3 observes a bifurcation in the preferred methods of criminology. One school of criminology, calling itself realist, endeavours to inject new life into the scientific empiricism of old. To feminists, the errors of the fathers are revisited by the sons. Another school (really a loose collection of writers variously influenced by Foucault and Derrida) becomes more conscious of the problems of epistemology, and so begins to examine the very conditions of the formation of cultural meaning: how we can say and know what we do within the constraints and the possibilities of language. Within this new philosophical criminology, some of the most fruitful work is done by feminists who examine and question the concepts of 'man' and 'woman' and their intimate linguistic and cultural relation.

The second part of the book shifts from the historical to the contemporary. Chapters 4 and 5 provide an indication of some of the techniques and strategies which can now be employed in a modern feminist criminology. All of the feminisms documented in the first part of the book are put to work here. Chapter 4 is a deconstruction of the crime of rape. It questions the orthodoxy that the sexual natures of men and women are necessarily complementary, and offers different, more dissident accounts of female sexuality. Chapter 5 similarly serves to undermine conventional understandings of the dominant male, drawing on the more subversive portrayals of women and men to be found in feminist crime fiction. Feminists have never been good observers of disciplinary boundaries and the benefits of their indiscipline are revealed here. Chapter 6 then considers the constituents of a more ethical relation between and within the sexes that does not depend on the sort of violent hierarchy always assumed by criminology.

Much of this book is about the effort of conventional science, criminology included, to preserve a distinction between the subject (in the present case, the criminological man doing the investigating) and the object (the criminal man who has been investigated), and what is wrong with this endeavour. My argument is that the one is never free of the other, and that the (usually male) identity of the knower matters because it always informs what is known. There is no way of wrenching the subject or the author out of the field of knowledge or writing, and so we should always acknowledge the effects of our identity on what we think and write.

As Edward Said observed two decades ago, 'No one has ever devised a method for detaching the scholar from the circumstances of life, from the fact of his [*sic*] involvement (conscious or unconscious) with a class, a set of beliefs, a social position, or from the mere activity of being a member of society.'[33] Attempts by writers to appear neutral or universal are often ways of disguising a point of view. Worse, the endeavour to speak in a neutral voice (and in criminology's case, a gender-neutral voice) paradoxically can serve to convey the message that the speaker can speak on behalf of everyone because everyone would see the point in the same way. This is an imperialist gesture that silences the others who fail to agree, but who lack the authority, or the opportunity, to express a different point of view. That women have often been in this position may serve to explain their excision from the standard criminology texts.

A willingness to engage in self-conscious, self-critical scholarship has been one of the manifest strengths of feminism. By contrast, such introspection has been singularly lacking in criminology. In a spirit of optimism, this book is a feminist endeavour to engage (yet again) with criminology as it is seen to be in its proper form. It is an effort to persuade the members of the discipline of the intellectual benefits of a more modest and self-reflective criminology which acknowledges its exclusions, its limitations and its silences.

Part 1

A Feminist History of Criminology

1

The Scientific Origins of Criminology

From Descartes onwards philosophers had thought of the human being as a subject in a world of objects, and because of that the central philosophical problems came to be seen as those concerning perception and knowledge. How do we as subjects gain knowledge of the objects that constitute the world?

Brian Magee, *The Great Philosophers*

In *A History of Western Philosophy*, Bertrand Russell examines the role of science in the making of the modern mind and the modern world. According to Russell, 'almost everything that distinguishes the modern world from earlier centuries is attributable to science, which achieved its most spectacular triumphs in the seventeenth century.'[1] What Russell terms 'the modern outlook' entailed a new commitment to science as a means of making sense of the world and with it a bold rejection of myth and superstition. The great men who heralded in the new way of thinking were Copernicus, Kepler, Galileo and Newton. The crucial effect of their scientific work was to transform 'the outlook of educated men':

At the beginning of the century [there were] . . . trials for witchcraft; at the end, such a thing would have been impossible. In Shakespeare's time, comets were still portents; after the publication of Newton's *Principia* in 1687, it was known . . . that they [comets] were as obedient as the planets to the law of gravitation. The reign of scientific law had established its hold on men's imaginations, making such things as magic and sorcery incredible.[2]

Through the 'patient collection of facts', it was now believed that one could arrive at 'scientific truth'.[3] The dominant epistemology, or theory of knowledge, from the seventeenth century until well into this century was to remain essentially scientific in nature. As John Jackson explains in a more recent account of the scientific outlook, it took as axiomatic that we gather evidence for principles about the nature of the world through an appeal to empirical data, 'to what is alleged to be fact; and we select, analyse and interpret material on the basis of principles'.[4] Scientific method was one of 'testing such principles by discovering to what extent matters that can be deduced from them correspond to the facts'.[5] From this method there follows a number of assumptions:

> First, it assumed that there is a world of facts which exists 'out there' as part of reality independent of the human observer, and the task of the scientist is to discover as much of it as he can by comparing this reality with his own theories and hypotheses. . . . Second, it is assumed . . . the complete truth is in principle capable of being revealed. . . . Third, knowledge of this reality can be obtained by using as a foundation the empirical evidence of our sense experience. Since this experience is value-free, science can be conducted in a value-free manner without the intrusion of value judgements.[6]

In other words, the identity of the inquiring subject did not matter.

Empiricism and criminology

Among the leading criminologists of the United States,[7] there is an enduring commitment to the sort of orthodox scientific method and quantitative research described by Jackson. As certain American commentators on the discipline have recently observed, 'Regardless of whether the causes of crime are viewed from the biological, psychological or sociological perspective . . . the scientific method still provides the chief means for testing hypotheses, checking results and approximating objectivity.'[8] Rigorous scientific method is thought to guarantee impartiality: for science 'has no loyalty to political programs or ideologies'.[9]

To secure publication in the prestigious journal of the American Society of Criminology (and thus to secure a high profile within the American academy and at the big criminology conferences), it is indeed wise to publish heavily empirical work that either documents criminal careers via 'the longitudinal research method' or that provides detailed measures of crime across the population 'especially using official records', but also through large-scale self-report surveys.[10] The more statistical the work, the more complex the correlations, the greater it seems is the chance of publication. The agile manipulation of very large numbers is highly esteemed, and concomitantly philosophical speculation or small-scale qualitative research is less highly valued.

This assessment of the scientific orthodoxy of the American discipline may be confirmed simply by scanning the addresses of the incoming Presidents of the American Society of Criminology. (This is not a difficult task because each year the lead article of *Criminology* is the Presidential address.) For example, in his 1991 Presidential Address, John Hagan declared that:

> Some of the greatest advances of criminology over the past several decades have involved its evolution into a more systematic and precise science. These advances have demanded greater clarity and testability of our theories, and these advances have occurred through the dedicated efforts of some of our field's most practiced contributors.[11]

In a similar vein, Joan Petersilia observed in her 1990 Presidential Address to the Society that 'to succeed under the academic model [of criminology] graduate schools must place science first.'[12] However, the problem then arises that scientific criminology becomes increasingly removed from the world beyond the academy. 'The further we move into computer analysis of large data files with more sophisticated methods, the harder it becomes for practitioners and policymakers to follow.'[13] Petersilia suggests that criminologists should not resile from science, but rather should ensure that their research is responsive to the needs of policymakers, 'without compromising the higher objectives of research'.[14] Modern American criminology should take the form of an applied and practical science. The implicit message is that criminologists should not engage in excessively academic and abstract speculation about the nature of critical theory and knowledge. Science should come first, and then its application to the real world beyond the university.

In his inaugural lecture as Wolfson Professor of Criminology at The University of Cambridge, England in 1986, Anthony Bottoms has offered some remarkably similar reflections on the nature of modern British criminology, endorsing its commitment to the methods of conventional science.[15] Bottoms speaks not unkindly, of the angry young British criminologists of the 1960s and 1970s who sought to transform the discipline (see chapter 2). Apparently, they had been charmed by the siren songs of phenomenology, of ethnomethodology, of Marxism and so they had strayed from the true path of criminology. In those passionate times, according to Professor Bottoms, 'it was legitimate to wonder whether anyone, other than those who had all along been committed empiricists, would, amid all the heady theory, return to the task of studying crimes, criminal justice and punishment.' With some relief, Bottoms then observes that criminology has come to its senses, 'that phase has ... been transcended, and empirical studies have been returned to with full vigour.'[16]

With these few words, Bottoms takes us to the intellectual roots of criminology. He reminds us that the discipline as we know it, both in the United States and in Britain, is the creation of nineteenth century men of science who were committed to the empirical scientific method described by Russell and that it is still men of science who assume a central place in the academy today.[17] In true scientific spirit, Bottoms (much like Hagan) also suggests that the criminological project is one of discovery and conquest over an unknown world which could, with enough sustained effort, be known thoroughly. He tells us that 'criminology is very much still at the beginning of its intellectual quest, and that our knowledge is still usually 'fragmentary and unsatisfactory' consisting only of 'scattered clues and glimmers of hope'.[18] Again, we are reminded of the nineteenth century scientific explorer who hoped through science to gain mastery over that which he did not yet understand and so reduce the things in the world to the objects of his understanding. In the case of criminological inquiry, those objects were criminals.

The first men of criminology seemed quite naturally to take their project to be the dispassionate and scientific study of criminal man. There was (almost) never any question of concerning themselves with women in any serious way. Caesar Lombroso and William Ferrero's work on women has come to be regarded as an interesting historical exception rather than an endeavour to incorporate women as subjects of equal interest into the scientific study of crime.[19] From the start, it was a given that criminology would be the study by men of men, though these men were not to be regarded as interesting because they were men, but rather because they were criminals. Criminology was the study of criminals who happened mainly to be men and so the male criminal was what was studied, though not as a man or masculine being, but as a criminal. This, it seemed, was simply the natural, logical starting point of the discipline. The assumptions underpinning this scientific selection were unexamined and remain largely unexamined today.

The idea that there was a certain inherent logic to criminology's brief for itself – the scientific study of criminal man – is certainly to be found in David Garland's recent account of the history of the discipline. He observes that by the end of the nineteenth century, 'the idea of a specialist criminological science [had] emerged – centred, *as it happens*, on the figure of the "criminal type" – and that . . . this subsequently led to the establishment . . . of an independent criminological discipline.' The term 'criminology' was generally adopted in the 1890s. Garland goes on to remark that 'Since the discipline was characterized by a . . . concern to pursue the crime problem *in all its aspects*, the subject is continually expanding to embrace all of the ways in which crime and criminals might be scientifically studied.' He suggests also that 'the tendency of the modern discipline [is] to embrace *everything that might be scientifically said* about crime and criminals' (my italics).[20]

In these statements, Garland describes and appears to endorse the assumptions of his predecessors: that the scientific study of criminal man was the quite natural and logical starting point of the discipline and that scientific criminology was and remains interested in everything that can be said about criminal man. Like the early men of the discipline he portrays, Garland is wearing gendered blinkers. Although he is discussing the very fact that criminology developed as the study of criminal man (he calls it the criminal 'type', hence, stripping criminal man of his maleness in much the same way as his predecessors), he does not appear to see that as a consequence there is something highly unscientific and skewed about the criminological enterprise from the outset. For criminologists are studying men (not women), and yet they are not interested in the maleness of their subjects. Thus, they are ignoring the 'man question' of criminology that is its most critical dimension – statistically and, I will suggest, socially and politically.

That Garland himself cannot see the distortions at work is evident from his observation that criminologists are interested in 'everything that might be scientifically said about crime'. This is patently not the case, for surely the most interesting first question of a scientific nature would have been, and remains still, the 'man question'. Even his own reference to the title of Lombroso's famous volume, *L'Uomo Delinquente* (1876), does not alert Garland to the masculine preoccupation and blinkers of the discipline. Then (and now) the sex specificity of the discipline was unremarked. Women were invisible, and so was the fact of their invisibility. Women were absent from the start (both as criminal subjects and as non-criminal subjects with whom the male criminal might be compared, and as victims of crime), but there was never anything to be made of their erasure from the fraternity of criminology. Criminology was simply the study of criminal man, but criminal man could be studied without reference to his gender. By necessary implication, men were beings whose gender was not crucial to their identity; it was only women who constituted a particular sex.

The idea that it is still possible and legitimate to study criminal men scientifically without referring to their sex is reiterated in the American and British criminology texts considered in the opening chapter. Recall that the editors of the Oxford volume referred to the study of 'gender and crime', quite uncritically, as a 'relatively new specialist interest'. Similarly, the American texts accorded a minor place to their discussion of women, gender and feminism, implicitly regarding them as marginal to the main discussion of (male) crime. What each of these texts are saying, in effect, is that scientific criminology can still be conducted in a manner which is free from the considerations of gender, and that it is still legitimate to produce vast modern tomes which glide over the sex of the offender under investigation (as long as he is a man). Garland too repeats this notion that there is a distinction between 'central' or 'substantive' criminological topics and the newer 'ideological' concerns, such as those of feminism. Again, the implication is that of an ideology-free (and so gender-free) substantive scientific criminology to which the ideologically-mounted concerns of feminism have recently been added.

In Garland's history of the discipline, we are brought up to the present day and told that criminology is now a robust scientific discipline which is continuing to expand. It has survived the onslaught of its detractors (considered in the next chapter) who were concerned about its 'atheoretical pragmatism', and who expressed the sort of intellectual and political concerns I am voicing in this volume. Indeed, we may discern a degree of satisfaction, even complacency, with the current state of scientific criminology.

This evident complacency with modern scientific criminology, the conviction that the discipline is happily on the right scientific course, also manifests itself consistently in the American Presidential addresses to the Society of Criminology. Recall the comments of Professor Hagan that criminology has now evolved 'into a more systematic and precise science'. Indeed, each year the message conveyed from the Presidential podium of the Society is that practical science (rather than abstract critical theory or conceptual analysis), is the appropriate way to go and that, if anything, criminology should become even more applied and practical. Policy-makers should be made to see the utility and relevance of scientific criminology.[21] If there is a problem within the academy, it does not reside within the scientific paradigm of its members (though inevitably there is controversy about which scientific methods are most effective),[22] but with the failure of American policy-makers to listen to scientific criminologists who can supply them with the essential data on crime.

A similar faith in the benefits of orthodox science is evident in the recent reviews of the state of British criminology (1988 and 1994) conducted by Paul Rock. He describes (approvingly) the criminologists of the eighties and nineties as 'empirical and policy-oriented'.[23] In world-weary fashion, he looks back at the heady but immature scholarship of the 1970s. Like Bottoms, he sees the radical writings of the early 1970s as 'bravura pieces . . . the bold creations of lone autodidacts' whose work was 'new, venturesome [and] eccentric'.[24] Things have settled down now and it is all to the good:

> The era of manifestos passed largely because an ageing group of scholars in the prime generation had no need repeatedly to fight the battles of its youth. . . . It has attained a satisfactory respectability and influence. . . . To be sure, there are always a few who lose none of their combativeness. . . . But the fortunate generation has come into its own. . . . Differences remain but there is decreasing profit in stressing them. . . . The central terrain of the sociology of deviance is no longer subject to bellicose dispute, most criminologists having become more conciliatory and catholic, engaging in a reasonably civil trade in one another's ideas.[25]

For Rock, the radicalism of the seventies has matured into a more sensible, often applied, criminology in which there is a general consensus about the aims and priorities of the discipline. 'The work that is being done', he suggests, 'is marked by a decelerating rate of innovation, a drift towards normal science and a new pragmatism'.[26] This account of contemporary British criminology is confirmed by Ian Taylor. He observes that it is the Home Office which now employs the largest group of criminologists, and that professional criminologists are also now in the employ of the local authorities. Their purpose is 'to advise on crime prevention programmes and policing',[27] a role which Joan Petersilia would like to see expanded even further in the American academy. Or, as a more recent President of the American Society has remarked, 'Our task as criminologists is to bring evidence and reasoned discussion to the [public] debate.'[28]

The empirical criminology described by the leading American and British criminologists is founded on quite traditional assumptions about the nature of knowledge. These assumptions make sense of, and serve to justify, criminology's faith in scientific method. For example, it is taken as given that language plays a quite particular role in our acquisition of knowledge. It is assumed that concepts and categories (such as 'man' or 'woman' or 'crime') describe and capture the essential meanings of things in the world, however imperfectly. They identify, pick out, picture, denote vital aspects of the actual world in a direct and pure way, unaffected by the particular characteristics of the knower. They directly label pre-existing things in the world, rather than constitute the world. (As we will see in chapter 3, these ideas about language and its relation to the world have come under serious challenge, but not enough to shift the attachment of criminology to conventional science.) The particular identity of the inquiring subject does not matter because language is clear and unambiguous and so allows each of us to apprehend the world in the same manner. In this view of knowledge-formation, each of us is simply naming or picturing the same world with a set of common linguistic tools which are essentially unproblematic. We are not actively creating and constituting the world as we go along through a medium (language), which is itself inherently uncertain, variable and creative. This is the view expounded by Wittgenstein in the *Tractatus*: 'there the claim was that the meaning of a word is the object it denotes, the meanings of words consisted in a denotative link with objects.'[29]

Criminologists of the empirical sort are, therefore, committed to a traditional ideal of objectivity. When they study an object, they must strive to get themselves out of the field of vision, out of the line of inquiry – and they believe that it is feasible to do this. The object of knowledge should have primacy and ideally the inquiring subject should be out of the way altogether. A related scientific, though rarely articulated, assumption is that inquiring subjects (that is criminologists studying crime) are interchangeable because they absorb, assimilate and constitute knowledge in essentially similar ways. This view may be traced to the work of Immanuel Kant and his notion of the 'transcendental unity of apperception'. Kant believed that we all possess the same conceptual structures in the mind that allow each of us to assimilate knowledge in much the same way. For example, concepts such as space and time are to be found in the minds of all human beings, they are *a priori* categories or laws of the mind which allow us to synthesize and organize our sensory experiences and so make possible objective observation. 'It is by means of the transcendental unity of apperception', this in-built feature of the human mind, 'that all the manifold given in an intuition is united into a conception of its object.'[30]

To Kant, the structure or scaffolding of the mind gives a constant form to experience. The important effect of this common mode of processing sensory data is that the particular identity of the person doing the particular processing is less critical as the laws of the mind are universal. What is important is that proper scientific rigour is employed so that experiments can be replicated by the next scientist who comes to the subject. (In chapters 2 and 3 I will consider some of the epistemological problems which inhere in the Kantian idea of scientific objectivity – that our minds absorb data in much the same way and that it is therefore possible to acquire objective, universally-valid, knowledge.)

Empiricist criminology, which to leading academicians such as Hagan and Bottoms is what the project is all about, assumes all this, though it often goes unsaid. It is simply the intellectual frame through which the criminologist views the world.[31] It entails a commitment to scientific, positivist methods of empirical inquiry into what is regarded as a distinctive criminal population. This is likely to involve, for example, the comparison of criminals and non-criminals with a view to isolating the peculiar features of the criminal group. The criminologist is a separate, uninvolved, knowing, inquiring subject: criminologists are therefore 'subjects in a world of objects'.[32] They are quite distinct from the world they study, 'subjects, spectators, observers separated by an invisible plate glass window from the world of objects in which [they] find [them] selves'.[33] They must therefore, take care to observe this distinction whenever their scientific minds are brought to bear on objects in the world – such as criminals, crime and the criminal 'justice system'. Whenever they wish to illuminate the qualities of an object under scrutiny, it is best that they establish a clear distance between themselves and it. Emotional detachment is necessary for scientific detachment. As John Hagan has observed:

> I . . . see [scientific] positivism as an opportunity to be as open-minded as is humanly possible – let the data fall where they may. Positivism is a system of thought that gives us our best chance to find out about how things are, independent of how we might wish them to be. This is the soundest foundation on which theories and policies can be built.[34]

The human world can thus be studied and understood in the same manner as the scientific world has conventionally been studied and understood. The later Wittgenstein and his new theory of knowledge does not get a look in.

The present assessment of empiricist criminology should not be interpreted as a blanket rejection of scientific empirical research *per se*. Clearly, there is an important place for scientific work about crime and the criminal, if only to enable law-makers to learn something of the effects of their policies. To this extent I agree with the Presidents of the American Society. For the moment, my particular objection is to scientific research of a certain unreflective kind. For example, it is not uncommon for criminologists to treat the data generated by all-male studies as of general value, rather than as quite specific information about men. Of course, this problem of extrapolating the male experience to the rest of the world is not confined to criminologists. Much medical knowledge, for example, has been acquired by studying male bodies, with the ensuing medical treatments regarded as equally suitable to men and to women.[35] It is also not uncommon to find in scientific criminology the absence of any critical discussion of the reasons why only men have been selected for study. The selection is usually noted, but little more is made of it.[36] It is simply business as usual.

For example, in his 1994 Presidential Address to the American Society of Criminology, Jerome Skolnick examines the connection between youth crime, class and unemployment. He observes that work is fundamental to social identity and that, as a consequence, 'people who have reasonably well-paying jobs are less likely to commit crimes than those who don't.'[37] The reason is that 'Work disciplines one's daily rounds. Work brings responsibility. Work supports . . . family life and moral values.'[38] Thus 'Jobless youth, who tend to be impetuous, to engage in male bonding activities that we call gangs – are likely to be free from ordinary social constraints.'[39] It is not difficult to see that Skolnick is making an easy slide from 'people', to 'youth', to young men, but without a moment's reflection on this shift from the general to the particular, from the gender-neutral to the gender-specific. When Skolnick thinks of offenders, he clearly has a mental image of men and of male working lives. But because much of his discussion remains at the general level, Skolnick never has to explore the implications of the sex-specificity of his subjects, beyond a passing reference to male bonding.

John Hagan and David Farrington who, with their skilful deployment of large criminal data bases, have made substantial names for themselves in American[40] and British criminology,[41] can be found committing the same errors of imprecision and of unwitting and unfounded extrapolation, in their case from the particular (that is men) to the general (both sexes). In his 1991 Presidential Address to the American Society of Criminology, for example, Professor Hagan spoke of 'the poverty of a classless criminology',[42] and implied that criminologists should not flinch from such a politically-sensitive issue. He identified 'a nonspurious correlation between unemployment and crime that endures over the life course' and suggested that 'Much important work remains to be done in establishing the direction and dynamic of this relationship.'[43] To illustrate the connection between unemployment and crime, Hagan invokes *inter alia* the famous longitudinal British crime survey of Professor Farrington and his colleagues.[44] He reports 'that nearly half the sample of 411 London males followed in their panel research from ages 8 to 18 experienced some unemployment, and the youths self-reported more involvement in delinquency during the periods of their unemployment.'[45] What Hagan omits to tell us, however, is that Farrington's work can only tell us about men. It has nothing to say about women because there were no females included in the study.

In the same article, Hagan refers to other all-male population studies of the relationship between class and crime, in the same unreflecting manner, never pausing to consider why the various criminologists he cites chose to examine only men and why they never chose to consider only women. This myopia becomes even more marked when Hagan starts referring to men as the very problem he wishes to solve. He observes that 'less-educated males are the core of the underclass'[46] (women have now slipped completely out of sight). Hagan keeps getting glimpses of the problem, but never grasps it firmly. Though he is telling a story which is basically by men, and about men (and very likely it is about men because it is men, as men, who are the problem), he never explicitly pursues this gender-specific line of inquiry. By the end of his paper, he has returned fully to (the more olympian?) gender-neutral position, cautioning his fellow criminologists 'to acknowledge the variety and complexity of the relationship between class and crime'.[47] At best, women have become, by necessary implication, simply a complicating factor in the male story of unemployment and crime.

In a more recent paper on crime and unemployment, Hagan repeats the same scientific errors of omission and commission. This time he is even more indebted to the findings from Farrington's all-male study that enable him to examine the relationship between crime and unemployment in working-class London. But again, he makes nothing of the fact that he is looking only at men (he never explains the scientific logic of doing so), nor does he limit the implications of his findings to the male population.[48] When he is studying men, it seems that Hagan is not attuned to gender, even though he is making some critical gender-based decisions about his subject matter.

All this is surprising when we consider that Hagan is also well-known for his work on women. In still another paper on the relationship between class and crime (which interestingly precedes the other two), Hagan and colleague, Helen Boritch, conduct 'a time-series analysis of male and female arrests in Toronto fom 1859 to 1955'.[49] Their important conclusion is 'that an adequate understanding of male and female criminality must give equal and simultaneous consideration to long-term gender similarities *as well as differences* in criminality' (my italics).[50] But only a year later, when he comes to give his Presidential Address to the American Criminology Society, Hagan has forgotten his own admonition. He relies on data derived from all-male studies in order to make general statements about the nature of crime, regardless of the sex of the offender: now men have been allowed to stand in for women.

One of the chief authors of the all-male London longitudinal study, David Farrington, has similar habits of mind. Not surprisingly, Farrington has put his vast and important piece of research to work a good many times but consistently the lessons he draws from it tend to be of a global (that is gender-neutral) kind. He conveys the impression that somehow it is rational, and perhaps even more scientifically controlled, to look at one sex only, but then he makes little of either the limitations or the interesting specificity of his research. Studying men, it seems, is just what criminologists do.[51] My objection (to the work of both Hagan and Farrington) is therefore to bad science on (conventional) science's own terms, such as treating the findings from one population as equally valid for another (without checking whether this is so), or failing to see that there is something quite particular about the people selected for investigation (they are all men).

My further concern is the deleterious effect on criminology of the conventional scientific goal of value-free research and, more particularly, how it has been interpreted (often tacitly, or unconsciously) by members of the discipline to mean that they need not consider the effects of their own identities on what they make of the work they do. The idea of value-free scientific criminological research has led to a paradoxical failure in criminology to scrutinize the values of the criminologist. (For example what is it about our criminological man that draws him so inexorably to the study of his own sex? And why can't he see what he's doing? Why these blinkers?)

The scientific tradition, as I have indicated, is based on the assumption that it is possible and desirable, to distance oneself from the object of inquiry. Paradoxically, this desire for value-free science, which in itself seems a good goal, has led to a failure among criminologists to inspect the effects of their identity on their inquiries. (This point will be pursued further in the next two chapters.) A more rigorous scientific approach might have led to more, not less, self-reflection. It might have involved a careful assessment of the characteristics of the criminological researcher to see what made them distinctive, what coloured them and so what assumptions or distortions might be colouring the criminological project. This did not occur in the formative period of criminology and it is generally still not happening today. Although there is research on the demography of criminologists, this is not being used to examine the particular orientation and the blind spots of the discipline. For example, Paul Rock has recently considered the sex distribution of the British population of criminologists, and concluded that it is male-dominated and generally unsympathetic to feminism, but then implicitly rejected the idea that knowledge is grounded in the (sex of the) identity of the knower.[52]

Instead, the ideal of the neutral scientific inquirer (an ideal which I will argue later has its own inherent difficulties) has led to sloppiness. The ideal that one should not bring one's prejudices to bear on a scientific problem has been taken too simply to mean that one should ignore the identity of the scientist in the quest for scientific neutrality. Instead of considering the characteristics of the inquirer and how they might entail a certain world view, the inquirer has simply been expunged. He has been deemed to be neutral. This amounts to the highly questionable assumption that the work of men who regard themselves as scientists must be scientifically neutral. Men of science, after all, do scientific work. Much the same assumption is at work today.

So far, I have presented a fairly stark portrait of contemporary empirical or positivist criminology. For the moment, I have skated over the fact that the 'progressive' criminologies (which will be detailed in the next two chapters) have had a lasting effect on the discipline, that contemporary criminologists are generally aware of these progressive movements and, to different degrees, have modified their scientific outlook. But the comments of the various Presidents of the American Society of Criminology also give us reason to believe that the prevailing attitude of modern American criminology is still essentially scientific or, at the least, that there has been a resurgence of traditional scientific thinking. This is also true of British criminology. According to Bottoms and Rock, the progressive criminologies have subsided (or grown up) and there is currently a benign mood of complacency among established criminologists. The suggestion is that the radical ideas of the seventies (see chapter 2) have now been assimilated into something which is more mature, more catholic, less theoretical, and more applied and 'scientific'.

Ian Taylor, one of the angry young Turks of the seventies, has recently commented on the present dominance of an atheoretical and unreflective scientific approach in criminology. He refers to the growth in the number of professional criminologists employed by the Home Office and by local authorities. Their express purpose is not to philosophize about the nature of crime but 'to advise on crime prevention programmes and policing'.[53] This mandate is hardly conducive to a theoretically informed or politically sceptical attitude to the discipline. Taylor describes the development of a 'very narrow and technical conception of the criminological task'[54] that is antithetical to creative and self-critical thinking about crime and how we conceive of it.

Vincenzo Ruggiero has similarly commented on the growing pressure on professional criminologists to produce 'immediate tangible results', the consequent concern with policy, and the 'tendency for conceptual and theoretical works to be discarded or regarded as indulgent. Because they are not measurable or immediately applicable', he suggests, 'they are denied the validity "scientific" or "concrete" criminological studies are awarded'.[55] And as we have already seen, the Presidents of the American Criminology Society positively applaud this trend towards a policy-oriented, scientific and technical criminology (and implicitly away from speculative theory) and would like to see the practical dimensions of the discipline expanded further still.

What we are observing is the reign of an often unreflective science of criminology, which neither examines its own particular ideologies (its own specific world view) nor speculates about the consequent intellectual and ethical value of the criminological enterprise (why it is doing what it is doing). We see, instead, a preoccupation with the scientific study of criminal man and how to correct him, much as the scientific men of the nineteenth century saw their task. But the gaze is unidirectional. Criminologist examines criminal man but does not look back at himself to discover the nature of his own identity and how it shapes the very nature of the scientific process, including the very identity of criminal man himself.

Feminist engagements

The feminist criminologies which form the subject of chapters 1, 2 and 3 constitute a series of engagements with (and departures from) this dominant scientific understanding of crime. In various ways, each of these feminist criminologies has questioned the conventional boundaries of criminological scholarship and fostered different understandings of the criminological project. In some cases, the approach has been to extend the ambit of study and the scientific methods deployed (chapter 1). In other instances, the significance of the identity of the inquiring subject has been more explicitly called into question. Such feminists have insisted that there can be no radical separation between the criminologist and the objects of her inquiry. Their point is that who does the inquiring matters, that who is doing the knowing affects what is known (chapter 2). Still other feminists have concentrated on the conditions of meaning. They have considered how central organising categories of thought (such as the concept of woman) operate and how those categories can be rethought and our understandings altered accordingly (chapter 3).

Throughout this volume, it will become apparent that none of the divisions between the different styles of feminism stand firmly. Though the feminist classifications imposed for the purposes of this book help us to organize and think about feminist writing on crime, they are simultaneously misleading (as are all categories which necessarily reduce the world) because of the refusal of most of these writers to observe strictly the canons of any one tradition of thought. Despite significant differences between the feminisms considered in this volume, however, all have one thing in common. The animating force of their scholarship is both political and intellectual. It is to think about women's lives in new ways, and so improve the lives of women. All of these feminist criminologies have therefore helped us to see crime differently – with greater intellectual rigour and with a sharpened sense of the political significance of the purposes and methods of criminology.

The intention of this book is not to undertake a major and comprehensive review of feminist criminological writing. There are already good review books and good collections of feminist writing in the discipline. My more limited purpose is to study a selection of writings which demonstrate the intellectual development of feminist criminology. The selection of feminist writing I consider in these first three chapters comprises important examples of different types of feminist thought. The juxtaposition and order of papers is intended to indicate some of the significant shifts which have occurred in feminist theorizing about crime.

Feminist empiricism

Much of the early writing of feminists in criminology assumed the methods and assumptions of empiricist criminology. The concern of these early feminists was that women had been left out of the researches of scientists (criminologists included) and the result was a necessarily skewed and distorted science. It accounted for men and explained their behaviour in a rigorous and scientific way, but it did not account for women, though it purported to do so. When it came to the analysis of women's behaviour, prejudice, ignorance and misinformation were the rule. Thus, when women made a rare appearance in criminological literature, their characters were distorted and denigrated.[56] Feminist criminologists pointed out the blatant sexism of this double standard and argued that women and men should receive the same scientific treatment.

Sandra Harding has provided a useful label for this style of feminist thought and research: 'feminist empiricism'.[57] This term denotes feminists who question the objectivity of so-called scientific work on women, while generally accepting that it is possible to be objective and neutral (in the Kantian sense). To feminist empiricists, scientific claims are thought to be realizable, but have not yet been realized in relation to women. In essence, the feminist empiricists were saying that the claim to scientific neutrality had been false. Criminologists had not considered the effects of their own biases and preconceptions on their work: on what they chose to do, how they did it, and what they made of it. This was especially the case in those rare moments when they turned their attention to women. And, as I have indicated, a good deal of the feminist literature in criminology is still of this empirical sort.

Feminist empiricism endeavours to develop a scientific understanding of women as the missing subjects of criminology, to document their lives both as offenders and as victims. It also points out the crude stereotyping of women that has represented the official wisdom on women in criminology and in the criminal justice system. It raises objections to the empirical claims made about women when those claims are based on meagre evidence, with a good sprinkling of prejudice. If criminologists and members of the criminal justice system are to deal with women with proper scientific rigour, with true objectivity, then they should document their subjects properly using the scientific methods which largely have been reserved for the study of men. In their review of feminist criminology, Loraine Gelsthorpe and Allison Morris effectively gather together the feminist criminologists writing within this empirical tradition and appropriately celebrate their considerable achievements:

> Feminist researchers have . . . made female offenders visible. They not only developed a critique of 'accumulated wisdom' about female offenders and victims, but illuminated institutionalized sexism within criminological theory, policy and practice. For example, they identified the way in which traditional gender-role expectations influenced the treatment of both female defendants and female victims. . . . Thus they showed that girls were penalized for behaviour which was condoned, if not encouraged, for boys . . . that being a good wife and mother governed courtroom decision-making . . . and that women who alleged abuse found themselves suspect.[58]

This volume offers only a small sample of the large body of feminist empirical writing in criminology. The work included here is mainly intended to indicate the range of scholarship which has been undertaken within this tradition. It should be said that few of these writers are simple, naive empiricists. In different ways, feminist criminologists have both worked within and worked on, or manipulated, the conventions of this style of scholarship. The reason that feminist scientific work represents an improvement on the older methods is that feminists have generally been more self-reflective than orthodox criminologists. They have been conscious of the political goals of their inquiry, and they have explored the idea that it is possible to develop specifically feminist scientific methods which are more sensitive to the effects of the relationship between investigator and investigated. What many have not tended to do, however, is question the possibility of doing research in a neutral fashion, of removing the effects of one's identity.

As Gelsthorpe and Morris make clear, feminist work has identified and underlined the misogyny of criminological theory and the policies and practices of the criminal justice system. Carol Smart's *Women, Crime and Criminology: A Feminist Critique* published in 1977, probably remains the most influential treatise. It did both jobs: it examined the caricaturing of women in criminological theory as well as the discriminatory practices of the agents of criminal justice. Smart's pioneering work was to stimulate further inquiries into the problems of women and theory. In *Female Crime*, for example, I observed that the supposedly gender-neutral theories of crime often did not work in relation to women because they were based on the scientific study of men, not of women.[59] Rather than attempt to make theory work for both sexes, by considering the lives of both women and men, the dominant practice was to regard man as the standard scientific case and woman as the unfortunate aberration, the special instance. The woman offender was the poor relation to the more interesting and somehow more authentic male offender.[60] She was regarded as lacking initiative, uninspired, incompetent; certainly she lacked the glamour of the male offender. She was driven by her hormones or her heart, never by reason.[61]

A host of studies have endeavoured to make male theories of crime, theories developed with male samples, fit women. Kathleen Daly and Meda Chesney-Lind refer to this as the 'generalizability problem'. The point of these exercises has been to adapt to the female case, theories of crime which purported to be gender-neutral but were in fact always highly gender specific. Not surprisingly, the results have been varied and generally inconclusive.[62] Perhaps the most time-consuming and fruitless exercise has been the endeavour to prove (and disprove) the thesis that 'women's liberation' causes crime in women.[63] This thesis was based on the assumption that if, as a result of the women's movement, women were acquiring the same opportunities as men, particularly economic opportunities, then one of the opportunities they would seize would be the opportunity to offend. The flaws in this thesis are not difficult to detect. To name but three: it assumed a simple, singular, reductive model of crime causation; it assumed, wrongly, that crimes associated with economic opportunity were rising dramatically among women; and it assumed that women are now financially emancipated, despite the considerable evidence of the feminization of poverty.[64]

More convincing were the endeavours to explain why women were so law-abiding. Frances Heidensohn, for example, considered how women's domestic role was paradoxically both a powerful control on women and a means by which women exercised power – the power to reproduce conformity in the next generation of women. 'Women, in short, in their roles as wives and mothers undertake the crucial basic tasks of care, containment and socialization, crucial that is to the maintenance of order in society.'[65]

What is generally missing from this feminist scholarship is a critical examination of criminological knowledge as it pertains to the male offender. As Heidensohn herself observes in her review of the literature, feminists have spent much of their time examining depictions and interpretations of women in criminology or trying to fit male theories to women's behaviour.[66] This is not at all surprising given the poor and meagre research on women that precipitated the feminist critique. But it does, however, leave the work on men (which purports to be gender-neutral) in place and generally unexamined.

Feminist empiricists also generated a literature on women as the victims of crime. They documented the experiences of women as the victims/survivors of violent men and then as the victims of the criminal justice system. The crimes of rape and domestic assault were central concerns. Feminists helped to bring to light the nature and extent of rape, challenging the once-dominant view that it was a crime mainly committed by strangers, rather than by friends and family. They also examined and criticized the misogynistic treatment of the rape victim as witness for the prosecution in court. Feminists helped to uncover, and then explain, the nature and extent of violence in the home. Much of this work was both practical and scholarly; it was associated with the setting up of women's refuges and rape crisis centres.[67]

Another major area of feminist research was (and remains) the treatment of the female offender by the agents of the law. Repeatedly, feminists have both rebutted the conventional wisdom about the treatment of women in the courts (that women are the recipients of chivalry) and have identified the continuing presence of discrimination against women. The considerable researches of Meda Chesney-Lind into the treatment of young female offenders, for example, have revealed that girls who are regarded as sexually active have received more punitive treatment than boys by the agents of the law who apparently object to sexual freedom in a young woman.[68]

Feminists have also reported the continuing effects of a traditional family ideology on adult female defendants. For example, in her study of a London magistrates' court, Mary Eaton examined lawyers' pleas in mitigation, social inquiry reports (reports on the social and economic circumstances of defendants prepared by probation officers) and the pronouncements of magistrates.[69] A highly conventional view of women and their role in the family emerged in a number of ways. In pleas of mitigation for both men and women, the nuclear family was presented as a stabilising and controlling influence on the defendant. In the social reports of probation officers, a clear picture emerged of the respective roles expected of men and women in a stable, and therefore desirable, family. Not surprisingly, it was considered normal and appropriate that the man provided financially for family members and the woman assumed responsibility for child care and housework. Where women were themselves the defendant, however, the focus became the quality of the housewifery. In what she refers to as 'magistrates' talk' (the comments on defendants issued from the Bench), Eaton gleaned further evidence of the legal view of women. Not only did her magistrates envisage and endorse a traditional sexual division of labour, but they also expected the man of the household to assert himself as head of the family.[70]

Another British study has revealed similar attitudes to women among members of the Scottish Bench. In her interviews of Scottish sheriffs (judges), Pat Carlen observed a disinclination to imprison women who were thought to be good mothers. As one sheriff put it, 'If she's a good mother, we don't want to take her away. If she's not a good mother, it doesn't matter.'[71] Like the London magistrates, Carlen's sheriffs also had faith in the husband as a disciplinarian. Thus, 'If she has a husband, he may tell her to stop it.' And, 'Not many women with steady husbands or cohabitees commit crime. They're kept occupied.'[72]

American research has yielded compatible results. Candice Kruttschnitt examined the probation files of over a thousand women convicted in California for various crimes in order to discover the main influences on the sentencing decision. For most offence categories, the economic dependency of the defendant emerged as the primary factor determining the severity of the sentence. From the comments of probation officers, it transpired that dependant women were regarded as safer bets because their family was thought to exert a degree of control over their behaviour and guide them into better ways.[73] Kruttschnitt concluded that 'the legal system prefers to exert little control over women whose lives presently contain an indicator of daily social control such as that entailed by economic dependency.'[74]

Feminists have also observed the complicating effects of race, class and age on the sentencing decision. Not only are women, it seems, divided into good mothers and bad, but they may also be judged according to other aspects of their identity. For example, Kathleen Daly has examined the relationship between family ideology and race, suggesting that judicial views of a woman's place in the family, and her consequent treatment by the court, may be influenced also by her colour and her class.[75] Kerry Carrington has similarly suggested that class and race influence the legal response to girl offenders. In her view, an exclusive focus on gender ignores the critical effects of these other dimensions of criminal justice.[76] In the next chapter, we will see how standpoint feminists have also emphasized the differences between women.

There is also a substantial feminist literature documenting the treatment of women in prison. In Britain, much of the critical feminist work on the contemporary treatment of the woman prisoner has been conducted by Pat Carlen who has sustained an interest in this topic since the early eighties.[77] Because of her unorthodox methodology, we will examine her work in the next chapter, when we consider the writing of the standpoint feminists. Lucia Zedner has also produced a prize-winning feminist analysis of Victorian attitudes to the woman in custody.[78]

Some critical thoughts on feminist empiricism

Feminist empiricism has added greatly to our understanding of the relations between women, crime and the criminal justice system. It has also received a good deal of critical scrutiny from other types of feminist. Some have objected to its tendency to treat the category of 'woman' as self-evident and so as unproblematic. Clear and obvious distinctions between the sexes which justify their treatment as two separate categories are simply assumed.[79] As we will see in the next two chapters, other feminists have paid far greater attention to the means by which the sexes are constituted as separate categories, refusing to treat them as brute facts of life, as pregiven or essential things in the world.

Objections have also been levelled at the tacit assumption of feminist empiricism that criminology has been ungendered (scientific) in its study of men but gendered (unscientific, guided by prejudice rather than by objective scientific evidence) in its study of women. This implication follows necessarily from the endeavours of feminist empiricists to apply universal (male) theories to women. For such feminist endeavours implicitly concede that criminological theory is satisfactory in relation to men but not in relation to women.[80] To obtain true objectivity, a goal which is implicitly conceded as a real possibility by the empiricist feminists, one simply applies scientific criminological research to both sexes.

A related objection to feminist empiricism is that it tends to accept men as the norm, as the human standard. It indicts criminology for its failures to treat women as equal subjects of study, as equal to men, the implicit demand being that women should be treated the same as men. Perhaps the clearest illustration of this assumption at work is the plethora of court studies which have compared the treatment of women with the treatment of men. Indeed, the entire chivalry thesis (the idea that women are accorded better, more chivalrous, treatment by the courts than men) and its rebuttal, turned on the question of whether women were treated the same as, or differently from, men, who represented the norm. Men were thus granted the status of universal subjects, the population of people with whom the rest of the world (women) were compared.[81] I know of no study which has posed the question of whether men are treated the same as women and thus established women as the human standard.

Similarly, the 'liberation thesis' posed a question which took men to be the norm. It asked if women were becoming more 'liberated' and so more like men, even in their offending. In this way, men were again constituted as the norm, 'the unproblematic, the natural social actor. Women [were] thus always seen as interlopers into a world organized by others'.[82] This then left unquestioned the effects of the maleness of criminologists and the maleness of their subjects.

Perhaps the principal shortcoming of feminist empiricism is its tendency to leave the rest of the discipline in place, unanalysed and unchallenged. It tends not to comment on the project and methods of the mainstream, that is, the way in which men's lives are documented and interpreted. The underlying assumption is that criminology is somehow competent and impartial when it is not dealing with women and so the gendered nature of criminal law and the criminal justice system remains unexamined. Feminist empiricism simply demands that similar scientific rigour and effort be applied to the study of women – that women be added to the criminological agenda. The empirical methods and the epistemological assumptions of traditional criminology are generally allowed to stand, as are its understandings of men. As Carol Smart explains, 'Under this schema, empirical practice is critiqued but empiricism remains intact. Such a perspective is not particularly threatening to the established order.'[83]

Traditional scientific methods are therefore accepted as the appropriate means of discovering the reasons for human behaviour (although a scepticism about the adequacy of these methods begins to creep in). This entails the retention of a distance between the feminist inquiring subject and the object of her study. Feminist criminologists therefore retain their role as inquiring, rational subjects in a world of objects of inquiry. As Smart observes, there may be greater sensitivity to the relationship of power between the researcher and her subject and a consequent adoption of ethnographic methods.[84] However, the idea of objective knowledge is retained: the epistemological stance of feminist empiricism is that it is possible to achieve a correspondence between theory and object of theory – between idea and the object of that idea, regardless of who is conducting the investigation.

Feminist empiricism, therefore, fails to ask about the significance of institutions which have been organized around men. It fails to ask 'What is man that the itinerary of his desire creates such a text?'[85] In fact such feminism (indeed this is true of most feminisms) tends to display little interest in the study of men as offenders or as victims on specifically political grounds. These grounds are that men have already had (and continue to have) so much time and effort expended on them. But, once again, this leaves the study of men to the men of the discipline who still tend to reiterate the conventional understandings of male crime and, most critically, to ignore the maleness of their subjects. In other words, a major problem with criminology proper is that though it is mainly about men, there is very little work done by men on men *as* men. As Judith Allen observes, 'Feminist criminology has been as much a prisoner as perpetrator of the discipline's longer-term disavowal of the place of men.'[86]

2

The Criminologist as Partisan

A good deal of criminology remains wedded to the empirical traditions of conventional science. Criminologists, in the main, are still committed to a style of science which places the inquiring subject at a distance from 'his' object of inquiry ('his' because these inquirers are mainly men). The objective scientist and the human object under inspection are quite distinct, and this distinction is considered necessary for intellectual rigour. In the last chapter, we saw the leading criminologists of the United States and of Britain applauding the continuing empiricism of contemporary criminology. Professor Bottoms, for example, was aware of the sheep who had strayed from the fold but felt confident that criminology was now back on a sensible course of practical fact-finding.

Though empiricism remains the rule rather than the exception in modern American and British criminology, there is nevertheless a long and respected parallel tradition of criticising precisely this style of dispassionate scientific scholarship. Some of the earliest research on crime in England conducted by Henry Mayhew involved the entry of the researcher into the world of the researched, though the sense was maintained of the social scientist as dispassionate observer.[1] In the early forties, with the publication of W.F. Whyte's *Street Corner Society*, American criminologists were exposed to a dramatically different way of conducting research into crime which was later to have its reverberations in Britain.[2] It was one which expressly rejected the idea of the impartial, scientific inquirer. Here, the researcher abandoned 'his' supposedly neutral role of expert observer and actively participated in the life of 'his' subjects. In order to learn about crime, the researcher explicitly adopted the viewpoint or standpoint of the offender.

This concern with the offender's standpoint represents an important epistemological shift. For one thing, it carries the necessary implication that direct involvement in a problem gives one the best understanding of it. It entails a rejection of the traditional view that the identity of the inquiring subject makes no difference to what is known and understood. On the contrary, where you stand in relation to the world matters very much to what you know and how well you know it. The Kantian theory that we all take in and process ideas with the same conceptual framework, regardless of our standpoint, is implicitly rejected. The reason that this rejection is implicit (and not explicit) is that direct links with philosophers of knowledge tend not to be drawn explicitly by criminologists. Criminology simply begins to reflect the shifts in thought which are occurring in the broader culture of ideas.

For Whyte, the adoption of the standpoint of the offender meant living for three years with the subjects of his study in an Italian slum on the East coast of America learning about life on the streets, in particular gang life and racketeering. The central characters of the story which emerged from this research were a group of young men: 'Doc', a heroic figure of street life, and his gang of boys. As Frances Heidensohn observes in her commentary on Whyte's research methods, 'Whyte's book is exemplary of its kind. He was both participant and observer and his account is sympathetic and analytical'.[3]

In Whyte's study, perspective matters. He implicitly assumed that who does the knowing affects what is known. By adopting the standpoint of the people most intimately involved in criminal activity, one acquired insights which were unavailable to the dispassionate and distant observer. Whyte gave us the lives of the boys of Cornerville with great effect. He humanized them and made sense of their lives. What Whyte failed to do, however, as he himself conceded, was to endeavour to give voice to the women and girls of Cornerville. For Heidensohn, 'the most important single thing about [Whyte's] work is that it marks the start of the long romantic attachment of sociologists of deviance to delinquents as heroes.'[4] The participant research methods of criminologists, such as Whyte, gave voice to the male offender but they did not do the same for the women who featured in their work. On the contrary, 'When girls do figure they are only observed through the eyes of . . . the gang and are not independent subjects.'[5] These women remain firmly in the place that more conventional social science located them. If women or girls appear at all, they remain the objects, rather than the subjects, of knowledge.

American sociologist and jazz musician, Howard Becker, also investigated the lives of men living on the edges of conventional society.[6] He was interested in the bohemians, the jazz musicians, the marijuana users of urban America. Becker's work was similarly premised on the notion that perspective matters, that one's place in the world affected what one could know and understand about the world. The best kind of knowledge of any given type of life came from those directly involved in it. While the criminologist adhered to his role of distanced scientific observer, he would necessarily remain oblivious to the most interesting aspects of deviance. Becker also believed that there was nothing essentially criminal or deviant about the criminal act. What really mattered was the power of the dominant social group to censure the acts of others by applying a criminal label to them. Crime, therefore, was better understood as a result of a process of labelling by those who had the power to do so. It was not an inherent quality of the criminal act. This labelling theory of crime was one which grew in importance and (as we will see in the next chapter) took on a new significance under the influence of the work of Foucault.

Like Whyte, Becker elected to enter the world of the deviant to find out how it worked by seeing it from the vantage point of those who lived there, from the viewpoint of those labelled deviant. Similarly, the method advanced by Becker to uncover the deviant experience was field research which required participant observation and also, for Becker, a positive moral commitment. In 1967 Becker posed the question, 'Whose Side are we on?' and opted to side with the offender.[7] As Colin Sumner observes, 'the very title of Becker's *Outsiders* expressed the . . . scepticism of a subterranean world he [Becker] had long been a part of.'[8] In other words, Becker was writing about himself as a man on the outer edges of society, as he viewed it. He was writing from his own personal standpoint. Sumner also remarks, in an admiring tone (one which he modifies later), that 'Becker expressed the spirit of defiance within social deviance and the commitment to disaffiliation from dominant values.'[9]

Becker did much to illuminate our understanding of life as, in some respects, an unorthodox American male. Again, this appreciative move towards the offender might well have heralded a more appreciative and thoughtful approach towards women. And yet the shift towards the standpoint of the male offender, and the desire to find value in his actions, entailed neither a reconstruction nor re-evaluation of the feminine. In his view of women, Becker remained highly orthodox. His endeavour to render the world-view of the male offender was predicated on the continuing exclusion of woman, and so the feminine in criminology was to retain its traditional negative associations. Thus, in his famous study of the lives of jazz musicians, Becker sympathetically revealed the 'outsider' status of the musician but then himself produced yet another class of outsiders: the women in the lives of the musicians.[10]

In *Outsiders*, women are there to represent the ties of conventional life. They are the unimaginative drudges of domesticity who fail to appreciate the artistic calling of the musician husband. In the following extract, Becker reports a conversation between Gene the drummer and Johnny the saxophonist. Gene says, 'Course, his wife wanted him to get out of the business. . . . [But] he'd rather be playing and it's a drag to him to have that fucking day job so why should he hold on to it?' Johnny replies, 'You know why, because his wife makes him hold on to it.' Gene responds, 'He shouldn't let her boss him around like that. For Christ sake, my old lady don't tell me what to do. He shouldn't put up with that crap.'[11]

Even on the rare occasions when women are referred to as musicians, rather than as wives, the viewing point remains that of the male musician, not the woman, and the man does not like what he sees. Thus, we are told of Eddie's suggestion to get a woman into a band. 'Well, you could have a sexy little bitch to stand up in front and sing and shake her ass at the bears [squares]. . . . And you could still play great when she wasn't singing.'[12] Becker offers no objections to this characterization of women. He is with the boys, not the girls. He is on the inside (paradoxically with the 'outsiders') and they, the women, are on the outside, shaking their asses but having nothing to say on their own behalf.

As Alvin Gouldner realized two decades ago, 'Becker's school of deviance is redolent of romanticism. It expresses the satisfaction of the Great White Hunter who has bravely risked the perils of the urban jungle to bring back an exotic specimen.'[13] We might add, in feminist vein, that Becker was the great white *male* hunter whose romantic flirtation with deviant culture had much to do with his own style of masculinity. He described the male-dominated world of the jazz scene, which he could slide into precisely because he was a man. This was a world whose attractions were peculiarly masculine in that they depended very much on the exclusion of women.

Across the Atlantic, similar concerns and loyalties were developing among British criminologists.[14] Many of the 'new deviancy' and cultural theorists of the 1970s set themselves against the men of the establishment (with their abiding faith in conventional empirical methods) and, despite an inherent problem of class difference, explicitly sided with and adopted the standpoint of the offender. The new deviancy theorists were white, educated, middle-class men endeavouring to give voice to their working-class brethren. Gouldner's idea of the 'Great White Hunter' observing and admiring the exotic clearly has purchase here too. The result was a host of studies which offered sympathetic accounts of the male offender 'from below'[15] and lent legitimacy to his criminal activities. As Phil Scraton explains, 'The search was for "social context" to define "delinquent action" from within the communities in which it occurred and to propose that the apparently mindless behaviour of boys could be part of the politics of "doing nothing".'[16]

The true sympathies of the new deviancy theorists could be inferred from the titles of their works. Howard Parker was most explicit about his loyalties in his *View From the Boys*. For other criminologists, there was a simple unthinking equation between working-class or bohemian life and the lives of men: one simply meant the other.[17] This point is nicely encapsulated in Heidensohn's observation about Paul Willis's *Profane Culture*: in the index 'the sole reference under "women" is "attitudes to".'[18] Women are cast only as the objects of male knowledge, not knowers in our own right, let alone knowers with men as our objects of knowledge.

Despite their good feelings towards the young men of their studies, one must question the extent to which they really ever got them right. The desire to impute rationality to the offender could just as well have been the projection of a male middle-class commitment to the value of reason of a certain sort.[19] It is, therefore, unlikely that these efforts of the new men of criminology to bridge the cultural gulf between themselves and the working-class offender were ever entirely successful. Certainly, there was no real sense of the criminologist going native, abandoning the privileges and cultural advantages of the academic male (and neither has this academic female). For example, Howard Parker's *View from the Boys* depicted young offenders who could make little sense of the criminal justice system. Parker himself emphasized the cultural distance between the sort of men who made the court room their place of work (judges, lawyers, police) and the young men brought before the law. The youthful defendants spoke of the intimidating effect of the courtroom, 'with the procedure quietly emphasising – you may not be guilty this time, but you're one of them, you look and speak like one of them and you'd better respect the court and take home your experience as a warning.'[20]

Nor was there necessarily a deep understanding achieved of the masculinity of young working-class offenders. The search for reason in the young male offender could easily be interpreted as a reflection of the value system of the academic male. In other words, the academics' desire to find rationality and purpose in the deviance of youth (despite its surface appearance of senseless crime) was possibly itself a desire to find in those youth the very qualities which the academic male still most admired in himself – intellectual reason rather than, say, animal spirits or something deeply alien, perhaps deeply different which could not be encapsulated in an academic treatise.

It is interesting to speculate about the thoughts of the corner boys as they encountered the criminologist. It is unlikely that the boys in the gangs, the street-corner lads, saw the world in the same way as their scrutineers. The academic life would have been profoundly foreign to them. Its sedentary nature, its preoccupation with words and theories rather than action, could well have been interpreted as unmanly, as effeminate – which is an interesting reversal of the standard scientific male's condescension (even when sympathetically inclined) towards the offender. In other words, the offenders' own sense of themselves was probably quite different from the official representations of them – which suggests the presence of a number of disparate masculinities all impinging on the criminological enterprise, though never clearly articulated.

Though they may well have got them wrong, the likes of Becker and Parker at least endeavoured to render their subjects faithfully. There were no such good intentions directed at women and girls. From the viewpoint of women, the new crime writing 'from below' did little for our understanding of female lives. It remained tightly focussed on the lives of men and boys, not of women, and thus it repeated the sins of its predecessors. (One important exception was Angela McRobbie's work on young female offenders.)[21] Women were once again on the outside, not the inside; they were offenders or deviants, wives or lovers or molls. The new deviancy theorists may have endeavoured to walk into the lives of deviant men. But the lives of women were to remain alien. Again, they were to be viewed at a remove, through the eyes of men, not through the eyes of women.

The new criminology

The emergence of explicitly Marxist writings on crime – in the late sixties in the United States[22] and in the early 1970s in Britain[23] – did little to alter the loyalties of male criminologists from the left. Although an important concern of this new writing was the economic, political and social structures which conduced to crime, what was variously termed the 'conflict',[24] 'critical',[25] 'radical' or 'new' criminology shared two important features with its predecessors. It remained firmly on the side of the (working-class) offender and it was concerned to give expression to the views of the offender in a manner which would render them rational and purposive, even political. In other words, the identification of the men of the left remained with the male offender.

American Marxist criminologist, Richard Quinney, for example, wrote of 'the everyday reality of the class struggle',[26] of the plight of the socially disadvantaged who pitted themselves against the powerful capitalists who constituted the true criminals.[27] The sympathies of the new radicals with the offender and 'his' plight and the concomitant desire to find rationality, indeed heroism, in the decision to offend are also made plain in *The New Criminology*. Here Ian Taylor, Paul Walton and Jock Young indicate their desire to strengthen criminology's sense of the offender as a rational social actor engaged in a process of positive change (rather than as someone passively labelled). For these writers, the offender has right on his side. In their own words, 'We have here shifted the focus away from the view of the deviant as a passive, ineffectual, stigmatized individual . . . to that of a decision-maker who often actively violates the moral and legal codes of society.'[28]

The new criminologists identified a two-tiered society. The truly offensive men were the capitalists whose harmful behaviour was beyond the reaches of the criminal law. As Russell Hogg explains:

> The genuinely harmful activities of the rich and powerful and those in positions of authority . . . benefited from the two faced nature of this system of justice, effectively escaping the reach of coercive intervention. . . . The political programme supported by these analyses tended to be one of abolitionism – the dismantling of coercive state apparatuses and the transcendence of the class society which gave rise to them.[29]

Working class offenders, therefore, were not the real criminals, but were to be regarded with sympathy and appreciation. For they were the true social critics. 'Deviance was now presented as a form of resistance by the ever-recalcitrant human spirit against the numerous structures of alienation.'[30] Again, we might question whether the new criminologists succeeded in taking the standpoint of working-class offenders, of seeing crime as they did. As Vincent Ruggiero has remarked, '[They] spoke on behalf of "criminalized" individuals who had probably never dreamt of appointing criminologists as their ideological representatives.'[31]

In the new criminology, the resisters were invariably perceived to be men, not women. The impact of crime on women had yet to be theorized. As a number of the critics of the new criminology were later to observe, the crimes of rape and domestic assault were either conspicuously absent from the new criminology's account of crime or documented in a largely uncritical manner.[32] Again, the desire to embrace the offender as outsider itself depended on the formation of another outsider group: it depended on the exclusion of women.

Shifting the viewpoint – from men to women

In 1985, Pat Carlen referred to 'the still dominant (and often ambivalently romanticized) conception of "crime" as an activity which is primarily the activity of males with an excess of masculinity'.[33] The effect of this male-centred view of crime was both to obscure the criminal injuries done by men to woman and to place the female offender in an untenable position. If the offender was a particularly masculine man, then the offending woman was of necessity a freakish female, or a would-be man. Carlen, like Heidensohn, criticized criminology for its identification with the offender as well as its characterization of women as the objects of the knowledge of offenders, rather than as subjects in their own right. Both argued that the offenders with whom the new criminologists sided were clearly men. They were men identifying with men; they were not describing or participating in the worlds of women.

For Carlen, the solution to this dilemma was to turn to women themselves and seek their own accounts of the criminal experience. She wanted to know how crime looked and felt if one were a woman. Explicitly, Carlen sought to invest the female offender with the sort of rationality and purpose which had previously only been found in the male offender. Carlen took an unusual step by making the 'criminal women' who formed the subject of her study literally the authors of their own stories. In the collection of essays, *Criminal Women*, Carlen generally takes a back-seat role as editor and places the female offenders to the fore. Their names appear not only as the authors of their own chapters but, more unusually, their names appear also on the cover of the book and on the title page. These 'criminal women' are the fully accredited authors of their own 'autobiographical accounts' of crime.

Carlen's explicit demand is that women be placed at the heart of the criminological project and allowed to become the knowing subjects of their stories. Carlen obliges us to view the world from the standpoint of the women whose lives we wish to understand. They, not us, become the authoritative speakers, the experts. In the opening story, for example, Chris Tchaikovsky talks directly to her reader about her likely misconceptions and sets out to disabuse her. For Tchaikovsky:

> Crime came in the shape of three ex-Borstal girls who had travelled to my home to pick fruit. But although these hardened three were the supposed bad influence upon me this supposition was untrue. It was their misfortune to happen upon a teenager who, bored rigid in the provinces, was ripe and ready to lead them into breaking their hard-won Borstal-licensed freedom.[34]

One of Carlen's stated purposes is to make us realize that the criminality of women is 'serious and intentional'. She wishes to lend dignity to the female offender by letting her speak for herself. An implicit message of her collaborative volume is that her co-authors, the 'criminal women', have the best insights into their own lives and their own offending. They are more expert than us (trained criminologists). Other feminists have taken further this idea of the woman's 'standpoint' and have suggested that the view-point of women provides a more secure grasp of certain aspects of reality, particularly the realities of disadvantage and political op-pression, than the standpoint of men. As Helen Longino explains, 'Feminist standpoint theory has been one of the most distinctive and debated contributions of contemporary feminist thought to the theory of knowledge.'[35] Its view of knowledge is that 'women (or feminists) occupy a social location that affords them/us a privi-leged access to social phenomena.'[36]

Standpoint feminism assumes a number of forms. It ranges 'from the romantic idea that women come, by nature or social experi-ence, to be better equipped to know the world than are men to the more modest proposal that a social science adequate for women must proceed from a grasp of the forms of oppression women ex-perience'.[37] Whatever its form, the intention is it to place women as knowers at the centre of inquiry in order to produce better under-standings of women and the world. As Sandra Harding observes, the adoption of the standpoint of women 'is fundamentally a moral and political act of commitment to understanding the world from the perspective of the socially subjugated.'[38] It assumes that the identity of the subject matters; the epistemological site of the woman 'from below' provides better insights into her condition. Thus, standpoint theorists endeavour to close the gap between the knower and the known. Their success at effecting such a closure, as we will see shortly, has been questioned by other types of feminist who doubt the very feasibility of such an endeavour.

To certain standpoint theorists, the value of drawing on women's experience lies in the fact that women are direct eye-witnesses to their own lives. They are reporters on their own experiences, telling their own stories. There is no expert intermediary putting a gloss on it, determining the shades of its meaning and its emphasis. Such feminism draws on the journalistic idea of reportage. A clear example of this style of scholarship is Blanche Hampton's book, *Prisons and Women*. This is an account of prison life for New South Welsh women as told by former 'inmates' and, so, has much in common with Carlen's British work, *Criminal Women*.

Hampton does not claim that it is because they are women that she and her contributors possess special, more accurate insights into the true nature of prison life. Her point is more circumspect. It is that direct experience is better than hearsay, that direct reportage is better than second-hand experience, and so to learn of life for women in prison one should talk to women prisoners. 'Grasping the realities of prison from the outside', she explains, 'is extremely difficult. Even those who work within the penal system are frequently blinded to what occurs around them by secrecy, subterfuge and something between the need to justify individual work practices and the need to believe in the "effectiveness" of one's work.'[39]

While criminologists might feel that they are recovering the truth about the criminal justice system through the application of scientific techniques, they are often poorly placed to do so. The reason is that the subjects of their inquiry do not passively accede to their interventions but often dissemble, fearing perhaps reprisals against family members, and, in so doing, elude the grasp of the criminologist, thus retaining their own separate and distinctive subjectivity. 'In this way, with the best of intentions, investigators gathering statistical evidence on prisons or interviewing inmates will almost invariably miss whole chapters of the penal story.'[40] Thus, Hampton herself shifts between a variety of roles and standpoints. She is an insider expert on prison life who reflects on the competence of the outsider expert (a nice turning of the tables). She is an expert on her own experience and a vehicle for other women to demonstrate their own expertise.

Hampton explains her project thus:

> Fearing a response of total incredulity, women prisoners are usually loath to discuss their experiences. . . . But who other than inmates have such an intimate understanding of Corrective Services and its policies, or lack thereof, with respect to women? Using this argument, I managed to persuade 13 other women ex-inmates to contribute their thoughts and observations on the major issues of prison and post-prison life.[41]

An important difference between the work of Carlen and Hampton is that there was no official criminological expert involved in the production of the Australian book. Although Carlen tries to get herself out of the picture as much as possible, she is still there as an important presence – the professional criminologist. Her influence can be felt at the beginning of the book where she supplies the introduction, which explains the book's purpose, and she is also a co-author of most of the chapters.

Because Blanche Hampton is herself a former prisoner, and not a trained criminologist, she does not encounter the same epistemological problems. She always speaks as a former prisoner (she cannot do otherwise), and she places her own personal biography in the same list as her contributors. Therefore, she can always speak with them rather than for them. As a consequence, she is always both subject and object, in the one person, never the dispassionate observer.

Hampton's declared mission is to alter our understandings of women prisoners (and hence of herself), and to challenge what she feels is the dominant view, which is that prisoners are 'uneducated and, by definition, unintelligent'.[42] Her tacit point is that criminologists have done little to correct these misperceptions. Not surprisingly, then, her tone is didactic. She questions the common view that, by implication, it is better having an expert explain women's lives within the criminal justice system rather than letting them do it for themselves. 'This book', she says, 'is not merely "testimonial" literature in which naive victims pour out graphic (if simple) descriptions of physical and psychological torture, although such descriptions are included. I like to think it is the result of 14 individuals with a common experience trying to make sense for you, the reader, of a penal system which is both vicious and extremely silly.' Hampton instructs her reader, 'As you will come to see, Corrective Services, as it stands, neither corrects nor serves.'[43] Her contributors document all aspects of prison life: arrest and interrogation, admission procedures, daily life in prison, health, families, sex and life afterwards.

Hampton's book serves several purposes. She does what she sets out to: she and her 'fellow' contributors document prison life with evident perception and considerable detail. They tell of the physical indignities, the shortage of information, the atmosphere of alienation and distrust, as well as the more mundane aspects of prison. It is a mine of information for the woman facing prison as it tells her what to expect – from an insider's point of view. Indeed, it sets up an implicit dialogue with other women offenders, thus granting to the woman criminal the subjectivity of a reader as well as author. The woman offender is talked to rather than simply talked about. Hampton also demonstrates the expertise of herself and her writers and so effectively shifts the status of the woman offender, from criminological object of inquiry to criminological inquiring subject. And yet the accounts remain direct, unpretentious, and not heavily theorized. It must also be said that, because Hampton eschews the role of the sceptical expert, these accounts of prison life are presented in a largely uncritical manner.

Paradoxically, the willingness of these prisoner/writers to expose themselves simultaneously disrupts the complacency of the reader, for we are led to see that what is ordinary in our lives is extraordinary in prison. What is mundane for us is precisely what is missing in prison life. Loss of personal identity does not depend on blatant abuse. Apparently trivial things, which we take for granted – such as clothing that fits – contribute greatly to our sense of our own dignity. For example, Elizabeth explains her reception into prison:

> I arrived in reception at 9.15 pm cold and ill from the journey in the meat wagon from Grafton jail. The only clothes left for me were size 10 and 12 and I was at that time size 18. I was told to 'make do'.... So I was thrown into the horror of remand with no clothes that would go on me except a dressing-gown which didn't meet in the front. I was left in that gown until ten the next morning after a night shivering with the cold, vomiting from car sickness from the trip down and covered in lice bites. Jail must be the most degrading and debilitating form of life for any woman.[44]

Standpoint feminism has also been used to highlight the injuries done to women as victims of crime. In some of the most disturbing writing, professional academic women have made themselves a part of the inquiry, describing their lives in an intimate and revelatory manner. Susan Estrich, for example, commences her book *Real Rape* with a vivid account of her personal experience of the crime and then of the criminal justice system. In *The Alchemy of Race and Rights*, Pat Williams examines perhaps the profoundest crime done to woman – her reduction to the status of property – through reflections on the slave contract of her grandmother. In a series of learned law papers, Martha Mahoney indicates her dissatisfaction with conventional understandings of domestic violence by revealing her own personal experiences of this crime and her own refusal to identify with the dominant view of the battered woman.[45] Each of these revelations carries a considerable impact, because the style of the confession is so unusual when undertaken by an academic. And yet, this is precisely how these feminists establish their peculiar authority to write about the topic. The idea of the uninvolved researcher is rejected as the researcher analyses herself and those similarly situated. Such feminism demonstrates the value of the role of victim as analyst of her own condition.

Standpoint feminism is by nature democratic. Its subversive potential does not depend on the academic credentials of the author – as Hampton made clear in her volume when she spoke of the expertise of her fellow prisoners. The writing of prostitute and writer, Peggy Morgan (not her real name), supplies a further example of such subversive feminism 'from below'. In 'Living on the Edge', which appears in a collection of prostitutes' writing about prostitution, Morgan talks about her life as an exotic dancer and prostitute.[46] She tells us from the start that we cannot tell her story for her because we are bound to get her wrong. She herself does not conform to type, and typing can itself be so misleading. (She is short and plump; a lesbian and a college graduate.) Morgan denies that she is a victim and that women outside the business have the moral edge. 'The fact is', she says, 'there's a livable wage to be made in the sex business, and we decide when, where and with whom we'll do it. Money talks, bullshit walks, and we don't have to put up with anything we don't want.' Morgan also claims to have a healthier view of her body than women not in the trade. 'Taking our clothes off in public, we realize there is nothing sacred or secret about our bodies. We don't have "private parts", dismembered from the rest; they are parts of the whole.'[47] Like Hampton, Morgan adopts a didactic style, seeking to work directly on the reader's prejudices, making the familiar unfamiliar, exposing the limitations of our own assumptions.

Hampton's book adopted the standpoint of the woman prisoner because she believed that the people who experience prison life directly are its greatest experts. To learn about life as a woman prisoner, you should talk to a woman prisoner. She therefore favoured direct, rather than second-hand, experience. This was also the message of Morgan. To other standpoint theorists, the reason why women should be given centre stage is not just that women have first-hand experience of their own lives. Rather, the larger epistemological claim is that women see the world more clearly, and more accurately, than those who view the world from other angles (that is, men). In short, women's expertise comes from being a woman.

This expertise is thought to be acquired in different ways and for different reasons. Many feminists are of the view that the angle 'from above', looking down, the angle from which the dominant class views the world, is one which provides a poor field of vision. Subjugation, and reflection upon that status, makes for a better appreciation of the world. To others, the source of women's superior insights is that they are thought to be mired in the facts of life; giving birth, getting their hands dirty, connecting emotionally with other human beings, nurturing others. In this view:

Women experience a lived reality of materiality, process, and change in the daily reproduction of life; a woman's 'immersion in the world of use', while a fact of her subjection, is also the condition which enables her to see more clearly the deeper reality of life.[48]

In other words, being close up to life, particularly in its oppressive forms, helps one to see better than when one is standing at a distance. As Carol Smart explains this version of standpoint feminism:

The epistemological basis of this form of feminist knowledge is experience.... Feminist experience is achieved through a struggle against oppression; it is, therefore, argued to be more complete and less distorted than the perspective of the ruling group of men. A feminist standpoint then is not just the experience of women, but of women reflexively engaged in struggle (intellectual and political). In this process it is argued that a more accurate or fuller version of reality is achieved. This stance does not divide knowledge from values and politics but sees knowledge arising from engagement.[49]

Women's view 'from below' is said to be superior because it supplies an understanding of both the oppressors and the oppressed.

It is a double vision, and binocular vision is considered better than monocular vision. For women must accommodate the needs of men and, in so doing, understand them. It is also said that women experience directly their oppression; they know and understand first-hand what it is like to be on the bottom. The view 'from above' is poorer because there are no incentives to understand the oppressed. Life is less problematic 'from above', so there are no reasons to discover other views. Indeed, 'from above' there may seem to be only one view – one which is regarded as neutral and objective – for there are no incentives to look down and see the lives of those living on the bottom. Maureen Cain summarizes this view:

> Women's bodies and women's life spaces make it easier for them to overcome the dualism between truth and falsity, subject and object, controller and controlled. . . . This overcoming is easier for women than for men. It is easier because their subordinate position gives them access to two worlds. In living they are forced to participate both in their own life world and in that of the dominant group.[50]

Clearly implicit in this feminism is the idea that women can acquire a more authentic, less clouded, view of reality. They can divine the truth better than men. There is, therefore, a certain romanticism and naiveté here about the nature of knowledge that other feminists have sought to challenge.

Criticizing standpoint feminism

A problem with advancing the standpoint of women, of demanding that women speak as women on behalf of women, is that of constituency. If I am speaking as a woman, and for women, on behalf of which women do I speak, or can I speak only for myself? And, if I think that I am capable of representing the experiences of other women, does this mean that there is some essential quality of womanhood which I can evoke simply because I am a woman? Am I therefore saying that all women are alike and so I can stand in for them? These are some of the dilemmas of standpoint feminism.

The problems associated with the assimilation of women into a single type ('woman'), or into a single voice (the 'woman's voice'), have not escaped feminists who have become increasingly concerned with the question of female diversity. Pat Carlen expressed this concern in *Criminal Women*, which she described as a book 'about four criminal *women* whose stories are important primarily because they deny the existence of the criminal *woman*. [her italics]'[51] Carlen also declared that:

> The essential criminal woman does not exist. Women who break the law come from all kinds of backgrounds though, as with male law-breakers, those women who land up in prison are much more likely to have come from lower socio-economic groups than from the higher ones.[52]

A. Brannigan has expressed this in a different way:

> The voice of women . . . is in fact, not a single sublimated voice, but a multivocality. Women do not form a class nor is their experience so common as to represent a coherent, all-inclusive point of view. Learning to listen to women raises a host of perspectives – women as victims of violence, women as agents of social control, women as censors and libertarians, women as heterosexuals, as lesbians, white women, coloured women, women as wives, parents etc. [53]

The most sustained analysis of the intellectual and political dilemmas associated with the notion of a single 'woman's standpoint' has been conducted by Elizabeth Spelman. In *Inessential Woman*, Spelman suggests that there is 'a paradox at the heart of feminism'. Feminist inquiry seems to possess a logic that demands that we treat women as a unity, for it is women as a group that forms the subject of our concerns. It is the collectivity of women whose interests we wish to represent and the iniquities of women's lives which draw us together, motivating us to engage in political action. But to treat women as an homogeneous group is to do women a grave disservice – to do something which does not work in the interests of all women. It is to erase the differences between women and so return to the sort of singular ideal of womanhood to which feminists first took exception, when men were doing the social analysis. From this it follows that the idea of writing from *the* standpoint of women is highly problematic.

Spelman also observes that the focus on the commonalities between women, at the expense of their differences, is to do a disservice to certain women, but not to others. The conflation of women in feminist theory has not produced a melting pot of different ages, colours and classes. Rather, feminists have extrapolated the condition of the most privileged type of woman – the white, the middle class, the heterosexual – to all women. As Spelman explains:

> It is not as if, in the history of feminist theory, just any group of women has been taken to stand for all women – for example, no one

has ever tried to say that the situation of Hispanas in the southwest-
ern United States is applicable to all women as women; no one has
conflated their case with the case of women in general. . . . This should
tell us that the 'problem of difference' for feminist theory has never
been a general one about how to weigh the importance of what we
have in common against the importance of our differences. . . .
[Rather] To bring in 'difference' is to bring in women who aren't
white and middle-class.[54]

The notion of *the* woman's standpoint, the suggestion that women
as a category possess a particular and superior view of the world,
is necessarily to select just one of the many viewing points from
which women look on the world, and then to impose that one view
on all. And, almost by definition, the woman who speaks for all
women is the woman who is least silenced, who is most articulate,
who is most advantaged. The woman who speaks for her sisters
colonizes them, assimilates them and shuts them up.

This point is well made by Marcia Rice about white feminist
criminologists. Although such criminologists have objected to the
'stereotypical representations of female offenders', they have had
little to say about 'black women and women from developing
countries'.[55] Rice suggests that black female offenders are 'the other
dark figure in crime'.[56] They have been included in neither 'black
criminology' (which is about black men) nor feminist criminology
(which is about white women). Having said this, Rice is concerned
that work on black women will be used simply 'to add an extra
edge to the victimization or offending patterns of women'.[57] Such
an approach fails to appreciate the significance of race for white,
as well as for black, women. That is, we all have a colour which
affects our lives in different ways, depending on whether our racial
group is associated with privilege or disadvantage. To fail to see
this is to reinstate the white woman's assumption that the problem
for women is always firstly one of gender, never one of race: that
race somehow comes afterwards as simply another layer of disadvantage and so is not always an integral dimension of experience.

We also need to bear in mind that categories of identity are always also relational in character, that they acquire their meaning
from their relation to that which they are not (as to be black is to
be non-white, the disadvantaged and repressed side of a binary
opposition) and also in relation to the other categories of identity
that constitute the individual subject. Thus, the black lesbian is not
simply a woman with double social disadvantage, but she also has
a particular intersection of identities that relate to each other in
quite particular ways.[58] In other words, we cannot take the idea of

'blackness' as a resting point, an unproblematic category with a self-contained meaning that can function in a pure way in order to assign identity. There is an important political reason for this continuing and vigilant scepticism about the constitution and stability of identity. 'Women who are aware that factors like race, class, gender, and erotic identity may be held against them are less likely to invest themselves completely in any single dimension and more likely to be attentive to the multiplicities within them.'[59]

The complex relations between race, gender and sexual violence have been explored by Barbara Omolade in an account of the case of Tawana Brawley, 'a fifteen-year-old Black girl [who] was discovered in an upstate New York community smeared with excrement and racial slurs.'[60] Although many expected this case to become a cause célèbre for the black community, Tawana Brawley refused to comply with the prosecution and say what had happened to her. In her paper, Omolade examines the reasons for Tawana Brawley's silence, and for the silence of black women generally as the victims of rape. They include the original right of the white slaver to the body of the black woman slave, the silence which continued to surround the rape of black women by whites after slavery, the black community's preoccupation with the lynching of men rather than with the rape of women in its own struggle against racism, and the ongoing denial of the rape of black women by black men. The black woman's history, she suggests, is one of layered silences. Omolade believes that 'only a black feminist political movement can enable black women to tell our story, in our own words, in a context that will bring justice and public vindication.'[61]

In their analysis of the film 'Thelma and Louise', Elizabeth Spelman and Martha Minow display similar concerns about the idea of white middle-class women representing the interests of other types of women, but this time focussing on the issue of class. 'Thelma and Louise' is itself very much a standpoint film. Louise saves Thelma from rape, by murdering her assailant, and then both flee the law. And we flee with them, egging them on in their illegal pursuits, for Thelma and Louise, we know, have little choice. Thelma is a flirt; they are uneducated women; they will not be able to convince a court that the act was justified. Female audiences, we are told, are known to cheer the outlaw heroines (while men are often offended by the depictions of men). The film portrays a number of misogynists from whom Thelma and Louise extract their revenge, but why do women feel so much satisfaction?

Spelman and Minow caution us to think carefully about our responses. Women might think they are operating within the standpoint of Thelma and Louise, but are they? Spelman and Minow suggest that the class of our heroines makes their status as outlaws 'more palatable to the middle-class audiences to whom the film is directed than if the heroines were solidly middle- or upper-middle class'.[62] And to drive home the point: 'One of the privileges of class dominance is to be able to admire what one sees as a courageous act without having to worry about the likely consequences of that act for the agent.'[63]

Spelman and Minow wish to draw our attention to the colonising tendencies of the woman-centred perspective, of the universal woman's standpoint, suggesting that, in truth, it can represent the viewpoint of privileged women. This is, in effect, an epistemological challenge to that brand of standpoint feminism that assumes that there is a prototypical woman's understanding of the world. Their argument is that knowledge (of women's condition) never resides completely in a single (female) knower, and that different knowers come to understand the world in quite different ways, depending on their location in the world. There is an explicitly political message in this. It is to ensure that the differences between women are recognized and respected. Different women have different subject positions, which create different world views that must be acknowledged and not subjugated. One type of woman, the most advantaged – that is, the white, middle-class, heterosexual – should not stand in for all women. For this is to repeat the sort of colonization or imperialism effected by the patriarchy (in which men speak for women).

As Christina Crosby observes, 'It is impossible to exaggerate the importance of the critique of feminism's (white feminism's) exclusions.'[64] But a further problem is that feminism's self-criticism often has not gone far enough. The problem of standpoint feminism is not simply one of a conflation of a multiplicity of female standpoints into a single one – the standpoint of the woman who is most privileged. The problem is also that standpoint feminism, even when transformed into the plural, tends to reject one form of essentialism only to adopt another. The unifying category of 'woman' is rejected as it is now appreciated that there is no essential quality to being a woman that unifies us all; and so we must respect the differences between women. But then those female differences are themselves endowed with certain essential qualities. There is, say, the essential experience of the black woman, or of the working-class woman, or the lesbian, or perhaps an essential quality residing in a permutation of these categories. In other words, there is the authentic, essential experience of the person whom this category describes. Knowledge fragments into a multiplicity of perspectives, each with equal epistemological value.

Put another way, once one has elaborated with sufficient specificity or particularity the site of knowledge (such as that of the black lesbian), reality can once again be apprehended in a direct, transparent manner.[65] True, one now acknowledges the limitations (or specificity) of one's knowledge of the world. But within one's specific site, the world can be apprehended authentically and clearly. From within this site, the individual knows their small piece of the world truly. As Crosby points out, this takes us from the question 'who am I?' to 'who are we?', but then tends to naturalize these differences between women. 'The problem is that differences are taken to be self-evident, concrete, there, present in history, and therefore the proper ground of theory.'[66] That is, social differences come to be regarded as brute facts.

A tendency to essentialize women's differences can be observed in the standpoint feminism of English criminologist, Maureen Cain. Cain rightly celebrates the new 'differences' approach. 'A triumph of the 1980s', she believes, 'has been that women have concerned themselves with differences from each other and with fractured identities, while maintaining a still recognizable women's movement. The identification of differences has led to sophistication, not to schism.'[67] But then she seems to suggest that, once one becomes sufficiently specific about the particular set of identities that constitute one's viewing point, about one's particular configuration of identity, then objectivity can reassert itself.[68] Thus:

> Black women in the West Indies are more aware of four centuries of denigration and oppression of blackness than they are of the problems of white women in Europe. What is important is to reflect upon a uniquely fractured site, reclaim it as a standpoint for knowledge and political work, and use this theoretical reflection to understand the relationships with other sites and standpoints.[69]

Knowledge is always partial, never complete, as it is always acquired in a manner that is limited and 'site specific'. Some things are known better from certain sites than from others. Objective knowledge is possible once one appreciates its limitations. However, this seems to set aside, as beyond analysis, the very concepts that are employed to piece together each complex identity creating a multiplicity of site-dependent realities. Thus blackness, for example, is more interesting as a pre-given means of constituting identity than as a particular cultural construct that obliges us to think about colour in a particular and political way. But, as Drucilla Cornell has explained:

> what 'black' signifies can only be understood through its asymmetric, differential articulation against whiteness. This is not a definition of blackness as the mirror opposite of whiteness, but as a signifier that only takes on meaning through the principles of condensation and displacement in which what is 'black' stands in for a whole series of negative metaphors associated with evil, and displaces very basic fear of otherness into the so-called reality of a color – black.[70]

In other words, the terms 'black' and 'white' are neither equal nor symmetrical. Rather, 'whiteness' derives both its value and its meaning from its ability to distinguish itself from 'blackness'. To be 'white' is to be not 'black' and it is also to be superior, more powerful, to have greater value. These are the long historical associations of the two colours and their intimate relation with each other. Or, as Kathy Ferguson remarks, we must always pay attention to the differences and instabilities within each claim to identity. These flow out of the fact that any given aspect of identity is never simply there in the world but is actively produced and negotiated through repeated social and political practices.

'Blackness', therefore, takes its meaning from the everyday repetition of mundane and ordinary acts which keep it in place. If we want an example, consider the depiction of sexual relations between people of different colour on television. Until recently, it never occurred; the first television interracial kiss can be dated.[71] Before that, every time a sexual move occurred on television, racial differences were implicitly policed, because it was always 'white' with 'white', or 'black' with 'black' (and incidentally man with woman, not woman with woman, in a similar policing of heterosexuality).

When we are vigilant to each constituting feature of identity (such as race, class, sex and sexuality), we then see that 'woman of colour and white woman become unstable categories, shaky representations, regulatory impositions concealing enormous turbulence.'[72] The categories of race and class as much as the category of gender 'are axes of power/domination/resistance'.[73] We must, therefore, always consider the manner in which each of these categories are produced, which is by force and imposition (for example, as a masculinist society imposes certain undesirable meanings on the category of woman) as well as by negotiation and by positive self-adoption (as, say, women renegotiate the meaning of 'woman' and adopt it politically as a basis of solidarity and organization).

Tamar Pitch provides a useful illustration of these standpoint problems of strategy in her account of the Italian feminist campaign to reform the law of rape. Pitch observes that Italian women deployed their shared identity (or standpoint) as 'rape victims' for certain political ends – in this case, to extend the rape law. Organising under the banner of 'victim' of rape, Italian women forged themselves into a political unit with a common collective experience that could then force legal change. But in the process of constituting themselves political actors (through their common standpoint as victim), these women simultaneously placed at risk that very group identity, for the success of their venture (the criminalization of rape) meant that once again they were separated from each other and reconstituted as individual 'rape victims' by a criminal justice system that (at present) can only deal with raped women as passive individuals who are not responsible for their victimization.[74]

Pitch does not believe that to claim the collective status of 'victim' is inevitably to lose 'full property of [our] grievances'.[75] In fact, she tells us how other victim organizations have managed to retain their political agency. Her paper stands as a warning, nevertheless, to feminists – that we must choose our collective identities self-consciously and strategically. Though we would press our own common understanding of a problem, in order to alter that which prevails, we are simultaneously always obliged to work within existing frames of meaning that are highly resistant to change and often antithetical to our aims. Pitch thus alerts us to the risks of the assimilation of women into a single standpoint, especially when that standpoint is not simply of our own creation.

As Christina Crosby says of standpoint feminism, 'What is foreclosed is the possibility of thinking differently about differences, yet that is precisely what is to be done.'[76] We must ask what the processes are which oblige us to think in terms of the categories that we do, when surely we could think in quite other ways. This requires us to examine the workings of all of our concepts, especially those that constitute our identity. How and why do these concepts compel us to think and act as we do? Or, to use again the Wittgensteinian metaphor, rather than simply looking through the frames of our thought, we need to examine the frames themselves. The assertion that there is now a multiplicity of frames through which we women look should not deflect us from the task of making sense of the frames. It just means that the task is a difficult one.

3

Examining our Frames of Reference: Realism to Derrida

One thinks that one is tracing the outline of the thing's nature over and over again, and one is merely tracing around the frame through which we look at it.

Wittgenstein, Philosophical Investigations

The concern of standpoint feminism was to shift attention from the criminological object (the criminal under the scientific microscope) to the criminological subject (the criminal as sentient being). More particularly, there was a desire to make women the subjects of their own criminology, to have women (in whatever capacity – as prostitutes, as survivors of rape, as prisoners) speaking for themselves, not to have others speaking for them. There was a move from the known to the knower. To standpoint feminists, the identity of the inquirer mattered, and the best sort of inquiry was conducted by the individual whose behaviour was in question. The conventional scientific stance of dispassionate neutrality, achieved by the apparent removal of the inquirer from the field of investigation, was thought to be a way of concealing the effects of identity. It obscured those aspects of the inquiry that drew their inspiration and understanding from the identity of the inquirer. It was also said to be a means of (the scientist) colonising the thoughts and actions of others (his subjects), of preventing people from speaking for themselves.

According to standpoint feminists, men and women saw the world in significantly different ways, and so it was important that women interpret their own behaviour. The differences between women were also a concern. It was said that, of necessity, women spoke from a variety of positions: the white woman, for example, should realize that she could not necessarily speak on behalf of the woman of colour (although often she had endeavoured to do just this). As a consequence, it was vital that (different types of) women be accorded a central role in criminology as the inquiring subjects of their own knowledge. The best sort of inquiry was forthright about the identity of the inquirer and what animated her research.

While standpoint feminists sought to reveal the diversity of womanhood, they did not necessarily examine critically the various aspects of female identity that were said to make one woman's perspective clearly distinguishable from another's. Cultural categories such as race, class and sexuality were, according to their permutation, said to be constitutive of perspective so that, for example, the white straight woman could not speak for the black lesbian. But those constituting categories which served to differentiate the community of women were often taken as a given. And yet, those categories themselves function in ways which are politically and ethically questionable.

Standpoint feminists also considered the means by which female understandings of the world had been repressed. In their view, it was through the power of others to define what constituted good research and so good knowledge. Power determined the ability of a class or group to extrapolate their point of view to the rest of the world and so silence those with different understandings. Standpoint theorists sought to undermine the conventional scientific (Kantian) view that knowledge was unitary. They also politicized the question of knowledge-formation, by suggesting that the impression of a unity of understanding was an artifact. It was the outcome of the positive repression of dissident views. Their work suggested that there was no one universal truth that could be discovered by science. Rather, there were dominant and subjugated knowledges.

To standpoint feminists, criminology's continuing preoccupation with the viewpoint of men was a function of power: (certain privileged) men as the (institutionally supported and funded) inquiring subjects still decided what mattered, what counted as good knowledge, and what they counted as good knowledge was still what (institutionally recognized) men thought. The new willingness of radical male criminologists to identify with the offender was but a shift to another male point of view in which women remained the objects of male knowledge. Because women still did not have the power to define the field of vision, women were once again relegated to the role of outsider, but this time by radical criminologists, rather than by the men of the establishment.

A fairly simple conception of power was implicit in much of the writing of the standpoint feminists. Power was that which was wielded by a particular group, in a conscious and instrumental fashion, to the disadvantage of other subordinate groups. Standpoint theorists had shifted the idea of power from the material to the epistemological. They suggested that power is not always a function of brute force or economic, or even political, advantage, but can also, and perhaps more importantly, take the form of the control of knowledge. It can involve the ability to impose one's understanding of the world on the world of others. However, the impression remained that (certain) men as a group had it all their way and were consciously manipulating the hearts and minds of others. The necessary implication was that (certain) men were somehow free themselves to define the world as they saw fit and in their own interests; that somehow they themselves were free from the constraining effects of social conventions (including the limiting forms and conventions of masculinity), and so could simply fashion the world in their own image to their own advantage.

Criminologists responded in at least two ways to the concerns of standpoint theorists. Some took up the point that crimes done to women were serious, and so it was inappropriate to identify with and romanticize the offender who inflicted them.[1] Thus, there was an apparent changing of sides, a shifting of loyalties. Others pursued the intellectual problems generated by standpoint theory, and so considered more carefully how categories of identity (such as sex, sexuality and race) are constituted, and how power relates to knowledge.[2] As Carol Smart observes, 'Feminism is now raising significant questions about the status and power of knowledge . . . and formulating challenges to modes of totalizing or grand theorizing which impose a uniformity of perspective and ignore the immense diversity of subjectivities of women and men'.[3]

Left realism and the return to empiricism

By taking the standpoint of women, by viewing the male offender through the eyes of the injured woman victim rather than through the eyes of male offenders, feminists encouraged criminologists of the left to take seriously crime and its injuries. The influence of feminism on left realism is explicitly recognized by one of its most prominent exponents, Jock Young. For Young, it 'constantly undermined the notion that fear of crime is largely irrational and without basis'. It was also 'morally entrepreneurial in its exposure of not only domestic and sexual violence, but in the areas of child physical and sexual abuse.' Young does not stint in his praise of feminism. It was, in short, 'the major contributor to the contemporary radical practice of exposing the invisible victim.'[4]

Thus is hailed a return to the sort of realism associated with empiricist criminology, but with a new set of concerns and sympathies. The manifesto of the left realists is that they accept the claims of feminists (and working class people) that crime is harmful and criminologists should help to eradicate it. They should get out of their 'ivory towers' and participate in the development of practical crime prevention policies. This is a return to the realism of the empiricists, but with a new mission. As Sharyn Roach-Anleu explains:

> Left realists criticise all previous criminology for being offender-centred and argue that the Marxist criminologists of the 1970s ignore the victim of illegal behaviour and present the perpetrators as victims of capitalist economics, disadvantage and unjust criminal law enforcement. They argue that crime is a real problem which is not reflected in officially collected data.[5]

Some of the young Turks described by Bottoms in his inaugural lecture, the Marxist-inspired criminologists of the early 1970s, therefore underwent a change of heart. Now under the banner of realism, they admitted that they had been insufficiently critical of the working-class offender. As Jock Young puts it, there had been a tendency 'to idealise oppressed groups and an inability to see anti-social behaviour and divisions within them.'[6] Feminists, they said, had shown them this 'dark' side of crime: as serious injury rather than as protest. Thus 'left idealists' (a label self-applied critically after the fact) transmogrified into self-identified 'left realists'.

The left realists describe themselves as empiricists. Their concern is to produce firm objective facts about crime victimization, especially as it is experienced within the working-class. Left realism is therefore responsible for a host of victim surveys conducted in some of the poorer parts of Britain.[7] Although left realism is mainly associated with British empirical work on crime victims (specifically designed to inform policy), its influence has also been felt across the Atlantic.[8] This is perhaps unsurprising given the current preoccupation with practical questions of law and order in both Britain and America, a preoccupation which has been repeatedly expressed by the Presidents of the American Society of Criminology.[9]

Left realists have produced a neat formula for the scientific explanation of crime. It comprises a 'square of crime' made up of offender, victim, state and society. According to Roger Matthews and Jock Young, '"crime" arises at the intersection of a number of lines of force' which connect each of these variables.[10] Or, as Young has observed, 'rates of crime are by definition a result of the interplay of actors and reactors: of victims and offenders, on one hand, and of formal and informal control, on the other.'[11] By studying the interaction between these variables, realists suggest that they can remain 'faithful to the nature of crime'.[12] Their approach, they suggest, is superior to that of their scientific forbears (who placed only the offender under the microscope) because it takes into account all of the dimensions of crime, it gets at crime in its 'totality'.[13]

Realists say they are sympathetic to feminist accounts of crime, but their approach is oddly naive. They suggest, for example, that although there might be some quibbling about the precise definition of crime, 'All groups . . . abhor violence against women.'[14] Violence against women is therefore used to demonstrate that there is a basic consensus about the meaning of crime: that crime is therefore a generally-agreed-upon-thing in the world which is susceptible to scientific measurement and explanation. Common sense dictates that we all basically see it in the same way, with only some disagreements at the margins. This ignores the fact that many men obviously derive positive pleasure from the depiction of sexual violence directed at women, witness the content of a good deal of pornography.[15] It also ignores the considerable feminist literature that has demonstrated the highly contested nature of the meaning of rape, one of the most analysed violent crimes against women. [16]

The legal definition of the crime of rape does not depend on the harm done to women but on the man's understanding of that harm. (I will return to this problem in chapter 4.) A woman who has non-consenting sex is only a raped woman if the man appreciates that she is not giving her consent[17] and, as feminists have repeatedly shown, often a man's perception of sex is very different from the woman's. The criminal law does not consider it a crime if a man proceeds with intercourse believing, no matter how unreasonably, that he has the woman's consent. Many feminists regard this as unacceptable for it suggests that the law does not condemn violence done to women from the woman's point of view. It only condemns the violence if the man appreciates the abhorrent nature of the conduct but proceeds anyway.[18] (It should also be said that some legal jurisdictions have responded to these feminist criticisms by seeking to provide a definition of rape that better reflects women's understanding of the crime. This will be discussed in chapter 4.) Feminist analyses of the crime of rape, therefore, serve well to demonstrate the disputed nature of the 'reality' of crime, not its consensual nature.

A related point has been made by Alison Young and Peter Rush. They suggest that left realists invoke the concept of the universal victim to establish a common concern about crime. The idea is that 'We are all victims now', and so it is thought to be legitimate for realists to join the fight against crime that was once considered the politically dubious preserve of the right. But in the process, the features of the victim blur and she loses her specificity, even though one of the major stated concerns of the realists is with the criminal victimization of women. The victim of crime could be anyone because anyone can be victimized.

However, there is already an incipient masculinity in this characterization of the typical or universal victim, and the typical crime. For 'the exemplary event . . . is street assault, which the realist understands as the minimal unit for the offender-victim dyad'.[19] This is the 'archetypal' interaction between offender and victim. For the realists, 'Assault is "a purely coercive act" which may occur "in the street, in a public house, or in some other public venue".'[20] It follows that assault is not domestic violence, although domestic violence is the form of assault that a woman is more likely to experience. Rather, domestic violence is one of the many other special classes of victimization. Again, we are reminded of Jonathon Culler's observation about the standard and the atypical case: public assault (which a man is most likely to experience) is the standard case;[21] domestic violence is the complication.

Left realism's preoccupation with crime in the public arena reduces the significance of crimes against women, and especially domestic violence, in yet another way, according to Young and Rush. It suggests that the proper object of concern is crime whose public nature offends and threatens local residents or passers-by. Authentic (usually working-class) victims are those decent citizens who do not give their consent to crimes occurring on their streets, such as drug-dealing or assault. Underlying this analysis is the old liberal assumption that only with public actions is consent required and able to be withdrawn. In the realist analysis, domestic violence almost seems to emerge as a victimless crime, precisely because it is embedded in the private sphere that is 'always-already articulated' with the consensual.[22] This underlying assumption is not only objectionable to feminists; it is also a curiously outdated view of private violence which has increasingly become the object of government attention. For example, in South Australia, domestic assault now carries a more severe maximum penalty than assaults of a public nature.[23]

The place of women in realist criminology is deeply traditional. Women are there to receive special protection, because they are considered especially vulnerable to crime, but their experiences are never allowed to set the defining conditions of the realist project. The realists' gaze never shifts from the 'unmarked'[24] man of the streets, and so women never appear as more than a special instance of victimization. The typification of crime (as street crime) employed by the realists, as Young and Rush suggest, implicitly gives the victim a male character, though that characterization is never made explicit. It is simply built into an analysis that takes street crime to be the paradigm case of crime.

The purported inclusion of women in the realist analysis, however, enables the realists to establish their radical credentials. Because they (say they) take crimes against women seriously, they must therefore be responding to the demands of feminism. But, in truth, it is difficult to discern any sustained engagement with feminist theory. In realist writing, feminist theorists are rarely referred to by name.[25] Feminism is merely a vague incantation; it is never treated as an extensive and detailed body of theory and knowledge that demands considerable application if it is to be deployed with proficiency and conviction.

An important illustration of the mistreatment of feminism by realists is to be found in some of their (slight) writing on the crime of rape. According to John Lea, rape is a 'crime of passion' which is concentrated 'among the poor and deprived and can be seen to arise from dynamics of relative deprivation'.[26] I suspect most feminists would wish to dispute him on every point: that it is appropriately regarded as a crime of passion (rather than cold-blooded sexual violence), that it is a crime of the poor (and not of the middle class), and that it is to do with relative deprivation (whatever that means).[27] And though they profess an interest in women, and their understandings of crime, left realists do not seem to respond to what women say about crime even in their own investigations. As Martin Schwartz and Walter DeKeseredy have remarked, 'Left realist discussions of fear of crime never make it explicit that women's fear of crime as found in victimization surveys is very closely connected to a fear of men. There are not only class problems to be considered when looking at women's fear, but the power and privilege given to men in a patriarchal society even within a particular class.'[28]

A major omission from the writings of realists who express a sympathy with feminism is any interest in the connection between men, masculinity and crime. The maleness of crime, and the maleness of those who study it, are again put to the side. One is, therefore, prompted to ask the very same question that was put to their empiricist forbears: 'What are the mechanisms ... whereby these men are able to evacuate questions of their sexuality, their subjectivity, their relationship to language from their sympathetic texts on "feminism", on "woman", on "feminine identity"?'[29]

Power and knowledge

> There is nothing mysterious or natural about authority. It is formed, irradiated, disseminated; it is instrumental; it is persuasive; it has status, it establishes canons of taste and value; it is virtually indistinguishable from certain ideas it dignifies as true, and from traditions, perceptions and judgements it forms, transmits, reproduces.[30]

To standpoint feminists, there was a vital link between men's power and the ability to control the viewing point of criminology and so define what counted as good knowledge. These concerns about the connection between power and knowledge were taken up by other criminologists, feminists and non-feminists alike. Much of this new work was explicitly influenced by the French philosopher Michel Foucault and his extensive writing on the constitution of knowledge and its relationship with power.

One way to appreciate the distinguishing features of this new work on power/knowledge (this is Foucault's conjunction of terms) is to compare it with what had gone before. For the empiricists, as we saw in chapter 1, the acquisition and application of knowledge was politically neutral. The role of scientific inquirer could be adopted by anyone and the same results would turn up. The adoption of rigorous scientific method to a problem, such as crime, would result in a discovery of the true causes of, and appropriate solutions for, that problem. The criminologist as scientist was siding with no one; he was an impartial and neutral man of science conducting experiments that any good researcher could replicate.

For the standpoint theorist, sides mattered. Criminologists had obscured their partisanship by calling themselves scientists. The criminologist as scientist had traditionally sided with the agents of the law and the state against the offender. This had led to a failure to appreciate the viewpoint of the offender, and a consequent tendency to regard the offender as either irrational or overdetermined.

American criminologists such as Whyte and Becker, and the British theorists 'from below' set out to remedy this; they took sides with the (male) offender and showed how the world looked from the perspective of the powerless and the marginal. They also made an important epistemological point. They said that crime was not an intrinsic evil that could be analysed and understood by the methods of science. Rather, crime was a constituted thing, a label applied by one group to another group. Positive power was said to reside in the application of the criminal label by powerful individuals to powerless individuals.

The workings of power were also a concern of the American and British Marxist criminologists (the new or radical criminologists) who identified a positive class struggle between the agents of the law (and the interests they protected) and the criminal class.[31] Crime was an epithet applied to forms of dissident behaviour that were thought to threaten the ruling class and its interests. Such criminologists, therefore, also saw a need to take sides. With both the standpoint theorists and the Marxists there was a sense of a free-standing, self-defining class of self-interested individuals who held power and wielded it, in an instrumental fashion, to their advantage. An important part of this authority was the ability to define a troublesome person as criminal, or to ensure that the viewpoint of the powerful was the prevailing or only apparent viewpoint. Other perspectives were suppressed.

A tendency in much standpoint theory was to give epistemological priority to the insights of the subject 'from below': to say that how she saw the world was how it really was, and that, 'from below', she in fact had a better grasp of reality than those who viewed 'from above'. This was true of the progressive male criminologists, such as Becker, as well as of the feminist standpoint theorists who objected to their masculinism. Immersion in the deviant culture or, better still, allowing the offender or victim to speak for herself, was thought to produce better criminological insights than could the distanced, dispassionate observer.

A second proposition advanced both by standpoint criminologists and by the 'new (Marxist) criminologists' was that the insights of the subjugated – the troublemakers – were somehow truer than those of the dominant class. Those who thumbed their nose at the system – Becker's American jazz musicians and bohemians, the British youth who revolted against the establishment through style, the social rebel of the new criminologists – as opposed to those who mindlessly conformed, could see more clearly than others. They saw life as it was and responded to what they saw with rationality and purpose (even though their protests might prove to be ineffectual). Their view of life and their response to it was somehow more authentic; it was truer to reality.

By contrast, the Foucauldian theorists of power/knowledge suggest that neither 'the powerful' nor 'the powerless' are free from the constituting effects of knowledge. Both are immersed in already-existing frameworks of thought out of which neither can simply step. Neither group can have a direct, unmediated grasp of some true authentic reality – to which the criminologist can have recourse through observing the correct, appreciative methods or by simply listening to the offender. As Foucault put it in *The Order of Things*, 'if there is one approach which I do reject . . . it is that (one might call it, broadly speaking the phenomenological approach) which gives absolute priority to the observing subject.'[32] The Foucauldian view of power/knowledge also entails an explicit rejection of the kind of power described by the new criminologists of the early seventies. They saw power as something possessed by certain individuals (capitalists) and positively wielded over others (the working class).[33] This could take the form of direct economic power of the capitalist over the worker, or the more devious ideological power of the capitalist to convince the worker that the capitalist's interests are identical to those of the worker (when in truth they are antithetical). For Foucault, power was not a coercive instrument deployed in an instrumental fashion, but rather that which constitutes our very framework of thought:[34]

> To Foucault, power and knowledge are inseparable. Humanism, good intentions, professional knowledge and reform rhetoric are neither in an idealist sense the producers of change nor in the materialist sense, the mere product of changes in the political economy. They are inevitably linked in a power/knowledge spiral: forms of knowledge such as criminology, psychiatry and philanthropy are directly related to the exercise of power, while power itself creates new objects of knowledge and accumulates new bodies of information.[35]

Power and knowledge have an intimate relation. It is power through knowledge that determines how we come to see things as we do, that establishes our norms, and neither 'the powerful' nor 'the powerless' are free from the constituting effects of power as knowledge. Power is imbued in conceptual systems, including the very idea of what we are as human subjects.

The account of male power implicit in much of the feminism described in chapter 1 is that men as individuals, and as a class, exercise power over women because men possess greater strength

– physically, politically and materially – and so can organize their world in their interests. This is a fairly static view of power in which men as a group are portrayed as generally possessing the resources to dominate women. We may contrast this with the Foucauldian account of power in which it is never fixed and stable and simply in the possession of an individual or group (say in his wallet or in the strength of his fist). Thus interpreted, power is not a thing permanently held by, and within the possession of, any one person or class that is deployed in their interests in a direct and unidirectional manner against another weak or powerless individual or group. Rather, power is more fluid. It moves around within relationships and its effects are felt not by people being bent to the will of others, but through the actual constitution of our thoughts and behaviour.[36]

We can illustrate Foucault's view of power (at least, as I interpret it) by seeing how it might work in relation to me as a female legal academic and my dealings with my students. A benefit of this example is that it demonstrates that male power over women is by no means a uniform or monolithic thing. It should also be said at this point that Foucault did not himself theorize the effects of gender on power, or power on gender, though feminists, as we shall see, were to do so. When I am counselling a student in my room (say he is male), I operate within a relationship of teacher to student, and whether I positively will it or not, these relations constitute me as the more powerful one within that relation. In this situation, I am cast as the expert. The student is the uninitiated outsider whose understandings are accorded less weight than mine, or none at all. I have institutional backing for my authority in the sense that I operate within an elaborate scheme of conventions (within the law school, within the university, across the disciplines, within the broader community) that ensure that what I say about the law is authoritative; what I say (generally) constitutes the truth of law because I am an appropriate mouthpiece for legal statements. I can impose my understandings and disqualify those of my student. I can silence him through direct disagreement, by quiet scepticism, or by simply refusing to listen to his account, because there is nothing which obliges me to do so. I can also encourage him to believe that there is no other way of seeing things and my institutional authority will help me to carry conviction.[37]

This disparity of power between my student and me may manifest itself in gesture (the way we sit, how we talk to each other, who leads the conversation, by how we look at each other), but more significantly it operates through understandings: our understanding of ourselves and our relationship to each other (which is the reason we are sitting, talking, and so on, in the way we are), and our understanding of the field of knowledge into which I am initiating the student, because I am the authoritative one.[38] Neither of us may be positively aware of all this happening. Whether we like it or not, we both operate within these institutional positions whose meaning is determined before we even assume them – and regardless of whether we reflect critically upon their meaning. I cannot overcome the inequalities that inhere in the relationship simply by an intentional act of my will, because I am already constituted within this position before I ever exercise my will – although my interventions may serve to counteract some of the worst effects. Thus, I am both shaped by, and (may endeavour to) shape, the relationship and its effects.[39]

The fact that I am a woman, as well as a teacher, and my student is a man, is likely to complicate further the relation and how power operates within it. It may, for example, lead to unconscious (or conscious) resentment in the student (because it is socially inappropriate that I as a woman am the more powerful person), and the student may, therefore, try to test me in a manner he would not contemplate with a male teacher. My understanding of our field of knowledge (remembering that what it means for me to be a teacher is part of that field) may convince less, may seem more open to challenge, because I am a woman. Thus power circulates between us, fashioning our thoughts and our gestures.

All this is not to suggest that the student and I are consciously acting parts, that we are somehow quite separate from the roles which we slip on, like cloaks, for the purposes of the situation. Rather, it is to suggest, in the Foucauldian view of it, that we both live and act through our understandings of what it means to be a student or a teacher in our society. And we do not ourselves invent these understandings but acquire them from our culture, which has determined them for us in advance. Thus, the understandings or meanings of these two parts, teacher and student, in a sense, precede us. This, to add a further qualification, is not to say that we cannot reflect upon our understandings of these roles: teacher and student. They are not so completely scripted that we simply think and act programmatically as teacher and student. Constantly, we are having to invent, as the situation develops between us, in both old and fresh ways. These complications, which always call for invention, are such things as our other identities (our race and age, for example, and the cultural meanings which attach to them), which add further dimensions to our relationship.

The different tensions set up in the relationship I have described require imagination in the way they are handled. As Foucault explains, 'The individual is an effect of power, and at the same time, or precisely to the extent to which it is that effect, it is the element of its articulation. The individual which power has constituted is at the same time its vehicle.'[40] That power is a dynamic thing, shifting between individuals and groups, also suggests that it is always subject to change. Its natural momentum can be pushed along different lines of direction, different lines of force. One can work on it, as it works on us. It makes possible the sort of manipulation of the cultural meaning of 'man', 'woman' and their relation with one another, which are undertaken in the second part of this book.

My example should also serve to illustrate the specific and local nature of power that was also emphasized in Foucault's account. To understand how it works in all its complexity, we need to get down to the level of the particular, rather than the general, for the workings of power depend on a multitude of factors that keep shifting, as first one person or group, then another, gains ascendancy. Say, at one moment I am a woman with a man, at another a teacher with a student, at another a colleague with a colleague – but then still a woman with a man. It is no longer acceptable, in the Foucauldian view, to talk generally about power used instrumentally by one group over another, as this distorts and simplifies the more complex nature of power.

This Foucauldian view of power as working within individuals and their relations with each other, as constituting their thoughts and deeds in the very moment that they deploy it, is why we cannot turn to any given subject, or group of subjects, to gain the direct and unvarnished truth of crime – as certain standpoint theorists seemed to think we could. It reveals the problem with the form of standpoint theory that says that the correct understanding of the world resides with the individual who is the eye-witness – for that subject's sense of herself as a subject, as an onlooker to the world, has already been constituted for her by the world she then apprehends. No subject is free from this prior constitution that affords the individual her very sense of herself as an individual with a particular view of the world she inhabits – that is not to say that she is incapable of reflecting on her position in the world. As Alec McHoul and Wendy Grace explain:

> Foucault thought of the human subject itself as an effect of, to some extent subjection. 'Subjection' refers to particular, historically located,

disciplinary processes and concepts which enable us to consider ourselves as individual subjects and which constrain us from thinking otherwise. These processes and concepts (or 'techniques') are what allow the subject to 'tell the truth about itself'. . . . Therefore they come before any views we might have about 'what we are'. In a phrase: changes of public ideas precede changes in private individuals, not vice versa.[41]

In short, neither the powerful nor the subjugated are free from the constituting effects of conceptual systems. Neither has a direct access to an authentic pre-conceptual or pre-social reality that the criminologist can tap into to acquire the truth. Conceptual frameworks order the thoughts of all – no one is free from them – and so represent power in its most potent form. They discipline, assign, define, control and cast certain individuals as insiders and others as outsiders, though from moment to moment, the insides and outsides can shift, as I showed in my illustration. At one moment, I am an authoritative lecturer (an insider), at another, a woman who is constituted as subordinate (an outsider). But I am never outside the schemes of representation which designate, from moment to moment, what is within and what is without. This is not to suggest that we can do without these schemes of meaning, since meaning always works by classification, designation and distinction. The important thing is that we reflect on the workings of meaning, not that we dispense with it (which would leave us with nothing to say).

Conceptual frameworks, therefore, tend to work to the advantage of some and to the disadvantage of others. Indeed, an important part of the feminist political project has been to show how Western concepts tend to work by repression and exclusion of the specific 'knowledges' of certain groups of people. In a statement on what he called 'subjugated knowledges', Foucault made clear his commitment to their resuscitation. He referred to:

a whole set of knowledges that have been disqualified as inadequate to the task or insufficiently elaborated: naive knowledges, located low down on the hierarchy, beneath the required level of cognition or scientificity. . . . It is through the reappearance of this knowledge, of these local popular knowledges, these disqualified knowledges, that criticism performs its work.[42]

The qualification of female understandings of crime forms the subject of the second part of this book.

Criminology and the discipline of the offender

In *Discipline and Punish: The Birth of the Prison*, Foucault employed the theme of power/knowledge in an account of the institutions of criminal justice, especially the prison, but also the institution of criminology, and, not surprisingly, it is this work which has been most influential among those criminologists who have taken up his ideas. *Discipline and Punish*, as its sub-title indicates, is a social history of 'the birth of the prison', but, in the course of his story, Foucault directs his attention to criminology and the part it has played in effecting a fundamental shift in the forms and the objects of punishment, away from the chastisement of the body of the offender and towards the control of his mind.[43] In Foucault's account, the discipline of criminology emerged in the nineteenth century (along with a number of other disciplines of knowledge) in order to effect discipline in the other more conventional sense. Criminology helped to discipline the criminal, not through the beating of the body (the old method), but by putting him under the criminologist's scrutiny – through explanation, observation and analysis. By endeavouring to explain and classify the offender, criminology could control his very thoughts. This was a more effective, more insidious form of power than the pillory and the stocks, which were only applied to the physical form of the offender. Thus, criminology was one of the new knowledges which served to alter the very nature of discipline in the modern West. Social control now took the form of a 'body of knowledge' about the person, rather than the manipulation of his anatomy.

Foucault's interpretation of disciplinary power as ever-expanding, and as assuming ever more indirect insidious forms of control of the mind,[44] was to be adopted and developed by a number of criminologists. It was perceived by some as a means of interpreting the shift away from formal justice (which occurred from about the late sixties) and the associated development of a range of alternative, informal and community-based mechanisms to deal with the offender. Stanley Cohen, for example, employed a Foucauldian account of power/knowledge in his influential book, *Visions of Social Control*. Here (and elsewhere), Cohen explained the paradoxical nature of the various 'decarceration' and 'destructuring' moves occurring in America and Britain. Ostensibly, they were intended to be a diminution of state control over the offender; but, in truth, they represented an extension and diversification of state knowledge and control over offenders who were now caught up in 'wider, stronger and different nets'.[45]

Other criminologists drew on Foucauldian reasoning in order to pursue further historical work on the nature of punishment. For example, in *Punishment and Welfare*, David Garland offers an erudite history of British penal strategies (focussing on policy changes effected in the Victorian period) that engages with Foucault, endorsing some aspects of his theory (his 'conception of knowledge ... always sees it in relation to power'[46]), and disputing other parts. Garland's *Punishment and Modern Society*, a critical study of social theories of punishment, contains a thoughtful exposition of Foucault's idea of disciplinary power that also suggests that Foucault has overstated the case. In Garland's view, Foucault pays insufficient attention to the various forms of resistance and opposition to disciplinary power, for example, by lawyers and judges.[47]

More recently still, Garland has emphasized the role of criminologists in offering a reply to power. In defence of modern criminology, Garland now argues, against Foucault, that criminology has set up its own 'counter-discourse' against 'these very themes'.[48] Foucault's interpretation of criminology as always complicit in the disciplinary practices of the state ignores 'the character and range of criminology', and its supposedly more critical and self-reflective nature.[49] This is a more sanguine view of the modern discipline than the one adopted in the present volume, for criminology has yet to reflect on its masculinism.

While Garland has helped to familiarise British criminologists with some of the work of Foucault, mainstream American criminology has been barely affected by Foucauldian thought. As Schwartz and Friedrichs have recently observed, such continental influences have only 'begun to touch criminology' in the United States.[50] However, on the critical fringe of the American academy, Stuart Henry and Dragan Milovanovic have written extensively on their own particular approach to the study of crime that clearly displays the mark of Foucault.[51] Their self-styled 'constitutive criminology' is difficult to characterise, partly because of the opacity of its exposition, partly because its constituting ideas perhaps have yet to be clearly realised, but also because of its curious eclecticism. Henry and Milovanovic endeavour to blend the realism of the left realists, the Marxism of the 'new' or 'critical' criminologists and the interpretation of power offered by Foucault. Given the doubtful compatibility of these different approaches to crime, this does not always make for a happy marriage of ideas.

On the one hand, Henry and Milovanovic seem to be suggesting, in Marxist fashion, that economic structures formed by the logic of capital (they call it 'capital logic') determine the fate of the individual.[52] Also in Marxist mode, they contend that 'law is created by classes or interest groups to maintain or increase their power'[53] and that '[c]rime is the expression of power'.[54] At this point their criminology appears to be pure instrumental Marxism. But then they endeavour to complicate their account of power by suggesting that the economic and social structures, which oppress, are the products of our imagination, which we can therefore reimagine. They are 'discursive practices . . . imaginary constructions . . . producing a particular image claiming to be the reality'.[55] And still further, 'These texts become the semiotic coordinates of action, which agents recursively use, and in so doing, provide a reconstruction of the original form.'[56] Here, Henry and Milovanovic seem to be drawing on the work of Foucault, but casting it in a rather different form.

While Foucault interpreted power as a discursive practice, he did not deny the reality of power. For Foucault, dominant forms of knowledge had perfectly real (and often oppressive) consequences. As Marxist materialists, however, Henry and Milovanovic evidently are not persuaded that the life of the mind can have real effects. It is the economy that is real, while our understandings of the world – our 'imaginings' – can never be truly constitutive of reality. So while they flirt with Foucault, at heart Henry and Milovanovic seem unconvinced by the Foucauldian account of power as knowledge, preferring an oddly-adapted Marxist formulation of power and its relation to crime.

Still another variant of Foucauldian criminology has been developed by British criminologist, Colin Sumner. In his work on 'social censures' (Sumner's term for the various disciplinary mechanisms which define and stigmatize deviant individuals and distinguish them from the morally acceptable), Sumner has generally remained loyal to Foucault but chosen to blend his conception of power with aspects of Marxist theory in order to produce a critique of the capitalist state.[57] Sumner, however, takes issue with Foucault in one important respect.

What Foucault failed to see, according to Sumner, was the highly gendered nature of power/knowledge – how it operates on men and women, and on the masculine and the feminine, in quite different ways, to produce different bodies and different understandings of the subject. It must also be said that the gender dimension of power/knowledge hardly featured in the work of Cohen, Garland, Henry and Milovanovic. Though these criminologists developed the ideas of Foucault in interesting ways, they generally failed to see that the operations of power/knowledge might vary according to the sex of the subject. Therefore, once again, the 'man question' of criminology was to remain muted. It was left to the feminists to consider the implications of these new continental ideas for the very constitution of men and women.

Feminism and Foucault: the regulation of womanhood

A substantial feminist literature has incorporated the insights of Foucault, especially his analysis of power/knowledge, while remaining sensitive to the fact that Foucault himself was not strong on the 'woman question'; it barely features in his writing. This insensitivity to the effects of gender on the part of Foucault (and some of his major exponents in criminology) is perhaps surprising given his preoccupation with the workings of power. It seems that Foucault himself could not get beyond the constituting effects of his own maleness and masculinity to reflect on its workings.[58]

Sumner suggests that the disciplinary power theorized by Foucault was distinctly masculine in character, though Foucault himself did not see this. It was 'rationalistic, militaristic, scientistic', entailed 'the social censure of homosexuality and effeminacy'[59] and, therefore, 'the censure of men who had "contracted the softness, habits and inclinations of women"'.[60] It was 'rooted in the economic conditions, political needs and ideological categories of dominant-class men'.[61] This gendered power, according to Sumner, was both positive and negative in its operation, both productive and repressive. It involved the censure of the feminine and was, consequently, negative and repressive in its workings.[62] But it was also positive in the sense that a specific masculinity was integral to the formation of the character of the modern state. What Sumner refers to as 'hegemonic masculinity',[63] that is rationalistic, scientific and militaristic masculinity, 'is part of a positive movement in thought and political economy, not simply an effect of the negativity of censures.'[64]

The production and the censure of the feminine have been examined by a number of feminist criminologists. The early writing of Frances Heidensohn on the social control of women by women – especially as mothers bringing up daughters – employed both themes, even though it was not explicitly indebted to the theory of Foucault. Recall from chapter 2 that Heidensohn described women as mothers both as controlled and controlling. They themselves were controlled by the strictures of domesticity, which set the limits of maternal life; but, at the same time, they exercised maternal

control over their daughters, by socialising them for the same con-
stricting role. Thus were women implicated in their own oppression. Heidensohn's work functions as a salutory reminder of the
dangers of idealising or romanticising women, of casting women
inevitably in the role of passive and innocent victims of patriarchy.
Her message is that the experience of women is more complex
than this, that in the one moment women can be both oppressors
and oppressed.

In her own contribution to her edited collection, *Regulating Womanhood*, Carol Smart considers some of the ways in which English
criminal and civil law, as well as the medical profession, defined
and understood women in terms of their reproductive practices
and sexuality in the latter part of the nineteenth century.[65] Smart
specifically examines the activities of infanticide, abortion, birth
control, baby farming and prostitution, and tells an elaborate tale
of state and professional repression (and production) of women.
Her focus, she says, is 'on discursive constructs/subjects and the
complex ways in which discourses of law, medicine and social
science interweave to bring into being the problematic female subject who is constantly in need of surveillance and regulation'.[66]

In Smart's account, women were deemed to be in need of greater
or lesser regulation depending on such factors as class and marital
status. Thus, some women were deemed to be more dangerous
and unruly than others. For example, it was the unmarried mother
who was singled out for specially punitive attention in relation to
the crime of infanticide. This suggests to Smart that the state was
less concerned about the welfare of babies than with the sexual
practices of the woman who had no man to support her. State
intervention in the working-class woman's practice of baby farming is also regarded by Smart as at least partly animated by a
desire to keep such women out of public life (because work and
babies were incompatible, as they are still today).

According to Smart, the legal and medical professions constructed
woman as they regulated her (and the regulation itself served also
to construct). For each intervention was based on certain supposi-
tions about the nature of women (assumptions that were also often
class dependent) and about women's sexed bodies. Because women
were taken to possess an unruly biology, certain interventions were
required to render them docile. As views changed about what made
women's sexuality problematic, so did the interventions.

Smart refers repeatedly to the resistance of women to these disciplinary discursive practices but does not fully elaborate the means
of this resistance. She asserts that 'the desired docility is not always

forthcoming as the continuing struggles over abortion, contracep-
tion, childcare and sexuality testify.'[67] We are, however, left wanting to know more about the ways in which women themselves
seized the means to define and redefine themselves in ways which
they found truer to their own sense of themselves. We are told that
women 'practised the agency of constructing [their] subjectivity as
well'[68] but we do not really discover just how this was achieved.
Smart's emphasis is (understandably) on the power to define and
so regulate, rather than on the power to resist.

Another example of feminist criminology which draws on the
ideas of Foucault is Anne Worrall's, *Offending Women: Female Lawbreakers and the Criminal Justice System.* This is a small but detailed
study of the various ways in which the agents of the law (judicial,
welfare and medical) seek to contain and control the female offender
by classifying, defining and so domesticating her behaviour. Worrall
observes of the legal profession, for example, that 'Its unspoken
goal is the "normalization" of the defendant through a process
which packages and re-presents the defendant as a coherent unity
which is recognizable by the magistracy'.[69] The impression to be
conveyed to the court is that these are 'normal, feminine women'.[70]
Like Smart, however, Worrall is unhappy with the idea that women
are fully defined by such professional discourses. She wishes to
incorporate the idea of female resistance into her analysis. However, her tendency is to emphasize the themes of the control and
construction of the feminine, rather than the means by which women
manipulate conventional conceptions of themselves.

Worrall locates female resistance in passive evasion and partial
non-compliance with officials such as probation officers. These
women remain 'nondescript', partly accommodating, displaying
only a muted anger. Many are 'not seeking to break out of the
ideologies that confine them to domesticity, sexual passivity and
sickness'. They are only trying to alleviate the worst effects of an
oppressive gender role, often by turning them to their own advantage.[71] And yet, the principal message we receive from this book is
that the orthodox classifications of femininity mainly serve to limit
and confine women; that there is precious little room to manoeuvre
within the strictures of the feminine.

My final example of Foucauldian feminism comes from Australia. In *Offending Girls*, Kerry Carrington employs the themes
of power/knowledge to explain how certain girls come to be
officially defined as delinquents. In this account, greater attention is
given to the fragmented, fluid and dispersed nature of disciplinary
power theorized by Foucault. Carrington wishes to emphasize the

complex and diverse workings of power, and is especially critical of the sort of feminism that depicts male power over women as direct, monolithic, coercive and repressive.[72] She observes that girls are not invariably subjected to the sort of moral policing identified by Chesney-Lind (see the discussion in chapter 1), for questions of class and colour complicate the matter. Often, it is not the girl herself who is being policed, but rather her vulnerability to male sexual abuse within the family (especially if that family is defined as incompetent and troublesome), and that intervention in the family may well be for the real good of the child, even though she is still the one who becomes the physical target of welfare intervention. To Carrington, there is no one source of discipline; it emanates from schools and families, from men and from women (as Heidensohn also stressed), and the result is not necessarily a programmed orthodox female. We are told of the girl who 'flouts the norms of adolescent femininity and chastity', but does not end up before the court.[73]

In short, there is no simple linear relationship between socially inappropriate behaviour in girls and the imposition of patriarchal (or maternal) disciplines, and, equally, the various disciplinary powers do not necessarily produce conforming feminine girls. Carrington's work is, therefore, perhaps more suggestive of the possibilities of resistance and change than that of Smart and Worrall. Carrington makes more of the Foucauldian idea that power/knowledge is neither simply repressive nor unidirectional. Rather, it is uneven, fragmented, contains internal tensions, and never works to a single effect. And yet one is still left wondering about the means by which young women ever develop distinctive and different understandings of their own, in view of the many forces lined up against them. These themes of resistance and change are also pursued by the Derridean feminists.

Feminism and Derrida

Foucault examined the workings of power at many levels. He considered how power operated positively to generate meaning, including people's very sense of themselves, through institutions, through bodies of knowledge, through classification – none of which were mutually exclusive. Feminist criminologists who drew on his ideas about power and knowledge focussed on the subjugation of women through various forms of state institutional power that defined, classified and constrained. It was the power to discipline, through classification, that was the particular concern of such feminists. Feminists under the influence of Derrida sharpened the focus on the workings of language – how it limits the way we think, and how it also provides the means of change. Textual analysis now consumed their efforts. What the two types of feminist shared, however, was a common desire to elaborate the limits of meaning and to find ways of transcending those limits. As Foucault himself explained:

> the question of knowing if one can think differently than one thinks, and perceive differently than one sees, is absolutely necessary if one is to go on looking and reflecting at all . . . what is philosophy today . . . if it is not the critical work that thought brings to bear on itself? In what does it consist, if not in the endeavour to know how and to what extent it might be possible to think differently, instead of legitimating what is already known.[74]

Derrida (in common with the later Wittgenstein of *The Philosophical Investigations*) stressed that we are always already immersed in a text, in a language, which supplies the very conditions of meaning.[75] It orders our thoughts and is the vehicle for their expression. In other words, by the time we get to thinking critically about our place in the world, who we are and what we want from the world (or, as feminists, who we are as women and what we want our lives to be like), we are already thinking in terms that have been supplied for us by the world that we wish to reflect upon (easily demonstrated by the fact that I have already been obliged to think of myself as a woman, with all the connotations associated with that term, even before I reflect upon the meanings of that term).

This approach necessarily entails a rejection of the empiricists' idea of a pre-linguistic world out there, outside ourselves, that can be studied at a distance by scientists/criminologists who are essentially interchangeable (their identity or place in the culture does not matter, so long as they are schooled in scientific method). The reason, as Wittgenstein made clear, is that we are always already present within a given network of social meanings, that no plate glass separates us from the objects of our concern (as the empiricists thought), which means that we are also always having to use those categories of meaning to explain them. As one interpreter of Wittgenstein explained it:

> there isn't any point of view from outside the language games where we can, so to speak, stand back and appraise the relationship between

language and reality... [we cannot] get outside of language to look
at the relation between language and reality from the side and see
whether or not language is adequately representing reality. There
isn't any non-linguistic Archimedean point from which we can ap-
praise the success or failure of language in representing, coping with
or dealing with the real world. We are always operating within some
language game or other.[76]

As a consequence, there is no way of making sense of the world
without language, and the language we acquire to enable us to
understand the world and to communicate with each other itself
creates the world. To use the jargon, culture is already encoded in
language and we are always obliged to use language to understand the world. As we acquire a language, so we absorb a particular appreciation of the makeup of the world. Thus it is that language
does not give us direct access to the world. Rather, language itself
divides up the world and invests it with meaning in quite particular ways. Different cultures divide up the world in different ways.
Within any particular culture, it is not possible to reinvent the
meaning we give to words according to our whims, for otherwise
we would make no sense. (Indeed the very way that I framed this
question, the very question itself, was a cultural product. It presupposes that there is such a thing as an individual subject who is a
meaning-maker – a very Western world view.)

It follows that our obligation as social analysts is to try to understand how our language games work. In a sense, we are always
interpreting ourselves – our own frames of reference – and so it is
quite impossible to get ourselves out of the picture, as the empiricists thought we could. Wittgenstein, himself, put it this way: 'A
main source of our failure to understand is that we do not com-
mand a clear view of the use of our words.'[77] Culture embedded in
language supplies the frame through which we look at the world.
To understand concepts such as 'woman', we must understand
their place within language and their histories. To speak as a woman
is therefore inherently problematic given that women have not
invented the meaning of 'woman'.

Though Derrideans acknowledge the constraining effects of concepts embedded in language, they also make much of our ability
to reflect on those concepts and so effect change. The reason why,
in the Derridean view of it, meaning is never fixed and change is
possible – in fact, always happening – is that meaning is metaphorical and works in a 'relational' manner. 'Simply put', as Drucilla
Cornell explains, 'the subject, including the masculine subject,
cannot be frozen into its gender role precisely because of the

performative aspect of language inherent in an understanding of language as a system of differences. It is always possible to play out gender roles differently.'[78]

What does Cornell mean when she says that language is 'a system of differences' that does not allow for closure? The idea of language as a system of differences or as 'a play of differences' has been most famously expounded by Jacques Derrida. In *Positions*, he says, 'The play of differences supposes, in effect, syntheses and referrals which forbid at any moment, or in any sense, that a simple element be present in and of itself, referring only to itself.'[79] That is, concepts are always referential or relational; they always take their meaning from something else. 'Whether in the order of spoken or written discourse, no element can function as a sign without referring to another element which itself is not simply present.'[80] The Derridean view of language may be contrasted with the conventional account in which it is supposed that what we mean precedes the formulation of our thoughts into words. Derrida, in common with the later Wittgenstein, accords to language a critical function in the determination of what we can and do think, and therefore say.

What Derrida is proposing is that language enables ideas rather than names them. The order of existence of ideas and language is not idea, then language, but rather language and then idea. Moreover, language enables ideas in a manner that makes for a great deal of fluidity and instability in meaning. For, language works by way of distinctions and differences, what Derrida refers to as the play of differences. The idea that language works by differences can perhaps best be understood by some simple examples. Here, Margaret Davies offers a demonstration of meaning-making through linguistic differences (which also shows that those distinctions determine how we understand the world: that there is language, then idea). Thus:

> 'Sheep' is defined in contrast to 'mutton' and 'lamb', and further opposed to 'cow', 'dog', 'hat', and so on. If the English word 'mutton' did not exist, then we might use 'sheep' to refer to what we eat. 'Sheep' is limited as a concept by 'mutton'. The concept associated with the word 'sheep' is derived purely from all the things which it is not. If without knowing English, I were to be given fifty sheep to look at and told in each case that the object is a 'sheep' and I am then confronted with a duck, I might also call it a sheep, because I would not know which concept – animal or sheep – corresponds to the object. Similarly if confronted with fifty sheep, and told they are all 'animals' the duck might get called an 'animal' or it might not.

I would have no way of knowing whether this was the appropriate word. I will only know if the sheep is systematically contrasted with other animals, mammals contrasted with non-mammals, and animals contrasted with plants, or inorganic matter. The system of classifications arises from a system of contrasting uses of words . . . . Thus concepts are a product of the oppositions in language, not of pre-existing ideas which just have names attached to them.[81]

Again, this account of language is to be contrasted with the conventional view of language in which it captures concepts in a positive, essential and fairly stable manner. On that understanding, language is a matter of naming, attaching labels, to that which already exists and so creating a taxonomy of things in the world. The implication that has been drawn out of this view of language as a system of differences is that meaning is never self-contained and complete, but is always referring onwards to something else that serves to define it, to give it its boundary of meaning.[82] Any term, such as the term 'man', therefore depends for its meaning on that from which it is conceptually distinguished, that is, 'man' depends on 'woman'. According to Derrida:

Whether in the order of spoken or written discourse, no element can function as a sign without referring to another element which itself is not simply present. This interweaving results in each 'element' . . . being constituted on the basis of the trace within it of the other elements of the chain or system.[83]

That which is pushed outside a concept is necessary to it. The inside (of the concept) depends on the outside (of the concept). Thus, to return to our illustration: the meaning of the concept of 'man' is neither pure nor complete in itself. Rather, it takes its meaning from that which it excludes from its meaning, from that which it distinguishes itself from, and that is 'woman'. The sex 'man' establishes its meaning by the boundary it sets up with what it is not: 'woman'. It is thus dependent on that which it excludes, and so always carries the trace of the excluded other, which is the logical and necessary condition of its meaning.

The political significance of understanding the interdependence of terms becomes apparent when we examine, yet again, the conceptual operation of the terms 'man' and 'woman'. For it transpires that their conceptual relation is not an equal one, but rather one which operates as a hierarchy. It is a binary opposition in which the term 'man' is regarded as the dominant, superior term, while the term 'female' is thought inferior; it is that which is positively cast out and excluded from the male term precisely because it is deemed inferior. This is a common way of organising concepts in Western thought, that is, in oppositions in which one side of the opposition is accorded greater value and the other is regarded as something lesser, or as the negative to the other's positive nature (think of reason and emotion; light and dark – an opposition which has been criticized by black theorists of language; culture and nature; mind and body).

Derrida tends to call such oppositions violent in the sense that the dominant term represses, excludes and denigrates the other. As Derrida explains, 'in a classical philosophical opposition we are not dealing with the peaceful coexistence of a *vis-à-vis*, but rather with a violent hierarchy. One of the two terms governs the other . . . or has the upper hand.'[84] It is only our failure to think differently, the snare of language imposing restraints on our thinking, that makes the present negative meaning of 'woman' (the female negative to the male positive) appear essential, inevitable and indivisible: 'our "belief that the picture forced a particular application upon us" consisted in the fact that only one case and no other occurred to us.'[85]

Deconstruction as a means of thinking differently

If meaning works in this manner, how is change achieved? The strategy favoured by feminists, under the influence of Derrida, is that of deconstruction. While explaining the approach to language adopted by such feminists, I have simultaneously endeavoured to deconstruct the conceptual opposition 'man' and 'woman' (a process I will continue in chapter 4 when I consider its operation within the crime of rape). I have suggested that the term 'man' should not be regarded as essentially dominant and self-contained; that, in truth, it takes its meaning from the term 'woman' that can now no longer be regarded as outside the concept of man, but utterly central to it. Viewed thus, both terms change because it transpires that neither are what they first seemed.

This strategy (or intervention into the workings of language) of deconstruction has been described by Derrida as 'a double gesture . . . a double writing. On the one hand, we must traverse a phase of overturning.'[86] That is, we must reverse the conventional order of terms in any given binary opposition. To turn again to our example, we must give priority to the usually subordinate term, 'woman', in the opposition which is man/woman by asserting the vital nature of the normally subordinate term, that is how it supplies the founding condition of the dominant term. But we must not stop at a simple reversal of the usual order. For, 'to remain in this phase is still to operate on the terrain of and from within the deconstructed system.'[87] In addition, 'we must also mark the interval between the inversion, which brings low what was high, and the irruptive emergence of a new "concept", a concept that can no longer be, and never could be, included in the previous regime.'[88] Once we appreciate the interdependence of the two terms, neither retains its original character, for that original character depended on a suppression of this interdependence of meaning.

Deconstruction thus reveals that the concept of 'man' is neither positive nor essential but rather functions through a process of distinctions, by contrasts, inclusions and exclusions. For example, male reason has always obtained its definition by way of an implicit contrast with the unreason of women. Equally, male vigour and potency has been contrasted with (and has set its limits against) the feminine condition of passivity. Deconstruction reveals that the term 'man' is always marked by this trace of its other: what it is deemed not to be, that is 'woman'. 'To deconstruct the opposition, then, involves showing how the "lesser" term is in fact absolutely essential to the "higher" term ... we cannot theorise ... "man" without "woman". .... Rather than being marginal then, the subordinated term in an opposition becomes central.'[89]

This is not to discard the terms 'woman' and 'man'. Deconstruction is not destruction, but rather a means of observing the manner in which terms work. 'To call a presupposition into question', as Judith Butler has observed, 'is not to do away with it; rather it is to free it up from its metaphysical lodgings in order to occupy and to serve very different political aims.'[90] The deconstruction of a concept, such as 'man' or 'woman', is not a negation or jettisoning of that concept:

> on the contrary deconstruction implies only that we suspend all commitments to that to which the term ... refers, and that we consider the linguistic functions it serves. ... To deconstruct is not to negate or to dismiss, but to call into question and, perhaps most importantly, to open up a term ... to a reusage or redeployment that previously has not been authorized.[91]

The inversion does not simply put what was low in the place of what was high. It also alters our appreciation of the original hierarchy and this altered understanding is the new concept. The original relationship (of dominant man to subordinate woman) ceases to appear natural and inevitable. We can observe that it was/is held in place in a political not natural manner. We see the dependency of the dominant term on the subordinate term, and we also see the damage done to the subordinate term in the very construction of this opposition. The idea is that after deconstruction we can no longer see the original term in the same manner – as autonomous, as essential, as positive.

Deconstruction, feminism and criminology

In the remainder of this chapter, I wish to consider the work of two feminists who have specifically employed the technique of deconstruction in their accounts of political protests, aspects of which came to be defined as criminal. One is describing (and deconstructing) the media representation of the protest of a group of British women against a Cruise missile base at Greenham Common, England. The other recounts her own involvement in a similar, though shorter-lived, protest which took place at Narrungar missile tracking station in South Australia.

In *Femininity in Dissent*, Alison Young studies the 'information coded within the news stories' on the women of Greenham Common.[92] She suggests that a series of 'dichotomies' were deployed to undermine and trivialize their protests. Contrasts were drawn (often implicitly) between the good woman and the evil hag, the sane and the mad woman, the reasonable and the hysterical, the clean and so pure woman and the squalid, the wholesome and the defiled, the heterosexual and the lesbian, between us and them, and invariably the protesters were associated with the undesirable side of these antinomies. The journalists who were sent out to report on the protest often understood implicitly that their duty was to entrench these divisions, to demonstrate the unreason of the women, and to represent them as the undesirable and, therefore, excluded other. To Young, the often unconscious mission of the reporters was to restore the order threatened by women being and behaving out of place, and the reporters did this by setting up a boundary between us (the good, the clean and the reasonable) and them (the dissident women who represented the forces of darkness).

The women of Greenham Common employed measures designed to counter and subvert these divisions and distinctions, according to Young. By leaving their 'homes', where good wives and mothers belong, and setting up all-women camps outside the base, they refused the conventions of orthodox heterosexual femininity. Young reads much into the women's protest. By casting themselves before military traffic, by protesting naked, by chanting and dancing, she feels that they defied the strictures of the clean, pure and passive female body. They blurred the distinction between the active male and the inert female. Conscious of the media depiction of themselves as hags, witches and hysterics, they parodied and 'overblew' these representations. They invested them with different, positive meanings, seeking to revitalize the idea of the witch by 'citing her independence, her resources of knowledge and her healing skills'.[93] In Young's account, they registered their dissent in a manner that was both literal and metaphorical. They endeavoured to convert the excluded and reviled into the valued and respected, reversing the usual dichotomies, and setting up new distinctions.

A point stressed by Davies is that considerable effort is needed to maintain the boundaries and distinctions which characterize Western thought. She suggests that the processes of exclusion which we customarily employ to define persons and institutions are unstable and keep breaking down. The boundaries between man and woman, black and white, us and them, are insecure precisely because there is such an intimate relation between each side of the opposition. Thus, for man to maintain his defining masculine qualities, he must work constantly to distinguish himself from the feminine, and when women (such as the Greenham protestors) refuse to accede to their place in the opposition, greater effort is called for still. According to Young, such women must be reviled as not-real-women, as witches. They must be distinguished from the acceptable face of woman who knows her proper place in the sexual opposition.

In her own personal account of the Narrungar protest, Davies also deploys the Derridean idea of the conceptual opposition. 'The whole experience', she reports, 'was a succession of barricades and frontiers, of insides and outsides, and of the collapse of the distinction.'[94] There were the police and the protestors, there was law and disorder, the wholesome and the clean. For Davies, the real challenge for the protestors was to resist these dichotomies. Though she felt the protestors were perceived as filthy outsiders, efforts were made to bridge the gulf between those who guarded the perimeter fence and those who sought to break through it – to bring the outside within. 'For instance, engagement with a police officer as a real person [was] a way of refusing the "otherness" which the police/activist division sets up.'[95] The positive (and alternative) order established within the peace camp also refuted the conventional distinction between the lawful and the lawless. For within the group that resided outside the fence and so outside the formal law, there was still law.

The limits of deconstruction

Deconstruction is an intervention into the workings of language designed to reveal the limits of concepts we often treat as unproblematic and so use unthinkingly. Delimitation of meaning is revealed to be an effect of exclusion. That is, concepts establish their limits by differentiating themselves from that which they are not (as 'man' defines himself against 'woman'), and, as a consequence, concepts are never autonomous and self-contained. They always contain an implied reference to that which they are not, to that which in truth contains them. Deconstruction exposes the problems which reside in the endeavour to keep meaning pure, to say 'just this' and not 'that', because 'just this' always depends on 'that' which it is not.[96]

Derrida, in particular, has devoted himself to a deconstructive reading of major philosophical texts, identifying the problems that inhere in the endeavour to close-off meaning. As David Wood has observed, 'Derrida's philosophical method is unashamedly second order. The core of everything he has written is a commentary on, reconstruction, analysis, dislocation of . . . another text . . . there are for Derrida no philosophical problems outside textual elaboration.'[97]

This preoccupation with the limits of textual meaning could well be regarded as a limit to deconstruction itself, for the concern seems always to be one of unravelling, of undoing the concepts that shape and constitute our thought processes. Of lesser concern are the robust economic, political and legal structures that help to keep that traditional meaning in place and make it appear natural and inevitable. This is especially true when we are talking about relations between the sexes. There are powerful institutional reasons why many continue to think that 'man' is quite naturally the dominant and more important term, even when deconstruction reveals the dependence of that term on 'woman'. As Richard Bernstein has pointed out, and 'Derrida himself acknowledges', Derrida's analyses, 'need to be supplemented by the theoretical and empirical study of societal institutions and practices'.[98] Deconstruction may do some of the job of effecting change, but alone it is insufficient to undo the institutional systems that have been built upon, and that help to sustain, the economic and political power of men over women.

In the second part of this book, a range of strategies will be used in an effort to think differently about women, men and their relation to crime. My debt to all the feminisms examined so far will soon become apparent. In addition, I will draw on literary and historical work on women and crime, which transcends the usual disciplinary boundaries of criminology. However, I will also make use of the strategy of deconstruction, despite its limitations, because it is a powerful means of revealing the instability of meanings that appear natural and so immutable. Even such apparently basic and original categories as that of 'man' and 'woman' are susceptible to deconstruction and, of course, this is of considerable import to feminists of all political and intellectual colours.

This short history of criminology has identified a largely uncritical approach to gender identity among members of the discipline. Consistently, criminologists have treated the concepts of 'man' and 'woman' as natural and given, the unproblematic starting point of any scientific study of crime rather than interesting objects of inquiry in their own right. But, in truth, these concepts are neither stable nor self evident. 'Man' is not a fixed, positive and essential term (a litany I will continue to repeat), but has been constructed within an opposition (with 'woman', the opposite sex) that always makes it dependent on that which it is said not to be. Every criminological reference to man's character has, therefore, by necessary implication, entailed a reference to woman's. Similarly, every reference to 'woman' has said something about 'man'. Each time a shift has been effected in the meaning of 'woman' – something that feminist criminologists have all been doing, one way or another, that is obliging us to think differently about women – so the meaning of 'man' has been changed commensurately.

Few orthodox criminologists have consciously attended to these changes in the meaning of their male subject wrought by feminist interventions. But just a little reflection, just a little historical sense, reveals this to be so. While conventional criminologists may believe that they have been unaffected by feminism (and certainly this is the implicit message of the Oxford handbook[99]), it is salutory to reflect on the traditional images of men and women in the literature that no longer seem so convincing after several decades of feminism. One simple illustration should serve as a reminder of the truth of this. Quite early in the piece, Howard Becker's jazz musicians who spurned the drudgery of domesticity were to lose much of their allure when feminists decided to take seriously the situation of the jazzman's wife. The jazzman's rebellious outsider status appeared less ruggedly bohemian when it was seen to depend on his female intimate becoming a reviled outsider to his world. Seeing her differently, making her central rather than simply a foil to her more-interesting man, changed our understanding of him.

Feminists have been unsettling the gender conventions for some time now, so that the old romantic notions of offending males, bucking the system, no longer have the same power to persuade. With each feminist inroad into a female stereotype, so a male stereotype has been similarly weakened. Or we might say that stronger women have produced weaker men. Increasingly, feminists have come to realize this fact – that their work on women has, at the same time, been work on men. As feminist criminologists have shifted our understanding of women, repudiating the female stereotypes, revealing the differences between women's understandings of their own lives and the orthodox (male) accounts of them, so man (whose meaning is so intimately linked with woman) has been altered too. This work of changing our understanding of the sexes in their mutual relativity continues in a more focussed manner in the second part of this book, which shifts the discussion from the historical to the contemporary.

Part 2

Effecting Change

4

Reinterpreting the Sexes (through the Crime of Rape)

We are now poised to do some of the work demanded of a modern feminist criminology that wishes to unsettle the most fundamental prejudices or prejudgements of the discipline – those associated with the meaning of 'man', the meaning of 'woman' and the supposed distinction between the two. In this second part of the book, I intend to examine more closely the precise way in which the term 'woman' has been used by theorists of crime to shore up the meaning of 'man', and to endeavour to alter that conventional female role (always the support act, never the star), by showing women in quite other positions – as other than man's complement, as more than the socket to his plug. But first, I wish to reflect briefly on the cumulative achievement of feminist criminologists, because the present work is so much a product of what has gone before.

Empirical feminists were some of the first to argue that criminology's view of women owed more to the male imagination than to the empirical realities of women's lives. It was not careful observation or good science that produced the (few) accounts of criminal and victimized women in the major texts. Rather, the existing characterizations of women were often informed by prejudice and simple female stereotypes – what male criminologists thought women were like, often based on precious little supporting evidence. It also transpired that what women were thought to be like had much to do with what men thought of men. Consistently, the tendency was to project on to women those characteristics thought unsuitable in a man.

Standpoint feminists not only questioned the scientific rigour of conventional criminology, but also questioned the very possibility of value-free research. They suggested that the identity of the inquirer always affected the nature of the inquiry and the findings that ensued; the knower determined what was known. Standpoint feminists disputed the idea that there was only ever one take on a problem, the supposedly scientific one. Necessarily, there were different ways of perceiving the one situation, for one's perspective on an event always determined what one made of it. The problem with men interpreting the lives of women was that men approached the study of women from their own male perspective, that is, from their own male experience with its consequent set of understandings. But men did not have the same experiences as women, and so were ill-placed to speak on, or for, women. The best understanding of women emanated from women themselves, and the best understanding of criminal women came from criminal women. Ideally, women should be afforded the opportunity to speak for themselves, and this would produce the best criminology.

Our third category of feminist, those loosely grouped as coming under the influence of either Foucault or Derrida, then considered the constitution of perspective. It was now suggested that there was no perspective or vantage point from which one could gain an authentic, unproblematic view of the world (as some standpoint feminists seemed to suggest) even when one was limiting the reach of what one said, by talking only about one's own experience of the world, and not the experience of another social group. For each perspective was itself already constituted by the world upon which one wished to reflect. Foucault believed that the sense we have of ourselves, as particular human subjects, is itself an effect of history, which has already determined what it is to speak as a subject. We do not personally invent the complex meanings of identity.

So, for example, if I wish to refer to myself as, say, a white middle-class woman, I could certainly speak of the experiences of such a woman first-hand, but I could not avoid the fact that the very categories of identity I had used to describe my place of enunciation (here I have chosen my colour, my class and my sex) have already been chosen for me in the sense that they have acquired their importance and their meaning in the very world I now wish to interpret. In a sense they always precede us, or as Richard Bernstein has nicely observed, 'we belong to traditions before they belong to, and are appropriated, by us.'[1]

This is not to say that I am unable to reflect critically upon my experiences of the world and my place within its traditions. But it does suggest a need for vigilance – for constant critical reflection on the nature and provenance of the various ingredients of identity that are said to constitute my viewing point. Those ingredients – say my sex, my class, my race, my sexuality – have a public meaning (and Wittgenstein would say only a public meaning) whose history cannot be ignored. Moreover, that public meaning is already tainted by the fact that it has taken shape within a hierarchy of meanings. Thus, historically, the meaning of woman has been defined negatively against the meaning of man. (It is not women who have invented the meaning of 'woman' with a mind to their own interests.) Similarly, the meaning of black identity has been defined negatively against the public meaning of what it is to be white. And so too with class identity. As Derrida said, meaning is relational and occurs within a 'play of differences'. A violent hierarchy is to be found in the formation of some of our most central concepts in the West.[2] And for many feminists, the most violent hierarchy is that of 'man' as it forms its meaning in relation to 'woman'.

And yet, we are always obliged to deal with the current set of meanings, however inhospitable they may be:

> There is no sense in doing without the concept of metaphysics in order to shake metaphysics. We have no language – no syntax and no lexicon – which is foreign to this history; we can pronounce not a single destructive proposition which has not already had to slip into the form, the logic, and the implicit postulations of precisely what it seeks to contest.[3]

Thus, we must start from here, and with existing categories, to move to yet other categories, which necessarily bear a relation to the old ones. This is all we can do as we cannot think outside the categories which frame our thought, including, and perhaps especially, the category of sex.[4] Or, as Monique Wittig has observed, 'sex is a category which women cannot be outside of.'[5] It is compulsory, it 'constitutes the first definition of the social being in civil status'.[6] To be a civil person, one simply has to be of a sex: sexual indeterminacy simply will not do.[7]

The epistemological problem, then, with which feminists are faced is how to work both within and without the existing frames of meaning? How do we effect change if meaning works in such seemingly recalcitrant ways? In a sense, we are stuck with present meanings and how they are constituted. But are women then obliged simply to *be* this set of negative associations? No, they are not. Though a woman cannot step outside the category 'woman', as a man cannot step outside the category 'man', this does not consign her (or him) to the mere passive object of a label. She can contemplate its meaning (as she can also contemplate the meaning of 'man') while at the same time always being a part of that meaning. And it is the knowledge that meaning is mutable over time and place and culture that assists her in this self-reflection. Moreover, at any given moment, the concept 'woman' does not fully encapsulate her (other identities always intrude), and so its negativity does not function with complete effect.

In fact, the very negativity of the term 'woman' suggests its incomplete nature, because it reveals its dependence on another term (that which is its positive term) with which it has an intimate relation. The recalcitrance of the existing categories of meaning turns out not to be such an impediment to change, once we realize the referential, 'relational' and metaphorical nature of meaning. For as we saw, the meaning of 'woman' is defined not positively and essentially, but relationally – in relation to its notional opposite: 'man'. And both these terms – the term 'man' and the term 'woman' – and their relations are constantly shifting, never pure and fixed. The category woman simply does not hold firm over time and place, but keeps assuming slightly new meanings. It is not absolute, but relative.

Therefore, we can work the meanings and so actually demonstrate how existing concepts and categories, which look so stiff and so hostile to women, can be changed, and how they are always subject to change. The very fact that we are obliged to work with inessential or non-positive bounded concepts (and must interpret, constitute and give meaning to our words constantly) in a world that does not provide us with a tight formula for interpretation, shows us that we are always manufacturing meaning and making sense of our lives. We are constantly bringing it all together into a coherent account of ourselves and the world. This is a remarkable act of creativity that tends to be disguised by the dominant idea of the positive and discovered nature of meaning – the idea (explained in chapter 1) that we simply name a pre-given world, rather than positively constitute the nature of meanings.

Rape as a case study

This chapter seeks to shift criminology's understanding of the sexes, drawing on the insights and the methods of all the feminisms described above. I am particularly indebted, however, to the work of standpoint feminists, though I am aware of the philosophical difficulties that reside in the idea of the authentic voice of women. I am also indebted to feminists who have indicated the value of deconstruction in altering perceptions of male and female identity, and their intimate and unequal relation with one another. My purpose is to see how these approaches might, in combination, help us to change conventional understandings of the sexes within the context of a major crime – the crime of rape. This crime is one of the most serious crimes systematically done to women, and one of the most analysed crimes in the feminist canon.[8] However, my reason for discussing it here is that rape is (generally) a crime about the explicit relation of the sexes to one another.[9] As a consequence, it is a crime which makes manifest criminological and legal orthodoxies about the respective natures of men and women, and the appropriate relation between the two.

Some might argue that if one is trying to unearth conventional understandings of the sexes, the crime of rape is a poor choice of study: rape is about human relations that our society finds unacceptable. That is, rape is not the paradigm of relations between men and women, but its very opposite. My point is, however, that the form of sexuality expressed in the crime of rape, and notionally prohibited by rape laws, is an extension of dominant (masculine) understandings of acceptable sexuality. It does not spring from nature, fully formed, but is a cultural (male) artifact. Or, put another way, there is an implicit view of the background 'facts' of ordinary consenting heterosexual life built into dominant understandings of the crime we know as rape. Prevailing accounts of this crime have been built upon a male understanding of heterosexuality, not women's experience, and yet that male point of view has often been presented as universal, as natural and as inevitable. It has been taken as a given that women stand (or lie) in a certain relation to men and that women have no different or dissident view of their own sexuality. So the study of the crime of rape tells us a lot about what criminologists and criminal lawyers think of men and women.

To reveal the limits and distortions of the male sexual imagination, it is necessary not only to expose its internal workings – to reveal its ordering premises and so to deconstruct it, it is also necessary to show how others (that is women) see it differently. To appreciate that the male perspective is a perspective, and not the world, we need a different imagination that shows man the limits of his world view – that his world view does not in fact reflect all the world. As Elizabeth Grosz explains, 'all knowledge is produced from sexually specific positions and with sexually specific effect.' As a consequence, 'what is needed is not just the inclusion of women within their [men's] various investigations, but also the acknowledgment that their works are also the effects of specifically masculine points of view and interests.'[10]

So my next step is to introduce a woman's standpoint, not only to delimit the masculine, but to show how the other sex interprets the same phenomenon. For this purpose, I have not chosen to consider the perspective of the rape victim, though there are many good studies of this nature. Instead, I have chosen to counterpoint the orthodox male understanding of their own and women's sexuality, with the quite different view of a group of women for whom sex with men is a business and who, as a consequence, have made it their life's work to explore (and exploit) the specific strengths and weaknesses of the (conventional heterosexual) male imagination.

What I find illuminating about this juxtaposition is that these same women, a group of courtesans, are also deeply sceptical of the very idea of a woman's identity, which lends authority to what they, as women, have to say about sex. That is, we are not simply contrasting a male view of this behaviour (which is not presented as a view at all) with a female view that contradicts it, and therefore reveals its limitations. The courtesans are acutely aware of the public and conventional nature of both male and female sexual identity – including their own. But, as we will see, this very awareness also allows them to manipulate both identities for economic gain. By the same token, these women are still courtesans, a social and economic role which carries considerable stigma and many social and legal constraints. These women identify themselves as courtesan women, but understand the limits and the costs of a public role that is not of their making and that is, in a sense, always in the service of men. The benefits of their self-reflection and their consequent manipulation of men are necessarily limited, for they are still using the 'weapons of the weak'.[11] So beyond their deconstruction of their role, there remains a need for more fundamental changes to the social, legal and economic order that would remove the need to resort to manipulation to achieve economic independence.

Questioning monolithic masculinity

My analysis of heterosexual relations within the crime of rape goes against much of what has been said on this subject, both by feminists and non-feminists. In particular, it disputes the common characterization of the crime as a hard fact that is to be found in much of the American feminist literature. For Susan Brownmiller, rape is a hard biological fact: the anatomical possibility of forced sex 'incontrovertibly exists. This single factor', she believes, 'may have been sufficient to have caused the creation of a male ideology of rape. When men discovered that they could rape, they proceeded to do it.'[12] Brownmiller maintains that 'Man's structural capacity to rape and women's corresponding structural vulnerability are as basic to the physiology of both our sexes as the primal act of sex itself.'[13] For Mary Hawkesworth, rape is one of 'the realities that circumscribe women's lives'. It is one of those things 'that can be known' in a clear, immediate fashion by women and so it is not susceptible to conceptual analysis and deconstruction.[14] Similarly, for Catharine MacKinnon the sexual victimization of women by men is a cultural fact so robust that it supplies woman's very definition: it ensures that our identity is that of sexual victim. MacKinnon suggests that the sexual dominance of women by men is so all pervasive that it 'is metaphysically nearly perfect'.[15]

Andrea Dworkin provides a similar characterization of men and their sexual victimization of women. She maintains that men annihilate women in the act of heterosexual sex, even when women are ostensibly consenting to it, for there is no freedom for women in their sexual relations with a man. For Dworkin, heterosexual women suffer a complete loss of their identity; they are subsumed into their men. This is the normal female condition. Dworkin regards male property in women and heterosexuality as much the same thing. To Dworkin, sexual violence against women is part of the very fabric of female heterosexual existence:

> Being owned and being fucked are or have been virtually synonymous in the lives of [practising heterosexual] women. He owns you; he fucks you. The fucking conveys the quality of the ownership: he owns you inside out. The fucking conveys the passion of his dominance: it requires access to every hidden inch ... getting inside you and owning your insides is possession. . . . Intimate, raw, total. . . . In the fuck, the man expresses the geography of his dominance: her sex, her insides are part of his domain as a male.[16]

Dworkin is trying to shatter our complacency about everyday life for women, to get us to see the daily criminal violence and injustice done to women that has been rendered utterly ordinary and so invisible. She says that we have come to eroticize male dominance and female submission; to see it as ordinary and as sexy. Although I think it is partly strategic and rhetorical, Dworkin's sexually overdetermined account of women sets (celibate? lesbian?) women against (practising heterosexual) women. It also attributes enormous power to men over women. Men have the capacity to reduce women utterly, and they do so as a matter of course. In *Intercourse* she writes:

> This reality [for women] of being owned and being fucked – as experience, a social, political, economic, and psychological unity – frames, limits, sets parameters for, what women feel and experience in sex. Being that person who is owned and fucked means becoming someone who experiences sensuality in being possessed. . . . Because a woman's capacity to develop sexual pleasure is developed within the narrow confines of male sexual dominance, internally there is no separate being . . . screaming to get out. There is only the flesh-and-blood reality of being a sensate being whose body experiences sexual intensity, sexual pleasure, and sexual identity in being possessed: in being owned and fucked.[17]

Although *Intercourse* is intended to serve as a trenchant critique of sex in a patriarchal society, simultaneously it helps to constitute, and to perpetuate, a certain view of relations between men and women, with man invariably as predator and woman invariably his victim. My concern is that this message teaches women to freeze at the predatory advances of the potent man. The encouraged identification of men as the subjects of female terror, and women as the terrorized objects of male sexual aggression, hurts women. It makes women complicit in the destruction of their own subjectivity. By learning to become objects of fear, women learn 'to identify with a state that does not elaborate our subjectivity, but dissolves it'.[18] The costs of feminine fear is 'a complete identification of a vulnerable, sexualized body with the self; we thus come to equate rape with death, the obliteration of the self, but see no way we can draw on our selves to save the self and stave off the rape.'[19]

The problem with this understanding of rape is that it treats the crime as an unnegotiable reality that defines and controls women. As Sharon Marcus has observed, it treats rape 'as terrifyingly unnameable and unrepresentable, a reality that lies beyond our grasp and which we can only experience as grasping and encircling us.'[20] In such a view, the masculinity implicit in rape is beyond deconstruction. The point of this chapter is to reject this view of rape as a transcendental disease or horror. Rape is a cultural construct, a masculine construct, which assumes a particular form. It can be deconstructed and, in the same moment, reconstructed.

This is not to say that rape is not real. It is to say, however, that rape takes its reality from cultural meanings and that we can begin to view it in new ways that reduce the vulnerability of women. Rape is not simply a function of the crude reality of the penis – of men having them and wanting to get them into women. Rather, as Marcus observes, rape is a language, a particular expression of sexuality, not a pre-given physical reality of penis-owning men, or of an all-encompassing patriarchy. The vulnerability of women, the aggressive sexually-proprietorial qualities of men, are not natural things in the world, the natural ingredients of a rape. Nor are they hard cultural facts that ensure that this is how things must be for women, or that this is how women invariably view their own condition. Or, to turn things around, as Marcus does, 'To take male violence or female vulnerability as the first and last instances in any explanation of rape is to make the identities of rapist and raped pre-exist the rape.'[21] Rape is not a hard fact. It can be deconstructed.

Why deconstruction?

In the last chapter, we examined the ideas of Cornell and Derrida about the instability of meaning and, particularly, the technique of deconstruction which demonstrates how meaning works and how it can be altered. This intervention shows how concepts are relational, that they depend for their meaning on other terms, which are often pushed to the periphery even though they provide the very conditions of meaning. Deconstruction is a means of showing how the dominant term works, how it depends for its meaning on a repressed term. Thus, it brings the outsider (term) to the centre.

Deconstruction is *inter alia* a political strategy that, as we saw in the last chapter, entails an inversion, which makes that which was subordinate, dominant, that which was marginal, central. This is a strategy that, when applied to relations between men and women, is highly compatible with feminism, for it serves to explain the operations of the masculine, and to bring woman to the fore. Deconstruction alters our perceptions of conventional meanings by showing how that which appears dominant, important and autonomous, is in fact dependent on that which is cast in a subordinate relation to the dominant term. Foucault and Derrida shared an abiding concern with those who are squeezed out – with the repressed 'other'. Their concern was for the fate of outsider groups whose very identity has been nearly destroyed by those with the power to mark them as outsiders: to colonize them, reduce them,

assimilate them, to cast them in a certain mould often by attribut-
ing to them certain essential, immutable characteristics. Feminists
have applied these insights to women in order to free women from
the dominant characterizations of womanhood which limit, repress
and injure.

Showing how concepts and ideas are formed through the subjugation of others is a powerful political act. This is why Simone de
Beauvoir's famous book, *The Second Sex*, was so important for feminists. It revealed to women how women had been cast in an inferior
human mould for certain purposes: to function as the second sex,
to the first sex; to reveal the comparative superiority of man; to be
his 'other'. Cornell has also made this ethical point. She has indicated how meaning operates by distinctions which confer priority
to certain concepts (such as 'man') and repress, while taking their
sense from, others (such as 'woman'), and that the way that meaning functions has served to squeeze out women (the repressed ones).
Through this demonstration of (male) priority and (female) repression, Cornell endeavours to change things. By showing how meaning works, we can help to change meaning. We can bring what was
on the outside to the centre.

Rape and the male imagination

My argument is that the sexual relations of men to women, and
women to men, implicit within orthodox understandings of the
crime of rape reflect a culturally dominant male view of heterosexual relations, including the culture of criminology. At this point,
I should add an important proviso. I am talking here of criminological orthodoxy, including orthodoxy from the left (in the case of
the left realists), but there are also to be found in the criminological
literature[22] more critical and reflective interpretations of rape that
have taken account of feminist criticism.[23] These exceptions not-
withstanding, the dominant understanding of rape is, I believe, as
expounded below. So how are we to characterize the conventional
(and so heterosexual) male imagination, as it reveals itself in the
crime of rape, and its official interpretation?

The sexual victimization of women is a theme implicitly animating the work of left realists. To these criminologists, the meaning of
rape is self-evident and agreed-upon. Rape is a brutal 'crime of
passion', something which because of their superior social and
physical power, men (can) do to women and from which women
must, therefore, be protected.[24] In realist criminology, generally, the

criminal victimization of women and, more particularly, women's susceptibility to male violence, appear as simple facts that are so obvious that they require little further elaboration. I have already indicated that what is lacking from the realist account of rape is any sustained engagement with feminist scholarship that has emphasized the highly contested meaning of this crime.

In fact, the slight treatment given by realists (and other contemporary criminologists more generally) to a subject which has greatly exercised feminists, suggests a felt lack of need to go beyond their own understandings to fathom this behaviour. The nature of the crime of rape is taken for granted and requires no further scholarly analysis. When John Lea trespasses a little into the work of others on this subject, he uses a reference which is nearly a decade old and then the work of a man, Stephen Box. Admittedly, this is a work of some sensitivity to feminist concerns, but then Lea makes little use of these feminists insights. Certainly, it does not prompt him to turn to the writings of feminists.[25]

As a consequence, there is no endeavour in realist writing to examine the particular cultural construction of these (legally defined) crimes of sexual violence. The impression conveyed is simply that the criminal law describes, and then prohibits, pre-existing and implicitly universal male sexual violence against women. Remember that violence against women was explicitly used to demonstrate a universal consensus about the meaning of crime that consequently demanded condemnation. 'All groups', according to Jock Young, 'abhor violence against women.'[26] Within this analysis, the potency of men is assumed (he is not referring to violent women). Also assumed is the vulnerability of women to men.

Even more explicit in his depiction of man's 'natural' potency in his relation with woman is the English jurist, Glanville Williams. In his commentary on the law governing rape in marriage (he favoured the continuing immunity of husbands from prosecution), Professor Williams does not mince words. He asks:

> Why is rape an inappropriate charge against the cohabiting husband? The reasons should be too obvious to need spelling it out. We are speaking of a biological activity, strongly baited by nature, which is regularly and pleasurably performed on a consensual basis by mankind. . . . Occasionally some husband continues to exercise what he regards as his right when his wife refuses him. . . . What is wrong with his demand is not so much the act requested but its timing, or the manner of the demand. The fearsome stigma of rape is too great a punishment for husbands who use their strength in these circumstances.[27]

In this account of violence against women, the job of the criminal law is to outlaw male behaviour that, once again, is taken to have its own inherent natural form. What we are not encouraged to see is that the violent crime in question does not possess an intrinsic, essential nature, but is an artifact of law (and of the wider culture of which criminology is a part) that constructs it in a quite particular way, casting men in a specific relation with women.

Williams is generous with his thoughts on the sexual natures of men and women. He tells us that 'The facts of life make consent to sexual intercourse a hazy concept' and so 'poses grave problems of proof and justice.'[28] Williams is himself vague about what he means by 'the facts of life', though his ensuing discussion throws some light on the matter. He suggests that in sexual relations, men may not be in a position to know what women really want, that women are given to changing their minds – and that they do so after the event. All of this makes heterosexual men particularly vulnerable to women.[29] Williams develops the theme of women's mendacity at some length. He explains 'That some women enjoy fantasies of being raped' and that 'they may, to some extent, welcome a masterful advance while putting up a token resistance.' He finds the verse of Byron illuminating:

A little still she strove, and much repented,
And whispering 'I will ne'er consent' – consented.[30]

Williams tells us that young girls lie about rape to placate their parents. Or they lie out of shame because they have engaged in sexual relations, and may even convince themselves that the lie is true. Women who are jilted may lie out of spite. Or, women may lie 'for obscure psychological reasons'.[31] To Williams, women are dissimulators who can neither be trusted nor understood. They are Freud's 'dark continent'.[32] In short, Williams' account of rape is very much a product of his male imagination. And so convinced is he that he is simply uttering the truth about the crime, that he feels no need to offer supporting evidence for any of his propositions. After all, he is simply reporting 'the facts of life'.

Prominent American interpreters of rape (and rape-related) law have offered remarkably similar accounts of women. In *Wigmore on Evidence*, for example, we discover that:

Modern psychiatrists have amply studied the behaviour of [sexually] errant young girls and women coming before the courts in all sorts of cases. Their psychic complexes are multifarious, distorted by inherent defects, partly by diseased derangements or abnormal instincts. . . . One form taken by these complexes is that of contriving false charges of sexual offenses by men. The unchaste (let us call it) mentality finds incidental but direct expression in the narration of imaginary sexual incidents of which the narrator is the heroine or the victim.[33]

In Australia's most prominent textbook on the criminal law, Brent Fisse sets the social context for his discussion of the crime of rape in much the same manner as Williams when he examines what he calls 'the realities of sexual courtship'.[34] Like Williams, Fisse implies that he has no difficulty penetrating the female mind, even when women dissemble. He tells us that 'Outward reluctance to consent may be no more than a concession to modesty or a deliberate incitement to D [the defendant] to persuade a little harder. The approach to and consummation of sexual intercourse is not usually made an occasion for detached self-analysis.'[35] As a consequence, says Fisse, the law has evolved various mechanisms to test the honesty and consistency of the complainant of rape. He goes on to discuss the various evidentiary protections which have developed to protect the man accused of rape from false witnesses. Now informed of 'the realities' of sexual relations between men and women, we are in a position to see the inherent logic and fairness of these rules.

What we are seeing at work is the male imagination on women. There is nothing here about how women themselves regard their own sexuality. There is no testamentary evidence from women. Neither the criminologists, nor the criminal lawyers, actually inquire into the modern-day facts of relations between the sexes that perhaps should include a discussion of changing sexual mores (less stigma is now attached to the sexually active woman). For example, the impact of the AIDS virus may well have encouraged greater sexual honesty, or it may have encouraged the opposite. Williams, in particular, holds to a view of relations between men and women that may owe more to Victorian notions of sexuality than to a knowledge of modern sexual practices. In this view, the masterful man exerts an erotic power, and women derive erotic pleasure from having their will overborne. This is a Romantic notion, in the literary sense, which is associated not only with the work of Byron but also with Pope (with *The Rape of the Lock*), Coleridge, the Brontes, George Eliot and Keats.

These male accounts of relations between the sexes are simplistic, reductive and masculine. They take no account of current feminist debates in the area. The French feminists, for example, suggest that women's sexuality may well be polymorphous and complex, that women experience sexual pleasure in many different ways.[36] Women's sexuality cannot be reduced to the simple story contained in the criminological and legal literature.[37] The prevailing masculine analysis of rape gives no hint of the complicated and contested nature of sexuality in which men and women act for a variety of motives. There is no sense here that a woman's experience of sex with a man can be other than the one that he projects on to her; that she might possess a quite different, distinctive, sovereign sexuality.

The male imagination in the law of rape

I now wish to turn to the legal definition of the crime of rape and consider just how this orthodox view of men, women and heterosexual relations retains a secure home within it. Rape is still 'the most gender specific of all crimes', as Temkin reminds us in relation to the English criminal law. '(O)nly a man . . . can be the actual perpetrator, only a woman the victim'.[38] The gender-specific nature of rape, however, is not simply a peculiarity of English law. Even in those (American and Australian) jurisdictions where the crime has formally become gender-neutral, so that, in principle, a woman can now perform the prohibited act and a man can now be the victim of a rape, the traditional heterosexual paradigm has been sustained.

By this I mean that the sex assumed by rape law takes the form of a sexual subject (a sexual initiator who is nearly always a man) who proposes sex to a sexual object (who is usually a woman, from whom consent is extracted). It is sexual intercourse when the offer is accepted; it is rape when the deal goes wrong and the man appreciates this fact.[39] The offeree either wants it or she does not. This is the only form the transaction can take. The sexuality of the offeree is always only either consistent or inconsistent with that of the offer proposed. It is never her own. The implicit form of the transaction is one of a proposal by an initiating party to the act of sexual intercourse (which is legislatively defined) to which consent must be extracted from the offeree. The law therefore casts the man[40] in the role of initiator (never the negotiator) of a sexual act (a singular, never a plural, thing which never takes the form of an engagement) that (usually) entails the thrusting of the penis into the vagina.[41] Sex still entails the (unidirectional) proposal of one party to take the body of the other party: the act is lawful when the other party agrees to be taken; it is rape when the other party does not.

Perhaps it might be said, in reply, that someone has to take the initiative in sex, and someone must consent to it. That is, it might be argued that rape necessarily assumes a contractual form of sexuality, in which there is an offeror and offeree (because this is the way of human relations), but that this contractual form does not in itself diminish the agency of either party, just as there is supposedly no loss of agency in a freely-bargained commercial contract. But, if we look more closely at the meaning usually given to 'consent' in the law of rape, we can observe the continuing objectification of one of the parties – the person to whom sex is proposed – in the contractual form of sex. For we discover that 'consent' to sex for the purposes of the law of rape does not mean free agreement. It does not entail a mutual transaction or negotiation on equal terms. Certainly, it is not about the mutual desires of sexual intimates.[42]

Legal interpretations of consent for the purposes of the law of rape of both a judicial and academic nature reveal that the sexuality presupposed is still a traditional compelling, coercive male sexuality. In the law of rape, 'consenting' sex is consistent with the application of a good deal of pressure on the part of the one who seeks sex to bring the other party around to their way of seeing things. In certain American jurisdictions, even manifestly non-consenting sex is not regarded as rape, if there is no additional 'forcible coercion' (while want of consent alone is formally sufficient to constitute the prohibited act of rape in England and Australia). Thus, the American woman who protests verbally but then 'passively' submits to sex (out of fear) is not raped at law because no force is discernible.[43] As one American commentator explains, 'Rather than asking whether certain sexual advances are inappropriate and sufficiently abusive to warrant penal prohibition, rather than asking whether there is any reason why various types of male sexual assertiveness should not be prohibited, we [Americans] have instead asked only whether such conduct is equivalent to violent compulsion.'[44]

The sexuality presupposed (and so left ungoverned) by rape law is one of strong seducers and of the ultimately willing seduced, the one who wishes (or who should wish) only to be taken. As an Australian judge was recently to observe about consenting heterosexuality:

> In the nature of things, men frequently bring some kind of 'pressure'
> to bear to obtain a woman's consent, 'pressures' in the way of
> compliments, blandishments . . . and the like, all of which may

legitimately be directed towards securing consent through her sexual arousal. This has always been the case and it seems too obvious to mention.[45]

The standard of consent in the law of rape is indeed much lower than the commercial one.[46] At common law, consent is destroyed only by threat or application of violence, or by fraud (as to the nature and quality of intercourse or as to the identity of the offender).[47] Blackmail, fraud of other kinds, even false imprisonment, are apparently all consistent with legally recognized consent to sex, so that sex achieved in such circumstances is not rape. The modern law of rape generally rewards the strong male seducer for his absorption in his own sexuality, his sexual needs, and his commensurate disregard of what a woman may want. In law, the man who can see only what he desires and needs, and who interprets a woman's reactions as invariably congruent with his own, whatever she does, has sex with the law's sanction. It is only the man who appreciates the difference between his own desires and those of a woman who commits (who has the necessary mental element to commit) rape.[48] The modern conception of rape reflects contemporary culture in which it is still the man who is expected to be the sexual agent. Just a brief scan of the romantic fiction in any bookshop will confirm this: Mills and Boon is still very much about strong possessing men, and women who wish only to form the natural complement to his desires.[49]

The law of rape, therefore, is conventional in the sexual form assumed. The modern crime remains committed to an idea of sexuality as a dyad in which one party seeks sexual access to the body and the being of another, and the other party is imputed to find pleasure in acceding to this proposal to be taken, to be had. In the crime of rape, sex entails the appropriation and possession of the other. There is a sexual subject and a sexual object. The sexual subject initiates and strikes the deal; the sexual object responds to the offer proposed, permitting herself to be taken on his terms. If she says 'no' it is (possibly) rape; if she agrees, or fails to convince him that she does not want what he wants, it is normal consenting sex. The sexuality of the offeree is never her own. This is a sexual form which depends on the idea of a vanquishing male and a woman for whom eroticism represents sexual surrender, not subjectivity, however we might interpret it. While she surrenders herself, he remains himself. She gives herself up to him, and he takes her and possesses her. The sex presupposed by the crime of rape does not reflect two sexualities, the sexualities of both men and women. Instead, we find the assertion of the sexual autonomy of men defined as appropriation and possession of the other, and the consequent denial and erasure of another sexuality.

The prevailing construction and interpretation of the crime of rape, and the background 'facts of life' which supply its logic, bring sharply into focus the male (heterosexual) endeavour to build autonomy through the denial of women as separate and distinct subjects. The means by which this erasure is achieved is through the depiction of women's desires as only more of his. The method of establishing male sexual autonomy is to presuppose that women's sexuality is not separate and distinctive. His sexual subjectivity, his heterosexual autonomy, is secured if women, by nature, always adopt the complementary role in sex; if they are invariably the negative to his positive.

The criminological (and legal) culture participates in the depiction of men as sexual agents, with women as their objects. Though it is generally insensitive to the significance of the maleness of crime, it is at the same time replete with messages to women that men are active and potent, and that women should be afraid of men. As I have endeavoured to show in this chapter, the very structure of the crime of rape incorporates this message – that men, by nature, are possessive, and that it is in women's nature to be possessed.

The female imagination

I have detailed, at some length, the nature of the (orthodox) male imagination as it interprets the crime of rape, as well as 'the facts of life' that give rape its logic. Conspicuously absent from these accounts has been the presence of women as sexual subjects with distinctive and different thoughts, not only about their own sexuality, but also about the sexuality of men. I now wish to shift the initiative, from men to women. For this purpose, I am reliant on a study of prostitution in past and present India, conducted by Veena Oldenburg, a feminist social scientist and social historian. Oldenburg came to her study of Lucknow courtesans with some common criminological assumptions. She was expecting to find women who had fallen out of, or who had been torn from, conventional society becoming victims (of their male clients) and offenders (that is, criminal prostitutes). Her feminist sympathies were with the prostitutes, but she had already cast them in the role of society's victims, rather than vigorous women adapting intelligently and creatively to the demands placed upon them by Indian society.

Oldenburg explains that women were at one time introduced to courtesan life after a kidnapping. This may help to explain why she expected to find women who had been thrown to the fates, stripped of their dignity, abject. Her interviews of thirty women living today in 'the Chowk area of Lucknow', however, were to produce 'a very different picture'. It was their conventional lives prior to prostitution that represented the true horror, not their present existence:

> (The) compelling circumstances that brought the majority of them to the various *tawa'if* households in Lucknow was the misery they endured in either their natal or their conjugal homes . . . three were sold by their parents when famine conditions made feeding these girls impossible. Seven were victims of physical abuse . . . Three were known victims of rape and therefore deemed ineligible for marriage; two had left their ill-paid jobs as municipal sweeper women, because they were tired of 'collecting other people's dirt'.[50]

Oldenburg was soon struck by the irony of the courtesans' position and how it functioned as a critical commentary on conventional female life in Lucknow. 'This assortment of refugees from the . . . respectable world', she observes, 'gave a completely ironic slant to the notion of respectability.'[51] If their former lives counted as respectability, these courtesans wanted no part of it. For these women, oppression characterized the lives of ordinary women, not the life of the courtesan. Oldenburg was told this, and yet she still held on to the notion of the courtesan as victim, as outcast. She was thus prompted to ask of one courtesan:

> Gulbadan, since you are a handsome woman, so well educated, with all this money and property and jewels, why didn't you marry a *sharif* [respectable] *nawab* [there are several descendants of noble families in Lucknow who use this honorific] and settle down to a life of respectability?[52]

She is given a sharp reply which obliges her to consider her own implicit prejudices about female life:

> Gulbadan: your use of the word 'respectable' is thoughtless. Is marriage considered the only 'respectable' alternative for women in America? Are married women not abused? Well let us show you what marriage is before you wish it on an old and respectable woman like myself, or any of us here. Let us dispel the darkness in your mind about the nature of marriage.[53]

It is here that the courtesans show the investigating scientist, with her supposedly dispassionate outlook, the lessons she can learn from parody; parody that reveals things about them and about ourselves and the limits of our thinking. Oldenburg tells us:

> Of what they then played out for me, I can offer an inadequate summary because it is difficult to capture the visual details of the half-hour-long satirical medley of song, dance, dialogue and mime that followed. Rasulan immediately took her *dupatta* [long scarf] and wound it around her head as a turban to play the husband. Elfin Hasina Jan took her cue as the wife, others became children and members of the extended family, while Gulbadan remained on the settee amid the bolsters, taking occasional drags from the *hookah*, presiding, as a particularly obnoxious mother-in-law, on a scene of domestic disharmony. The wife/mother first surveys the multifarious demands on her energy and time: the children squall, ask for food, drink, and want to be picked up; the mother-in-law orders that her legs, which have wearied from sitting, be massaged; the husband demands food and attention; the father-in-law asks for his *hookah* to be refilled. . . . Hasina is defeated, harried. Muttering choice obscenities under her breath, she begins in a frenzied way, to do the job of a wife. . . . She finally collapses, her hands striking her own brow as she croaks . . . 'never more'.[54]

Oldenburg discovers that the courtesans also make use of drama and parody in their working lives. They take care to disguise their hard-edged business acumen, by putting on the airs of foolish, emotional women. Their avowed purpose is to put the stereotypes to work in order to extract more from their customers. Thus, they exploit the interval between the conventions of femininity and their own sense of themselves as something quite other than this. They are well aware that the hold of patriarchy is metaphysically not nearly perfect, and take open advantage of those who think it is.

Precisely because the fine art of being a woman is not natural, but learned through constant tuition, repetition and rehearsal, the more experienced courtesans spend some time training women new to the business in their evocation and manipulation. The new women have to learn to feign the modes of femininity until there is no pretence discernible to the male eye:

> These well-practiced ploys – the feigned headache that interrupts a dance or a song, feigned anger for having been neglected, a sprained ankle, tears, a jealous rage – have beguiled generations of men to lose thousands of extra rupees or gold coins to these women. The . . . refusal, at a critical juncture, to complete a sexual interlude with a

favorite patron is a particularly profitable device, because feigned coital injuries or painful menstrual cramps involve expensive and patient waiting on the part of the patron. Gulbadan said she often carried the game a step further by 'allying herself' with the patron against the 'offending' courtesan to set the seal of authenticity on the scene. She would scold and even slap her till the patron begged her not to be so harsh.[55]

Gulbadan, the matriarch speaks of the 'gambit' which is 'the game of love that makes these men come back again and again, some until they are financially ruined. They return every evening, like the flocks of homing pigeons, in the vain belief that it is *we* who are in love with *them*.'[56] Conscious use is made of the men's own sense of their masculinity. The courtesans research their client's 'public reputation, his finances, his foibles and vanities'.[57] His blindness to the limitations imposed on him by his own sex is exploited. Thus, a double game is played with gender. The courtesans deploy both the masculine tendency to reduce woman to a foolish stereotype as well as the tendency of man to overlook his own sex specificity and foibles. They exploit the masculine belief that man (but not woman) can transcend the trappings of his sex. And, in both aspects of the double-play, women remain the subjects of the game and have the man as their object.

In *Gender Trouble*, Judith Butler suggests that parody is a highly effective means of undermining oppressive forms of femininity. Butler feels that this dramatic art is one that women do not even have to be schooled in, as they are already doing it. The reason for women's proficiency, according to Butler, is that gender is always a performance. It is not prior to culture, a pre-given, natural thing that women inevitably assume or become, as it often seems to appear and as it is generally represented. Rather, gender is utterly within culture and, within culture, it is repeatedly constituted and reconstituted by acts, by performances, by practices, by positive tuition and learning. In her analysis of mothers as agents (and objects) of social control, Frances Heidensohn made a related point. Bringing up daughters in the ways of femininity, she said, was a demanding occupation because femininity did not come naturally. It involved extensive socialization. Or, as de Beauvoir declared, one is not born a woman, but becomes one.

In other words, women have to keep sustaining the meaning of their female identity by positive acts that keep that identity in place, though never in the same form. With each repetition, change is effected. The feminine gesture, the feminine dress, the feminine smile are all means by which being female is, through positive social effort, invested and reinvested with old and new meanings. As Gulbadan made plain, it takes energy to sustain femininity because it does not spring out of nature, complete and perfect, fully-formed. The feminine is constituted by endless acts of repetition. 'Gender is the repeated stylization of the body, a set of repeated acts within a highly regulatory frame that congeal over time to produce the appearance of substance, of a natural sort of being.'[58] Because it is an endless performance, the drama can be changed, the story line developed in new directions.

This is not to say that I can suddenly decide to abandon all this, to be a woman utterly differently or not to be a woman at all. The culture I have entered has already constituted me as a woman through teaching me what I am to be; by shaping my gestures, my walk, my dress. There is a force, a compulsion to my femininity, one which is imposed from without although always refashioned by me. The compulsions of femininity also stem from women's enforced place in the polity and the economy. As Gulbadan revealed, the grim economic realities of life for the conventional Indian woman had made the courtesans appreciate the attractions of their alternative way of life. We might regard their choice as the lesser of two evils, though I suspect Gulbadan would resent and reject this analysis. 'The naming of "sex"', according to Butler, 'is an act of domination and compulsion, an institutionalized performative that both creates and legislates social reality by requiring the discursive/perceptual construction of bodies in accord with principles of sexual difference.'[59]

But, there is no 'master' template of womanhood, no complete programme for the mind and body that preordains it all, which says 'this is how everything is to be done if you are a woman.' We have already examined how meaning works – through the play of differences, through metaphor, which is always incomplete and, therefore, always open-ended, always changing. We have also seen that there is no single template of femininity, but rather many femininities. Women are always working with/in a range of possibilities of femininity, whose very multiplicity demonstrates the potential for, and fact of, change. Femininity is never a constant. It is constituted and reconstituted differently across and within time, place and culture.

The woman who is proficient in the art or practice of the feminine is, therefore, a practised actor in that she is always performing a part which entails invention, imitation and parody; she is never simply expressing an original essence. Through the generations, the feminine arts are passed on – and with each passage they are

modified and reconstituted, making Butler's point about constitution and reconstitution. Contrast the ways of the Victorian woman
and the ways of women today. We are speaking of significantly
different femininities though, of course, there is also a line of con-
tinuity between past and present woman.

The writing of Luce Irigaray is also replete with themes of female parody, performance and dissimulation. Irigaray describes
Western culture as monosexual, as male. Women's sexual distinctiveness, she feels, has yet to find positive representation. At the
same time, Irigaray also speaks of the irreducibility of woman, of
femininity which always remains beyond masculine culture. This
is femininity that is excessive to male culture, which is unrepre-
sented but remaining still. It is not the femininity that woman is
obliged to perform to satisfy the masculine, to give it form (the sort
of femininity depicted by MacKinnon and Dworkin). It is something beyond this. In writing which is itself playful and parodic,
Irigaray suggests that this femininity, which is other than that to be
found in Western culture, always remains elusive, without a positive presence, but never extinguished.

To Irigaray, women discern the difference between this other
woman, the woman who escapes the dominant schemes of representation, and the woman who appears to know her proper place.
The (so-called) feminine arts of seduction and dissimulation – precisely the arts in which the courtesans were so practised – are means
of marking the difference between the two women. 'Woman', says
Irigaray, 'is so artistic. . . . So well disguised, made up, masked. . . .
The comedy of the other that she plays so artistically only because
she "is" not in it, has no personal involvement.'[60] The fact that
woman is often known for her wiles and her seductions, indeed
suggests that the dominant culture senses that there is more to
woman than meets the eye. To Irigaray, woman puts herself out to
be something which she is expected to be, but remains alert to the
act of acting. 'The most powerful effect of woman: to double for
men. . . . To give body . . . to their ideals . . . to give them voice,
foundation . . . [woman is] the perfect doubler, faultless mimic. . . .
An exemplary echo chamber.'[61]

Women appreciate that they are more than they are putting themselves out to be. 'Beneath all those/her appearances, beneath all
those/her borrowed finery, that female other still sub-sists. . . . And
as she is dis-tant – and in "herself" – she threatens the stability of
all values. In her there is always the possibility that truth, appearances, will, power . . . will collapse. By mimicking them all more or
less adequately, that female other never holds firm to any of them

univocally.'[62] And so, the courtesans of Lucknow always maintained a distance from conventional femininity, while mimicking it so well.

What Irigaray appears to be suggesting, and what Butler says in a more direct way, is that imitation and parody are positive, political and subversive acts that women can employ in the interests of women, not just in the interests of men. We have witnessed the subversive acting of the courtesans. Butler gives another example of subversive acting with the culture of 'drag'. 'The notion of an original or primary gender identity', she suggests, 'is often parodied within cultural practices of drag, cross-dressing. . . . As much as drag creates a unified picture of "woman" . . . it also reveals the distinctness of those aspects of gendered experience which are falsely naturalized as a unity. . . . *In imitating gender, drag implicitly reveals the imitative structure of gender itself – as well as its contingency.*'[63] And, as Butler further clarifies her strategy for change, 'The notion of gender parody defended here does not assume that there is an original which such parodic identities imitate. Indeed, the parody is *of* the very notion of an original.'[64]

The courtesans in Oldenburg's story literally acted out a drama for Oldenburg and also engaged in further dramatic acting for their clients. They satirized and exploited the conventions and practices of 'respectable' female life. But my point about the benefits of parody are broader than this conscious theatre of the courtesans. My suggestion is that women are constantly engaged in ironic acts of negotiation with female life: that they both function within the apparatus of conventional (and less conventional) female life and treat the apparatuses of femininity (and masculinity) with scepticism. And yet, we do not hear of this other side of women in the criminological and legal literature about rape and its relation to consenting sexuality. Oldenburg reveals the parody of her subjects, she exposes herself to their satire, and then engages in the subversive feminine act of writing a feminism that mocks conventional understandings of male and female sexuality. It is precisely this critical self-reflection and openness to the different understandings of others that is missing from the criminological and legal writing on women. I will take up this theme of the ethical relation – in which each is open to the other – in the last chapter of this book.

Some thoughts for the non-possessing man

Before closing this chapter, I wish to consider, briefly, how men are themselves disadvantaged by the concept of the strong possessing heterosexual male, and its complementary idea of the feminine and feminized object of that possessive sexuality – and why it is, therefore, also in men's interests to think about masculinity (and femininity) differently, beyond these cultural stereotypes. I should say immediately that I do not wish to diminish the seriousness of the damage done to women by the sexual violence of men. Nor do I wish to deny that men, as a category, can always be said to benefit from the prevailing view that they are the stronger, more powerful sex. Not only does this confer on them a superior status, but it actually seems to make men as a sex more confident than women, and less concerned about the dangers of violent crime.

Consistently, the evidence reveals that men, as a rule, are less afraid than women to inhabit the public sphere, that as a consequence they feel freer and more willing to take risks.[65] This public confidence is to be found in men, even though it is also true that in the public sphere a man is more likely than a woman to be the victim of a violent crime. So men are more risk-taking than women, even though they are more likely to experience the violence of another man (no doubt partly as a consequence of this greater risk-taking), and yet they are, generally, less worried about it. In their study of men who had experienced criminal assault, Elizabeth Stanko and Kathy Hobdell discovered that for most of their male subjects, 'the likelihood of intrusive physical violence had never worried them'.[66] These findings contrast starkly with the available evidence on women's fear of crime.[67] The powerful cultural belief that it is men who are the predators, not the predated, seems to be an important ingredient of the greater public confidence of men, and the reduced confidence of women.

Having said this, I now wish to acknowledge the not inconsiderable costs for many men that flow from the idea of the powerful heterosexual man who puts fear – a fear which smacks of the erotic – into the hearts of women. For one thing, the ideal of the strong male (and the complementary idea of the weak one as feminine) makes it unacceptable for a man to be afraid of violence and to admit that fear.[68] The real man is the man who can hold his own, and so it is culturally inappropriate for a man to be reduced to a state of abject feminine fear by the actuality or potential of violence. As Stanko and Hobdell have observed, 'Physical injury due to criminal injury is an affront as much to a masculine order of things as it is to the individual man.'[69] The man who has been injured through criminal assault may well feel that he cannot look after himself, as a man should. The ideal of the strong man poses an even greater problem for the man who succumbs to male violence of a sexual nature. The man who has been raped simply does not accord with our culture's understandings of the sexual victim. As a consequence, and as Monique Plaza has argued, the raped man becomes culturally a woman. He has lost his manhood. He is feminized.

Law and the broader culture, similarly, denies the existence of the powerful, violent woman who subjects a man to her physical authority. (Certainly as yet English law has no concept of a female rapist.[70]) There is evidence to suggest that men are, at times, the victims of female violence in domestic circumstances, although it is women who are almost invariably the victims of extreme and injurious abuse.[71] The man who is beaten and controlled by his wife, however, is generally regarded as a laughing matter, for he has suffered a complete fall from grace. Not only has he failed to demonstrate the possessive masculinity of the strong man, but he himself has become the possession of the very person whom he is supposed to dominate. The powerful cultural denial of the woman as aggressor (barring the occasional and self-consciously freakish representations of sexually violent women by Hollywood) must surely place the man who is the object of such violence in a completely untenable position.

The masculine ideal of the strong man, who can take charge of a woman, also functions, obviously, as an implicit rebuke to gay men. There is a clear cultural history of condemning and reviling the 'queer' man and assigning to him those undesirable qualities which are normally associated with the feminine.[72] The dominant heterosexual masculinity necessarily leaves the gay man 'queer', beyond the straight and narrow – feminized. Some gay men have themselves responded to this repression through the sexual performance of 'drag'. Drag can be interpreted as a form of protest against conventional masculinity, and as a conscious means of highlighting the artifice (and violence) that is entailed in conventional masculinity and femininity.[73] In short, it is not only women who suffer from the culture of the strong man, though it is women who are the most consistently dispossessed by it. When Glanville Williams describes the rough passions of the possessing husband, when John Lea interprets rape as a 'crime of [male] passion', there is a range of other masculinities which are simultaneously implied, and then cast out. They are, by implication, rendered unnatural and undesirable. Thus are the men who depart from the masculine ideal rendered silent.

5
—

Relocating the Sexes
(Through Crime Fiction)

Storytelling, it might be said, makes visions that today have no existence except as possible alternatives real to us, give us an image and challenge us to respond.

Sandra Berns, Concise Jurisprudence

An epistemological problem, which still exercises modern philosophers, is how to effect change within a language that has already defined for us the conditions of meaning, and hence how we think about the very problem of change. We are always to some extent bound to the current meanings of woman and man, even though these are deleterious to women and to many men. These concepts precede us; we do not invent them, and so cannot easily reinvent them. How do we think differently about women, and our relations with men, given the hold of the present?

In the last chapter, two strategies were employed. My first strategy was to examine some orthodox criminology and criminal legal writing on a major sexual crime against women. My intention was to show that a quite particular cultural construction of sexuality was lodged within the crime of rape; that its logic was a male logic; and that it took little account of women's understandings of their own (and men's) sexuality. My second strategy was to present an alternative view of the same possessive male sexuality, to show that it failed to tell the full story. In this female account of male sexuality, strong men became the butt of female satire. Men's failure to see the limits of their sexual powers over women made them vulnerable to manipulation. The courtesans turned the tables on their clients, but always within the larger political context in which their clients retained their superior economic power – the power to range of current definitions of women, noting their malleability and porousness, and speculates about the possibilities of change. The raw materials we have at our disposal, I suggest, are not all that bad. Certainly they allow us to conjure up richer, more persuasive images of women than conventional criminology has ever allowed. Women as offenders, as victims, even as inquirers into the nature of crime itself, form the protagonists of this chapter. My intention is to develop more convincing images of women in each of these guises. I will consider a victim turned offender, a crime investigator who often offends, and a crime pathologist who spends much of her time investigating the effects of male violence on women.

This chapter also reflects on the nature of differences between woman and woman, between woman and man, and between now and the future. It endeavours to generate some new thoughts on the different natures of women that take us some way from the stereotypes. These new thoughts about women are not intended to be fantastic, to have no grounding in truth, even though I will have to resort to the use of crime fiction. Rather, they represent extrapolations from current realities of women's lives, which have never been adequately reflected in criminology, and they flow also from imaginative writings about how women might inhabit new worlds, were current conditions of female life less constraining.

The women crime writers I consider in this chapter quite consciously work within a well-accepted formula, but then shift its component parts, in particular by putting the normally marginal woman at the centre, and letting her experience the freedom of a man. The disruptive effects of this feminist manipulation of meaning are particularly apparent precisely because the rules of a blatantly masculinist genre are so well established. That is, as a form of fiction, and as a highly stylized form of fiction, we are well aware that we are dealing with a construction of a quite specific kind which has, until recently, explicitly favoured men and disfavoured women (in much the same way as criminology has generally dealt with the sexes). When feminists tamper with the convention, by introducing a prominent woman who does not act according to type, the misogyny of the orthodox appears in sharp relief.

Feminist crime fiction actually gives permission for this latitude, for this play of ideas. It draws on a pre-existing genre, a constraining formula for how things should be written, but then it also encourages, and indeed derives, its very fictitious nature, from imagination and creativity. There is, thus, a natural convergence

buy a woman's sex. Thus, the courtesans resorted to 'the weapons of the weak'.

My third strategy of effecting change, while working with the materials at hand, is simply to invert or reverse the existing roles assigned to men and women in relation to crime, and crime fiction provides an effective means of doing this. The immediate consequence of fictitious reversal is to render the familiar unfamiliar, to show that what is ordinary and mundane in the life of a man is extraordinary in the life of a woman. The freedoms that many men take for granted can be remarkable to women who are accustomed to constraints and limitations that are quite foreign to many men. With sex role reversal, the point is not just to show that a woman can do what a man can do, that the two roles can be reversed, but also to show that once one effects a reversal, everything changes. The man's role can no longer be seen as natural and inevitable, and nor can the woman's. Inversion allows us to see the commonplace freshly and critically because our viewing point has altered. The normally marginal woman, or woman outsider, is given the opportunity to offer her understandings of the ethics and injustices of conventional relations between the sexes. We see male actions and experiences in a new light because they are seen through the eyes of the one who is usually cast as man's other.

Sex role reversal requires a flight of the imagination, for it depends on a suspension of the usual limiting conditions of female life. Fiction supplies the means of taking such a flight of fancy, of suspending the realities of the female condition (the shortage of money, the physical risks associated with both public and private life, the demands of wanted and unwanted reproduction). In large numbers, women have already responded to the appeal of fiction as a means of shifting the sexes around and letting women experience aspects of the lives of men. This is more than a simple, even clumsy, literary device that can carry little conviction and so achieve little. Its present significance lies in the fact that it allows us to see both sexes differently. It de-naturalizes the female condition as well as the male condition, showing how things could be different. And, as we will see, because a woman always brings her womanliness with her, even when she is allowed to live as a man (the category never lets go and perhaps we do not want it to), the inversion is never simply an inversion. Rather, woman is transformed, retaining qualities of the old and developing qualities of the new. Thus are all changes made.

Our current concern is criminological, and we are fortunate that there is already an abundance of crime fiction by women, on women, in which women are allowed to enter the world of crime, much as men do. The verve and imagination of these female crime writers show us the value of moving outside the criminological canon, which is still dominated by male criminologists who dress up the study of man as the study of humanity. Women have achieved a great deal more recognition as writers of crime fiction, than as writers of crime fact. This may partly be due to the fact that it is not essential to gain a foothold in a formal male institution to make a mark as a writer of fiction. For centuries, women have been writing from home, rather than from the institutions of government or from the universities.

There is a further reason for this decision to look to fiction for new meanings of womanhood, and this reason is already to be found within the thesis of this book. It is that meaning does not reside in the world, natural and given, but is actively constituted by meaning-makers. We, as meaning-makers, are obliged to deal with meanings already constituted (by others) for us, but we also play an active part in reconstituting those meanings as we pass them on. If the making of meaning is already a creative process, then there is no hard division between the creative nature of writing about crime fact and the creativity involved in crime fiction. It will no longer do to say that one is an act of scientific discovery (in which creativity plays no necessary role), and the other a flight of the imagination. Both are products of active creative minds making meaning.

To understand crime is to engage in a positive act of creation – something requiring invention and imagination. The feminist criminologist is not simply reporting on the phenomenon of crime, but positively constructing that body of knowledge. For example, as I endeavoured to show in the last chapter on the crime of rape, our understanding of this crime depends on certain critical assumptions about the nature of relations between the sexes, and so our understanding is a product of a certain way of looking at heterosexuality that can be constructed quite differently from a feminist perspective. As Cornell explains:

> the reality of Woman cannot be separated from the fictions in life and in theory. When we [feminists] write of Woman, we are indicating the 'not yet'. Feminist theory, in other words, cannot be separately maintained from fiction. Feminist theory, insofar as it involves an appeal to Woman, demands poetic evocation.[1]

Cornell's point here is that feminist appeals for a better world for women, for a better idea of woman, already entail acts of creation

involving imagination. So, once we view the study of crime process of invention rather than the simple discovery of wh already in place, then the division between fact and fiction b to break down, and perhaps in a highly productive fashion. It in fact, already breaking down when empiricist feminists tol men of criminology that the women in their accounts of crime a poor relation to reality. They owed more to the male imagin than to anything to do with actual women. The social dis between traditional male empiricists and the subjects of their s meant that stereotypes – that is invention – predominated. En cist feminists tended to adhere to the view that it was possil discover the real nature of women – to portray women accur through the methods of empirical science. With the entry of philosophically-minded feminists to the debate, there was a fundamental questioning of the bases of knowledge, and a r nition that the world view of the inquiring subject helped to c the objects of her investigation. Cornell's further point abou concept of woman and the need for creativity is that any fer move for change must also require a construction, an imaginir how things could be.

So to alter the meaning of the term 'woman', we may ha invent. We cannot think without the existing categories, but w employ the instabilities in the existing categories to imagine c ent worlds. We must start here, but we can then manipulate n ing because meanings are not bounded and essential, but c operating metaphorically and subject to alteration. Thus, an related justification for moving outside criminology proper i search for new and different ideas about women lies in the r nition that disciplinary boundaries do not hold in a firm or ab manner. Therefore, it is always an act of creation that hold boundary, an act of creation from without that defines wl within (if we accept that meaning is always relational, that t 'just this' is always to say that it is 'not that'). And anyway, has the authoritative status, the right pedigree, to say what inology is?

Criminologists have rarely thought imaginatively about wc Concerted efforts have been made to enter the mental world c male offender, even to ennoble him, though perhaps not alwa a manner which carries conviction (recall that in chapter 2 I tioned the success of this endeavour). But interpretations of wo lives, when they are touched by crime, have generally been and pallid. This chapter is another effort to think differently a women and our relation to crime. It contemplates the conside

between feminism, which seeks to imagine a different world for women based on a transformation of existing categories of meaning, and fiction, which shows us how life could be different and, in so doing, throws light on how life is at the moment. To imagine difference one must always trace the contours of the familiar, and then retrace them along another line.

There is a tension in feminist writing generally that feminist detective writing may specifically help to overcome. The tension is that feminists are always trying to render women the subjects of our own lives, but as we write about women we simultaneously objectify women. That is, we turn women into the objects of our knowledge, imposing our own interpretations on the multiplicity of an entire sex. Is it possible to write about women – their lives and visions – and not objectify women? In one sense, we never can because, as soon as the subject of woman is down on the page, we have made her an object. But there are other senses in which feminist detective writing retains women in the position of knowing subjects, rather than as known objects.

Feminist detective literature works at several levels. It is about women seizing the role of knowing and inquiring subject, both as writer and as the subject of the story written. It also turns the woman reader herself into an investigator as she is required to solve the problem along with the female detective. It creates female subjectivity on three levels: woman as writer, woman as investigator and woman reader who reconstructs and solves the crime as she reads. Thus, the reader engages in an act of creation as she reads, and is not the passive recipient of the words on the page. In fact, my own writing here about the feminist crime writer and reader could be said to form yet another layer of female subjectivity that is not available to the male criminologist. As a woman inquirer into the feminist detective writer, I organize and interpret the feminist writing before me. I am a feminist inquirer who endeavours to retain the subjectivity of her three subjects: the detective writer, her female investigator and the female reader, even though, in a sense, it remains true that as I write about them, they become the objects of my inquiry.

The emergence of feminist crime writing

It was a man, Sir Arthur Conan Doyle, who popularized crime fiction late in the nineteenth century, but a woman who perfected the 'crime puzzle' in the 1920s. Agatha Christie went on to become the biggest-selling English crime writer which suggests that she has exerted a considerable impact on popular conceptions of crime.[2] Clearly, the business of writing creatively about crime was not considered an unsuitable job for a woman. Indeed, a woman was permitted to establish the terms of a genre and was embraced by the populus. Meanwhile, the business of theorising crime fact was to remain a male pursuit: witness the male preserve that was the university in the twenties, which prompted Virginia Woolf's reflections on the need for a room of her own. I have already reflected on some of the institutional reasons for the different fates of women in crime fiction and crime fact. Crime fiction writers have not depended on institutional support. They have been able to launch their careers from the kitchen table, rather than from places of power within the university.

According to Bird and Walker, the 'crime puzzle' novel had its golden age in the 20s and 30s, but was then superseded by a different style of book. There emerged the 'hard-boiled' American crime novel that was to take the form of either 'the classic detective story [or] the private eye story'.[3] This is the genre with which many contemporary feminists engage. There is a particular set of conventions that defines this style of writing, which may be seen to echo those of crime 'fact', that is, of criminal law and criminology, for such books are about 'the investigation of intention and action', a division of human behaviour that also occurs in criminal law. These books assume 'social confidence . . . in the individual investigator and in principles of justice or at least retribution', which repeats the view of an ordered world, a world of law and order, implicit in criminal law and implicit in mainstream criminology.[4] Feminists have entered crime writing by self-consciously playing with the strict formulae of the genre, developing unusual characters and relationships, plotting in new ways.

It has been suggested that a vital difference between feminist and orthodox crime writing concerns the representation of sexuality. 'In hard-boiled crime fiction, a woman who is sexually active is by definition wicked and must be disposed of.'[5] Early women writers, such as Agatha Christie, desexualized women. The newer writers, such as Sara Paretsky, have strong female characters who also have an active (though not always active) sex life. Feminist crime fiction therefore conveys a very positive message to women. 'It presents the fictional possibility of controlling events. . . . The female heroes are strong and capable but not invulnerable or afraid to admit their limitations.'[6] These positive portrayals of women contrast dramatically with those thin and insulting clichés that not only pervade conventional crime fiction, but that (as we saw in the first part of this book) feature consistently in the conventional scholarly writing on crime fact. As Judith Butler says, women become a problem for men 'with the sudden intrusion, the unanticipated agency, of a female "object" who inexplicably returns the glance, reverses the gaze, and contests the place and authority of the masculine position'.[7]

In the new feminist crime writing, violence and its relation to justice is never taken as given. Nor is the characterization of men and women ever entirely orthodox:

> Violence and justice are problematised in these American women's worlds, where the [female detectives] struggle to deal with them while retaining their own decency and integrity... all these writers are revolutionaries, seeking to change the homophobia, the sexism, the perpetration of stereotypes and validation of violence that are so often a part of male crime writing.[8]

The paradox of feminist crime fiction is that it works within a genre that has traditionally depended on a hard-boiled male detective as central character, and that has cast women in the role of sexual sirens or sexual victims, but not subjects in their own right. Almost by definition, crime fiction has entailed this relation of the sexes: the strong man and the weak or corrupted woman. As Bird and Walker put it, 'Action and authority in the conventional detective novel belong to men. At one extreme of the genre, women are victimized and alluring: worse, their victimization is part of their allure.'[9] The feminist wishing to enter the world of crime fiction faces much the same problem as the feminist writing about crime fact, which creates an illuminating parallel for current purposes. The problem confronting both creative and academic feminists is one of entrenched stereotypes, which seems utterly fundamental to the project at hand. 'In the crudest tough-guy school of crime fiction women appear as victimized, manipulative or simply distracting.'[10] That is, they appear in much the same guises as they have in criminological writing. Think, for example, of the women in the work of Howard Becker.

The problem of the masculinity of the genre is one for both the feminist writer and the feminist reader. The inbuilt masculinity of the detective novel caused me to respond to my first feminist detective novel with incredulity. At the first reading, I did not believe a woman could be a detective, someone paid to solve crime. Because I had absorbed the conventions of the genre, a detective for me meant a male detective. By the time I was on to my second feminist detective novel, I was beginning to see things differently: I was becoming a convert and a believer in the woman detective. My way of viewing women and our relation to crime was being changed by these novels; they worked. This is why I think these books of fiction have something to teach us as criminologists. They show women in new ways: threatened but not terrorized, intellectually engaged rather than confused and befuddled, self-reliant rather than looking to a man. And so they help us to question the inevitability of the old ways. They also take a sharp look at the violent forms of masculinity that have become acceptable in the more orthodox literature. One prominent feminist who has led us into new ways of seeing women and our relations with men is Sara Paretsky.

Sara Paretsky and V.I. Warshawski

Sara Paretsky was a visitor to Writers' Week during the 1994 Adelaide Festival of Arts. She was one of the prominent international authors we were given a chance 'to meet' and whose life we heard about. The meet-the-author sessions at the Festival can be highly personal. The writer may decide to tell us what gets her up in the morning, what pen she uses, what impels and sustains her as a writer, about her muse, about her sense of her self. Dr Paretsky was a particularly intimate and affecting speaker. With sad-eyed eloquence, she spoke of the men in her life and their failure to treat her as the capable woman that she so manifestly is. There was her father, who put her brothers through university while she was obliged to pay for herself. There were her male colleagues in the insurance business before she was a writer, who found pleasure in reducing their female associates to tears. And she spoke of her decision to reply to these indignities by an act of creation: by giving life to her outspoken, American, feminist detective, V.I. Warshawski. For Paretsky, fiction is a means of coping with what she sees as the despair and loneliness of the modern female condition.

Paretsky turned to the detective genre as the one she knew best, but found herself with the genre problem I have already described, for the heroes and anti-heroes of this medium were men who did, while their women were done to. Paretsky's protagonist, therefore, did not begin life in her current guise. Paretsky's first thoughts for her character had her as a sort of 'Philip Marlowe in drag': a hard-boiled, wise-cracking woman of the world. Paretsky found it hard to see a real woman running the crime agency until she thought about herself, and her friends, and how they might behave in such a role. They would stick together, and they would question male authority, but they would also be vulnerable at times, and unnerved by a world hostile and violent to the independent woman with opinions. They would not always be in charge of the situation. Humphrey Bogart they were not because Bogart never had to inhabit the world in which women are obliged to live.

With these disclosures about the birth of her subject, Paretsky revealed the dilemmas of feminism and crime fiction. A danger for the feminist detective writer is that her concerns about assimilation into a genre with such an unsatisfactory pedigree will kill the story (and not just the murder victim) stone dead. She is not allowed to depict women as sex objects, and her leading character must be both tough and caring. In short, she must be true to women and yet entertain, a requirement which has never been imposed on the criminologist. Can this be done? Sara Paretsky has shown us the possibilities by creating a feminist detective with courage, humour and foibles who is also convincing as a woman.

In Paretsky's own account, V.I. is 'not a parody of Spade or Marlowe but just a woman doing a job that ha[s] traditionally been done by a man'.[11] She is overtly feminine: attuned to fashion, favouring silk blouses and high heels. But her fashionable attire does not indicate weakness; her pleasure in silk and linen is not a sign of frivolity but rather an indication of style. V.I. is intrepid (though also convincingly anxious and at times neurotic) and will employ violence to defend herself and others. She has a strong social conscience and is particularly engaged by political problems associated with women. For example, her close friend Lotty, a medical practitioner, falls victim to the violence of anti-abortionists in one story. In another, V.I. deals with homelessness and a woman's fear that her failure to provide will mean that her children are taken into care.

Though intrepid and compassionate, V.I. is also a hard nut who does not take lip from her clients. She examines them with a cool, critical and often humorous eye, especially when they have underestimated her talents, that is, by treating her simply as a woman. In Paretsky's writing, we are always allowed to reverse the usual line of gaze. The belittled woman appraises those who normally condescend. It is her expertise to which they turn, though often with reluctance, and as a last resort.

Paretsky depicts the female condition beyond the embrace of the conventional family circle. She shows us a woman who lives an independent life alone (which is increasingly a reality for women, often by choice) and enjoys the fact that she need accommodate no others. V.I. suits herself, pursues her own conception of the good and honourable existence, though often at the cost of feeling raw and up against the odds. The mix of discomfort and pleasure in the single female existence strikes a chord of truth. However, as Paretsky herself concedes, there are aspects of her story that require us to suspend disbelief. Quite deliberately, she stretches the limits of current realities for women, but thereby allows us a vision of life which is less constrained. Thus, V.I. walks the streets at night, inhabits the most dangerous of places, but is never sexually assaulted – a fact which makes her an acceptable read for many women. 'In a way', says Paretsky, 'V.I. acts out what I idealize; she's someone who doesn't have those fears, which is really not true of any woman I know.'[12]

Paretsky depicts a strong woman who can handle violence, who indeed enjoys the odd act of retribution against the evil doer, but the author tends not to dwell on serious violence against women. For Paretsky, the representation of especially sexual violence against women is a harm in itself, and so she has made it a deliberate policy not to portray cruelty inflicted on women by men, especially cruelty of a sexual kind, which is widely available outside feminist detective fiction. The crime that generally concerns Paretsky is corporate crime, not personal crimes of violence. When the reader retreats into a Paretsky novel, she knows she can feel relatively secure.

In fact, the detective form provides its own safety net. We know that our heroine will not die and that she will persist in her self-assigned role of investigating (and so helping to stop) crime. Security for the reader comes from knowing that the crime will be solved (and thus order restored at least in that respect) and that our heroine will live to fight another day. Neither assumption, of course, can be made in the real world, which is simply not susceptible to such neat closure, to such tidy endings.

Patricia Cornwell and Dr Kay Scarpetta

Patricia Cornwell adopts a very different approach to the female encounter with crime, and so alters our perception of women in rather different ways. In each of Cornwell's books, she obliges us to look directly at the physical injury done to women's bodies, in the course of a brutal murder, so there is a level of security Cornwell refuses us, even though she is arguably a feminist writer working within the detective genre. Anxiety and fear run through her novels, even though we know that we will still have the catharsis of a solution, and one that is offered by a woman, not a man. Again, in the real world, such resolutions and catharsis are by no means assured and so, like Paretsky, we remain within the realm of fiction, but a fiction which alters our perceptions of the real.

Cornwell portrays a woman expert who discovers what crime has been done to women, and why. She is Dr Kay Scarpetta, Chief Medical Examiner for Virginia, who examines the dead body of the murdered woman, who dissects her and ultimately explains her death. The reader is told of the medical examination in unflinching detail. In each novel, Cornwell lingers over the form of the murdered woman and contemplates the terror that has preceded her death. Given her subject matter, which seems designed to instil fear in women, it is perhaps surprising that Cornwell has a strong following of women readers. In her critical feminist reading of Cornwell's oeuvre, Sue Turnbull offers several suggestions why this is the case.[13] One is the scientific finesse of Scarpetta that is disclosed as she examines the body and then recounts her findings to her detective side-kick, Pete Marino. Marino and Scarpetta form an unlikely partnership. He is a course-grained, but discerning, police officer with integrity who plays 'the Watson to her Holmes'. There is obvious satisfaction to be had here for the woman reader. However, the satisfactions run deeper than this and are to do with the way Cornwell alters conventional understandings of women and their relation to crime.

It has been suggested that the appeal of the detective novel lies in its sense of law and order.[14] Although crime is invariably committed, that crime is invariably solved, the offender brought to justice and order restored. Though these ingredients might appear to be present in the Cornwell novel, there is always a prevailing sense of unease. This is not the safe detective read because, in various ways, the medium has been altered. Cornwell reworks the genre, 'placing women and their concerns centre stage, questioning the workings of official justice and law and suggesting that the world is anything but a safe and ordered place'.[15] There is a raw realism here, a sense of the uncertainties of life, especially for women, which is often missing from the conventional crime novel as well as from the work of crime fact, that is, from the criminological treatise. Cornwell's killers are not glamourized. They are unmemorable, ordinary men, that is, like real killers.[16]

In Cornwell's crime writing, doubt and danger are heightened by the sex of the central character. Female life is portrayed in all its complexity, indeed, in a manner which is foreign to the criminologist. 'Scarpetta constantly fears betrayal, often by the man with whom she is sexually involved. She is assailed by anxiety about the masculine on all sides. There is her fear of the killer, realized and relived, as she contemplates the horrific injuries he inflicts, particularly on his female victims, anxiety about her colleagues who appear to conspire against her, and anxiety about her personal relationships with men.'[17] Throughout her novels, Cornwell reminds us that her subject is a woman, that women have no natural home among the experts on crime, and so she must forge one. Scarpetta is never allowed to relax into her profession but is always having to manufacture herself as something novel: a woman who deals coolly with the dead while her male colleagues are revolted; a woman who is a senior scientific expert, not a subordinate; a woman who is regarded as an odd fish, without children and living alone (in truth not an odd situation at all). By contrast, Scarpetta's predecessor, Cagney, is in every way a man, and Scarpetta is made to suffer for her female differences:

> People were constantly reminding me of him. . . . He rarely wore gloves while doing a post. He was known to arrive at scenes eating his lunch. He went hunting with the cops, he went to barbeques with the judges. . . . I paled by comparison and I knew comparisons were constantly being made. The only hunts and barbeques I was invited to were courtrooms and conferences in which targets were drawn on me and fires lit beneath my feet.[18]

We are discomforted both by the professional situation of Scarpetta and by the plight of the murdered women. Turnbull suggests that what Cornwell is giving the woman reader is not the usual escape from her own anxieties, by immersion in the unreal anxieties of the novel, but a direct exposure to them. Women are allowed to examine their 'own anxieties and ambiguous feelings about men',[19] as colleagues, as lovers, as our potential assailants.

A related function Cornwell serves for the woman reader, is in providing a compassionate woman's interpretation of the horrors of violence done to women, while keeping faith with the dignity of the murdered woman. As a woman, with a woman's body, Scarpetta has an intimate appreciation of the significance of the mutilations of the bodies she examines. When she reconstructs the crime, she does so from the point of view of the woman, imagining the scene as if she were the victim. And, though the women victims in her stories are dead, and so cannot speak for themselves, they are not accepts that she is 'nothing-Bella, this rubbish-Bella'. In chapter wever, Zahavi's story takes a turn. All along we have only reading the prologue to the more important story, which begins Bella's assertion of her freedom. Zahavi shifts from Dworkin's pia (which, for Dworkin, is the present) to a new era in which emerges with a fresh persona and so begins to fight back: r the butcher than the lamb'.[29]

e should have worn a balaclava. . . . But balaclavas are made for e close-cropped head. They're made for the lads. . . . But the boys their balaclavas could not imagine Bella in her basement. Tooling p, pulling on gloves, zipping up the jacket.[30]

s Zahavi makes plain, women are not supposed to be the dark eless shadows in the night and so 'Bella in her basement is ond their [men's] imagination. She's beyond belief.' But Zahavi brought her into being. Though a work of fiction (or perhaps ecially because of this), her richly-drawn Bella enters the read-s imagination. 'She's a video nasty in velvet gloves. Mad-dog lla has slipped her leash.'[31] For the first time, Bella leaves her flat night. 'This is something new for Bella. . . . One small step for lla, but a huge leap for womankind.'[32] She breaks into his flat, mmer in hand, intent on revenge:

He stared at the hooded figure by his bed. The horror in those eyes, was something she would hug to her heart through many a long night. For the first time in her life, she looked into a man's face and saw fear flickering back at her.[33]

In the black comedy which unfolds, Bella becomes an avenging ngel. She now frequents the streets and with each man she en-counters, the new Bella appraises his transgressions (which are both considerable and quite ordinary), and then gives him his due. First, she reduces him with her withering gaze and her sharp tongue, then with the brutal but measured act. Take the story of Norman, the senior lecturer (who 'almost made professor'), who meets her in a hotel bar and invites her to his room. Norman slips into some-thing more comfortable and emerges:

Indeed his lack of self-consciousness was extraordinary, given what he'd been given. . . . The nonchalance with which his generous breasts lay on that swollen belly unnerved her. She would have killed for a pair like that.[34]

simply reduced to female flesh. Nor are their bodies eroticized, for Scarpetta always treats her bodies with respect. Cornwell familiar-izes us with the wrongs done to the female body and, through Scarpetta, expresses her outrage.

Cornwell is revolted by the eroticization of woman as crime victim, which she exposes as a commonplace in the masculine world of criminal justice. In the opening pages of Postmortem, her first crime novel, Cornwell takes us to the scene of the crime and de-scribes in detail the unclothed body of a murdered woman. The dead woman is surrounded by the men of the police force, per-forming the standard forensic tasks. Dr Scarpetta foreshadows what will happen to this woman as the investigation proceeds, provid-ing a critical but realistic appraisal of the criminal law at work. She reflects on the fact that:

The dead are defenseless, and the violation of this woman . . . had only begun. I knew it would not end until [she] was turned inside out, every inch of her photographed, and all of it on display for experts, the police, attorneys, judges and members of the jury to see. There would be thoughts, remarks about her physical attributes or lack of them. There would be sophomoric jokes and cynical asides as the victim, not the killer, went on trial, every aspect of her person and the way she lived, scrutinized, judged and, in some instances, degraded.[20]

Cornwell merges the role of crime investigator and crime victim when Scarpetta discovers that the dead woman is a physician like herself. The woman victim is also a woman expert, but her exper-tise has afforded her no protection from brutal crime. Scarpetta observes the victim's 'recent editions of the Annals of Surgery, Lan-cet and the Journal of Trauma'[21] and is 'thoroughly unsettled'.[22] She cannot objectify the body and so put the crime at a distance. Corn-well has described her approach to Scarpetta and the bodies she examines thus:

I show it to you through Scarpetta's eyes and there is never a time, not even once, where her observations would be voyeuristic. She is looking at it from a humanitarian point of view, from [the position of] a physician, a scientist, somebody whose job it is to investigate violence and reconstruct what happened to somebody and take care of the problem. So she is never looking at a victim and focussing on the attractiveness of their anatomy, for example. I mean that would just never enter her mind so . . . there's really no room for any kind of voyeurism because it would be so out of character for her which is very different from the writers, particularly men, who write these crime novels ... they're very obsessed with what the woman looked like and they even make her sexy in death. . . . You can answer this, how many women would look at another woman who's been raped and strangled and be focussing on what a good body she has?[23]

So, we are led to see the worst, but through the eyes of a compassionate woman for whom the often sexual brutality has intimate meaning, not through the eyes of the usually dispassionate, or worse, voyeuristic, man. We are afforded the protections of a woman's standpoint, in a situation in which women are most vulnerable and which is nearly always in the control of men. Scarpetta cannot objectify the female body, nor does she wish to. As a consequence, she cannot shut out the images of violence, and so her nightmares are peopled by the featureless faces of the killers.

The shock of disorder outside the genre:
Helen Zahavi and Bella

Cornwell dwells on the dangerous and the uncertain, but Dr Scarpetta always gets her man. In each novel, there is the expected resolution, hence Cornwell remains, in this aspect of her writing, within the detective genre. In the work of Helen Zahavi, however, there is no wish to displace the reader's anxieties, but rather to play on them. In *Dirty Weekend*, Zahavi steps outside the genre to provide a convincing, though satirical, picture of the danger and uncertainty of women's lives, and a vindicated female serial killer. Violent men are made to face the sort of horror they normally inflict. Though this is ostensibly a work of fiction, there is a realism to this novel that is often missing from academic writing on crime, for Zahavi describes the dangers and risks of life for women, with its indeterminacies and with women's realization that the state does not protect them. Zahavi's initial premise is that brutal crimes against women are often unreported and, even if reported, they are not necessarily solved or understood.

Though she dwells on violence directed at women, Zahavi depicts a woman replying to this violence. Her protagonist is satirical, dangerous, ungovernable and unpredictable. She encounters danger but creates further danger and so unsettles the *status quo*. Zahavi's novel responds to the imaginings of Sharon Marcus in that her character makes men know what it is to be afraid of the other sex, as a sex:

In the place of a tremulous female body immobilized cavity, we can begin to ima subject to change, as a potential object of f Conversely, we do not have to imagine the weapon ... we can take the temporality of sideration and bear in mind the fragility of ability of male genitalia.[24]

Zahavi tells a disturbing story of repetitiou time of intimidation by men, her central back and then keeps striking back, but alway protagonist makes a moral judgement prior so this might be regarded as a modern mor

Dirty Weekend 'is the story of Bella, who and realized she'd had enough'. Bella represen confines her life, closes her doors and windo ments, but still lives in fear. Bella lives alone i basement flat in Brighton, England. She has b but has found herself a corner where she hopes Her flat lets in only a small square of light, tho sun. She then discovers that she is being watche opposite and so she draws the curtain and shuts locks her windows, and breathes stale air all nigh Bellas of the world do. They lock their windows, air. . . . Putrid air and bars. Men riot over less.'[25] B it, however. Next, the man telephones her and tell see her through the curtains and asks her 'to touc feels 'the fear churning and the nausea rising', sh lessly in the empty room'.[26] Bella stops answering tl he approaches her in the park and tells her of his d her: 'Think of the worst thing I can do to you, an doing it.'[27]

He never touched her again. He didn't have to touch he knew he'd already forced his way inside. He'd already space and set up camp. Squatter's rights. Possession is of the law, and he already possessed her. All she could crouch in a corner and wait for the day he would come tl window.[28]

The fable of Bella starts in Dworkinian fashion, with Be of all dignity, the embodiment of all women who have cc life because of men. Recall that Dworkin depicted wome mutilated (physically or psychologically) and as overde

Despite herself, Bella is interested and takes down her pants. Norman tries to perform, grunting and sweating, but fails. 'Percy remained in his slug-like state. He didn't care. He wasn't bothered. He couldn't give a toss.'[35] Norman attempts to rationalise his failure. His therapist has told him that failure to achieve erection is not important. Yet Bella is sceptical; she observes, 'But he would, though, wouldn't he?'[36] And then she cannot control her laughter and, so, according to Zahavi, breaks the rules:

> And they are not arbitrary rules. They are not random rules. They are rules grounded in what each fears most, the most devastating thing a man might suffer from a woman, or a woman from a man. He fears her ridicule. She fears his rage. She might laugh at him. He might kill her. There is no balance in the fear. Justice demands balance. Balance demands Bella.[37]

Norman rears back 'in shock and horror, as if she were a foul heretic'.[38] He kicks her in the face and Bella apologizes. He hits her another time for good measure and she agrees to make amends by acceding to his request for bondage and ties him up. She then announces her attention to kill him (she suffocates him by placing a plastic bag over his head), explaining that 'it's nothing personal'. Her final message before she despatches him on his 'final sabbatical' is that 'the rules have changed'.[39]

Zahavi's brutal and satirical inversion of gender roles serves several purposes. It sharpens our sense of the current gender imbalance. It shows how an underlying fear of men modifies women's behaviour, and it does this perhaps more so than the dark passages in the writing of Dworkin. It employs humour, showing that feminism does not have to be bleak nor lacking in irony. Though it is, I think, intended to be a gothic tale of horror, it is also anchored in everyday reality for women. In particular, it expresses the 'heretical' thoughts I suspect women often have about men, but do not express, except perhaps among themselves in safe company. It is, therefore, a reply to the writings of feminists and non-feminists alike that women are overdetermined by patriarchal culture. It shows that the hold that men have over women is not metaphysically nearly perfect, as MacKinnon puts it, but is constantly questioned and subverted.[40]

Paretsky gives us a somewhat romanticized reversal of the sexes – woman steps into man's shoes as detective – which is, in fact, quite liberating for her female readers. Warshawski is a lone, rugged, detective type, identifiably a woman, but still not a long remove from, say, Parker's Spenser or Corris's Hardy, despite Paretsky's statements to the contrary. With Cornwell, there is greater subtlety and realism, and we are disconcerted to a greater degree. And yet, Dr Scarpetta, steeped in blood, in man's dominant role, is also in some ways a simple reversal of the sexes. She remains in the role of detective who observes the rules and respects them. Zahavi gives us a more satirical and violent inversion that strays off into anarchy. We have a heightened sense of the claustrophobic nature of conventional female life, its indignities and terrors, when a man is made to experience them. We also have an enhanced appreciation of male freedoms when a woman assumes them – when Bella hits the streets. Unreflecting male freedom no longer appears innocent. Zahavi shows us that what many men take for granted – fresh air through an open window, leaving the house at night – is highly problematic for women, and that it is problematic because of men.

6

An Ethical Relation

Traditional epistemology has increasingly come under challenge this century, and yet it retains a secure home within criminology. Across the other disciplines, there has been a questioning of conventional science as the means of discerning truth. The conventional scientific outlook described by Bertrand Russell (in chapter 1), and many years later endorsed by the leading men of British and American criminology, treated as axiomatic that facts were things to be discovered in the world with the aid of rigorous scientific method. However, for the new thinkers, such as the later Wittgenstein, it could no longer be assumed that 'the facts we find are ... plucked out of reality ready made. [Rather] They have to be stated and this requires language.'[1] Facts and language are, therefore, intimately related. The one (facts) cannot take form without the other (language). Thus, facts are utterly dependent on language.

As we saw most clearly in chapter 3, the vital consequence of this dependent relationship between facts and language is that facts take their colour and meaning from the conventions of the language that is used to denote them. Statements about facts in the world must, therefore, always ascribe properties to those 'facts' according to the conventions of the given language, rather than according to a self-given, self-evident world that forces its nature on us. As Jackson explains:

> These ascriptions do not come out there from the world, but from the conventions of the language that we have adopted to reflect the conceptual frameworks or frames of reference that make sense to us. To determine whether something is to count as a fact, therefore, we

do not dip into some linguistically naked reality, but instead we
must ask whether it can be justified within the conventions of a
language which are grounded in what Wittgenstein calls our 'forms
of life'.[2]

In short, we do not discover the world, in its raw essentials, through
the rigorous use of scientific method. Instead, we constitute the
world and we do so linguistically. We come at the world already
with a language, and within that language there is already encoded a particular way of looking at the world, a philosophical
framework.

Wittgenstein proved this point ingeniously by the use of an arrow to denote direction. In the first instance, it might seem that the
arrow speaks for itself, that it tells us directly, without any medi-
ating interpretation, that it indicates a direction. But how do we
know this? It is a previously-established convention that tells us to
read the arrow from shaft to point. Indeed, it is a convention that
tells us that this sign is a sign for direction, and not simply a
meaningless, or perhaps only a decorative, mark. 'The arrow points
only in the application that a living being makes of it.'[3] But we are
so immersed in a way of thinking about the arrow, in a particular
interpretation of the arrow, that it is difficult to see it only as a
mark on a page or as something other than an indicator of direction. For us it is already a sign with meaning. (So, too, when I look
in the mirror I see a woman who is already invested with meaning.
She does not look back at me in her raw essentials, except perhaps
very early in the morning! In many ways, she is already interpreted for me. Like Wittgenstein's arrow, I am obliged to see her in
a certain direction.)

From this, it follows that theory and viewpoint precede observation, rather than our senses directly informing us about the world.
It also follows that it is impossible to view the world in a neutral,
value-free manner. As the standpoint feminists made clear (in chapter 2), who is doing the viewing matters. And, as I have made plain
throughout this book, in criminology, the viewpoint that has mattered most has been masculine. The (male) subject of criminal law
and criminology is a creation of (Western male) culture. He does
not spring into the world direct from (man's) nature, nor is he simply a fact in the world that has been discovered in a neutral fashion
with the aid of science. He is a feat of the Western male imagination and he can be reimagined, even dislocated. Chapters 4 and 5
were endeavours to unseat him, or at least to turn him around.

Similarly, the qualities attributed to women in criminology are imagined things with endless permutations. The feminists discussed throughout this volume have done much to question the masculine viewpoint of criminology, and so to alter our thinking about both men and women and their relation to crime. They have indicated that women do not recognize themselves in the subject of criminology and they have brought to our attention the refusal of women to accept their outsider status in a passive manner. They have shown us that the sexed roles that are allotted to women[4] never function in a tight or bounded way. Irigaray, for example, has shown us that women are always transforming our ascribed statuses through imaginative parody and mimicry. Or, as Silvia Vegetti Finzi observes, 'woman has always resisted "normalisation", she has never completely entered the place assigned to her by the masculine economy.'[5]

Feminist empiricists said some time ago that there was a dire need for criminology to document the lives of real women as they are lived now in their particularity,[6] and then to reconsider the adequacy of its model of humanity. They pointed out (and continue to stress) that criminology's failure to do this undermines all its claims to treat women as its subjects. It marks women as outsiders and deprives them of the benefits of an understanding of real women's lives. Feminist empiricists continue to do important research that reveals how women experience criminal justice both as offenders and as victims. They persist with the point that it is simply unsatisfactory and unscholarly to base our understanding of crime on the lives of men, and then implicitly to deny the presence of a sex bias. It is both unethical (to women) and unscholarly to push women to the margins of the discipline. And, given that this is where women have largely been, there is a lot of catching up to be done.

But considerably more than this is needed, more than the documentation of women's current relations with crime and criminal justice. Though a first step is for criminology to recognize the workings of real women's lives, the second is to move beyond those trappings and imagine how we might live quite different lives. According to Elizabeth Grosz, 'Feminist theory must always function in two directions if it is to effectively challenge patriarchal knowledge:'

On the one hand, it must engage in what could be called a *negative* or *reactive* project – the project of challenging what currently exists, or criticizing prevailing social, political, and theoretical relations. Without this negative or *anti-sexist* goal, feminist theory remains unanchored in and unrelated to the socio-theoretical status quo. It risks repeating problems of the past, especially patriarchal assumptions, without recognizing them as such. But it remains *simply* reactive, *simply* a critique.[7]

The courtesans of Lucknow, were a salutory reminder of these socio-political realities. Despite their percipience in assessing critically the daily grind of the lives of conventional Indian women, and their consequent rejection of that way of life, they were still, in a sense, always victims of structured economic inequalities. It would be to ignore the underlying problem if we were to assume that the courtesans could, through an act of will, evade the ills of patriarchy. But as Grosz continues:

> To say something is not true, valuable, or useful *without posing alternatives* is, paradoxically, to affirm that it is true, and so on. Thus coupled with this negative project . . . must be a positive, constructive project: creating alternatives, producing feminist, not simply anti-sexist theory. Feminist theory must exist as *both* critique and construct.[8]

We need to move beyond critique because critique on its own 'leaves one in a permanent opposition, where one does not have to take responsibility for one's mistakes'.[9] We need to begin to construct the visions of the lives that women want. A close appreciation of real women's lives, lived now (work already done and continuing to be done by feminist empiricists and by standpoint theorists) is the beginning of the female sexing of the criminological subject, of getting women, as women, into the discipline. But what men have always also had is a vision of their ideal selves (as rational, self-possessing creatures of the mind) to inspire them and guide them. Women also need guiding visions. Such visions try to 'imagine the unimaginable – namely, where we're going before we're there'.[10]

The task of even sketching lightly a female utopia is in a sense always undermined by the fact that we can never extract ourselves from our present sexual category.[11] Because, like Wittgenstein's arrow, a woman is always constituted a woman before she considers whether she likes it (as a man is constituted a man), and whether she might not prefer something else, a woman is compelled to start from here, with the present meaning of 'woman' and all its connotations, before exploring the way that present meanings are susceptible to manipulation. But there is another reason why we should work with, and within, the existing categories of meaning, and why we should not jettison or reject the current meanings of being a woman. The reason is an ethical one, for to reject the word 'woman' is also to reject the people associated with the term – that is, it is to reject women. As Drucilla Cornell has observed, 'a challenge to the gender hierarchy... must ... involve the affirmation of the feminine within sexual difference ... without the affirmation of feminine sexual difference, we will unconsciously perpetuate the gender hierarchy under which the feminine is *necessarily* devalued.'[12]

A related point is that to reject the idea of 'woman' because of its mainly negative constituent meanings, is to drive woman towards her 'opposite'. We have two sexes only, no more subtlety than this in our present sexual division of humanity, and so within the current, but not inevitable, frames of meaning, to be not-woman is to be man, both culturally and biologically.[13] We cannot escape the fact that woman has been constituted within an opposition (why opposed?) of male/female, even if we question the fact of this opposition. So, if we reject the appellation 'woman', there is a sense in which we are necessarily embracing the appellation 'man'. But do women want to be men? Is this progress?

Having said that we should not jettison 'woman' for ethical reasons, our problem is still one of robust and inhospitable definitions of the female sex that form the background (and foreground) of change. Were women obliged to form their existences only within the existing category of 'woman', then that would seem to leave them stuck with a very negative characterization of themselves – in criminology and, of course, well beyond into the other disciplines and into the world beyond the various university academies. But, as I have consistently suggested, neither women nor men simply collapse into the dominant conventional definitions of their sex.

To advocate utopian thinking is not to romanticize and idealize women as they are now. Rather, it is to reach beyond the current stereotypes of woman, and beyond the current real lives of women, to think of women differently. Feminists are already engaged in this imaginative project. In a sense, all the feminists discussed in this book have been doing this one way or another. Perhaps the writers of crime fiction have been doing so most explicitly, but equally the feminist empiricists needed a vision of something better in order to say what was wrong with the existing empiricism of criminology. 'Feminist utopian visions ... are mostly of the dynamic, rather than the programmatic kind; they do not seek to offer blueprints of the ideal future, still less of the steps toward attaining it. They are intended more to bring about shifts in consciousness (paradigm shifts).'[14] To Drucilla Cornell:

> it is precisely because the feminine, as it's lived, can never be reduced
> to its current definitions that [she] can advocate an affirmation of the
> feminine within sexual difference.... [For] The affirmation of the
> feminine within sexual difference operates within a ... contradiction
> that explicitly recognises that the feminine is precisely what is denied
> the specificity of a 'nature' or a 'being'.[15]

Cornell asks us to affirm what is 'other' to the current gender order, which is not a reversion to the old ways, but an imagining of the new.

Women currently lack a significant presence as subjects in criminology. If the discipline is to maintain its credibility, there is a pressing need for mainstream criminologists (not just feminists) to recognize the sexed particularity of women's lives, something which the empiricists have been working at with considerable success. The discipline needs also to recognize the right of women to participate in new positive visions of themselves. How is this to be done? The specific philosophical problem for criminologists is how to think differently about women, crime and criminal justice when, as criminologists, we are already steeped in a discipline which has a certain view of its (implicitly male) subject and a certain view of women (which is a part of the broader culture's view of women, a culture in which we are also steeped). In fact, the very condition of being a criminologist is to have this insider point of view. To practise criminology is to think within the frames of reference of the criminologist. One is not recognized as a criminologist if one does not engage with the existing range of theories, deal with the subject matter of criminology as criminology defines it, publish in criminology journals, go to criminology conferences. To have any authority and recognition as a criminologist, we must do these things, for these are the very conditions of meaning of being a criminologist. So, one is always already working within the frames of meaning of criminology. Contamination is absolutely essential and inevitable. This puts the feminist criminologist in a curious position in that she is required to operate within the discipline to have any voice at all, but that discipline is premised on the maleness of both its academicians (because the role of knower is assumed by a man), and of its subjects of inquiry.

Constructing an ethical non-violent relation between the sexes

I began this book with a reflection on what I see to be a fundamental problem of modern criminology. The problem is that criminology continues to take the male as its standard case, and so continues to regard woman as simply not-man. By regarding man as the human norm, the sex specificity of man in criminology (both man as inquiring subject, that is, as criminologist, and man as subject of inquiry, that is, as criminal man) is eliminated. This tendency to see man as the standard case and woman as the particular, as her own special case, has made the discipline remarkably blind to the political and intellectual significance of one of its most central features: that crime is largely an activity of men.

I have also suggested that it is only with the recognition that woman exists as a separate subject who can herself make man the object of her understanding, that criminological man will be able to appreciate his own limits, the contours of his own sexual difference. As Richard Bernstein has explained:

> it is only through an engaged encounter with the Other, with the otherness of the Other, that one comes to a more informed, textured understanding of the traditions to which 'we' belong. It is in our genuine encounters with what is other and alien (even in ourselves) that we can further our own self-understanding.[16]

A concerted endeavour to engage with the Otherness of Woman would serve more than one purpose. It would help criminologists to develop a greater appreciation of the particular nature of the enterprise in which they have engaged: that is, the study of men, rather than the study of the two sexes. And, when they understand the specificity, rather than generality, of their enterprise to date, then the discipline should become more reflective about itself and its project. Different questions would arise about the genesis, and the perpetuation, of the social practices that produce men and women, and how those practices conduce to, or discourage, different forms of social and anti-social behaviour, and even determine what is to count as social and anti-social behaviour (see chapter 4 on the very meaning of the crime of rape). We might, therefore, consider more seriously the implications of those practices for the creation of a good and ethical society. A greater appreciation of the social methods by which men and women are encouraged to inhabit their sexual categories may also give us the means of effecting change.

The prevailing belief that the current sexing of humanity is natural and inevitable impedes progress towards different constituting practices. A greater awareness of the means by which man has enhanced his sense of autonomy, of his self-completeness (through the repression and exclusion of the feminine), might help us to think differently about how men could be. We need to consider the damage done not only to women, but also to men, by conventional masculinity. We need to consider the qualities men have repressed in themselves and in other men (such as gay men) in order to ensure their difference from the feminine, and how we might bring those excluded qualities to the fore, for the benefit of both the sexes.

Saturated with the familiar, utterly at home with themselves, (heterosexual) men are perhaps poorly placed to appreciate their own defining qualities (while gay men have always been obliged to consider what makes a man a man). It is a female understanding that, perhaps, can render the familiar unfamiliar, the normal strange, and so show up the constituting qualities of the dominant masculine. Centuries of female accommodation to men have taught women a great deal about the specific character of the masculine, its needs and demands. While men have not needed to monitor their borders with the feminine (because the feminine has not been something to which men have had to accommodate themselves), women living on the borders of male territory, at the male margins, have needed a finer appreciation of sexual cartography. By listening to women, by according women expertise in the masculine, men might learn more of the contours of their own natures. They could, thus, benefit from an idea emerging in much of the new post-colonial literature, that 'of the exile as bearing witness'.[17]

With a better appreciation of the making of the sexes, we might think of different avenues of criminological inquiry, and perhaps new policies would emerge as a consequence. At present, for example, women are encouraged to fear men and to circumscribe their public behaviour. The customary association of men with the use of force is not confined to the criminal population. Our culture also draws a close connection between men, physical coercion and the legitimate exercise of authority, usually in order to assert control over another, to extract obedience. Virtually every time we see the imposition of authority, with either a veiled or explicit use of physical coercion, it is a man in this role. Often, this authority is depicted as perfectly appropriate: it may be familial, as in the rule of the father, or it may be political, as in the rule of the head of state or his functionaries. By contrast, vulnerability to force is nearly always given a female form. It is not invariably the case that a woman must assume the role of the weak one, the one in need of a man's protection. However, when it is a man who assumes this role, when he is threatened and humiliated, he is often in the same moment reduced to the feminine, considered an object of pity, effeminate.

Female vulnerability is often invoked to strengthen both our sense of male power and the need for its considered use, that is, paradoxically, to protect women. Indeed, women seem to play a vital role in the demonstration of male potency (an idea which has played a central role in this book). The adequate, strong male is one who performs strongly, and who is potent (with a woman, though not with a man).[18] When these positions are reversed, when a woman is seen to be physically, sexually or psychologically dominant, even violently aggressive, it is interesting as a curiosity, and the woman in question is often treated as unnatural, as a freak of female nature.

Instrumental aggression in women, both of a legitimate and illegitimate nature, lacks a place in our culture. (By instrumental aggression I mean that which achieves a desired result, rather than aggression as a manifestation of hysteria, of female loss of control, which in fact we do see portrayed.) What is seen as normal in a man, as a means of maintaining status and authority, appears unnatural and inappropriate in a woman to the point that it is redefined as something else. Hence, the angry woman is defined as the hysteric, but there is no equivalent concept of the male hysteric.[19] Women are not expected to use force when their femininity is impugned; in fact, the use of force to assert one's status is seen as the very antithesis of conventional femininity.[20] Nor is it thought natural for a woman to use force to maintain authority over another person, especially for a man to be the object of her authority.[21] The man who is the target of female violence is unmanned and positioned as a woman, as is the man who is raped by a man. The position of victim, especially the victim of sexual violence, is culturally sexed as female while the assailant is sexed male.[22]

As a consequence, women who behave in a manner inconsistent with either male authority or female vulnerability are poorly represented in our culture and are often derided when they do appear. Conventional depictions of the family have a man present as an authoritative head of household, despite the fact that many women choose to live alone, or with children, or with other women: that is, without a man's 'protection'.[23] Such women do not organise their domestic (nor necessarily their sexual) lives around the needs of a man, and so they could be said to threaten the dominant order, for they deny the centrality of men to female life. Such women refuse to play the Jill to his Jack, the Dora to his Dick. As Richard Collier has observed, one of the principal objections of the 'pro-family' right to the single [and lesbian] mother is that it is 'motherhood without men'.[24]

Also poorly represented in our culture are the men who dispute the messages and the demands of muscular, dominating masculinity, wishing to dissociate themselves from the portrayals of potent and (at least potentially) threatening men.[25] Many men decry the violence against women with which such masculinity is often associated. Some gay men choose to parody it.[26] Some men feel the force of it directed against themselves when they refuse to conform to the muscular male type.[27] The most provocative thing the British comic actor, Stephen Fry, could do in a recent episode in which he was heckled (by 'boys' from his old school, not by working-class youth) was to blow his hecklers a kiss. It precipitated an immediate response of violence involving the breaking of fingers. Men who transgress the rules of muscular masculinity are likely to elicit violence in men who hold it dear. There seems to be almost a desperate desire to preserve men from associations with the feminine and its supposed weakness and subordination.

Perhaps it would be appropriate to see whether there is something positively dysfunctional about certain forms of masculinity. Perhaps we should be trying to encourage greater social responsibility in men, rather than getting women to adapt themselves to the fact of male violence (as Bella – see chapter 5 – did in the first instance, and as judges have so often suggested to raped women who, by their very presence on the streets, 'provoked' men). It is here that the identification of an ethical relation with the Other assumes particular importance. It may also be appropriate to encourage in women a more realistic appraisal of the degree to which they need fear men, and so encourage greater risk-taking in women. After all, men are encouraged to feel they have a right to inhabit public spaces, even though they are also at risk as the main targets of non-sexual assault. Perhaps Bella should be taken as more than metaphor – as an explicit message to women.

Another purpose served by an appreciation of the Otherness of Woman would be to develop a more ethical relationship between and within the sexes. The importance of this exercise cannot be overstated. Although I have objected to Dworkin's characterization of the relations between men and women (which I think accords too much power to men and too little to women), it remains true that men are still the vast majority of violent offenders (indeed of offenders generally) and that women are the main objects of their sexual violence. I think it is also true that much of our culture is pornographically anti-female, though I would question Dworkin's view that women are saturated with these representations of themselves and can barely free themselves from them. We also need to question the monolithic characterization of men as, inevitably, only interested in the repression and sexualization of women. It is not necessarily in the interests of men to deal only with such degraded objects and not with vigorous sexual agents.

In *The Philosophy of the Limit*, Drucilla Cornell has endeavoured to write about a relation between the sexes in which neither appropriates the other: in which Bella is neither had, nor simply has. Cornell endeavours to depict an 'ethical relation', by which she means 'the aspiration to a non-violent relationship to the Other, and to otherness more generally, that assumes responsibility to guard the Other against the appropriation that would deny her difference and singularity'.[28] Cornell is immediately up against a problem. If the non-violent relation is one of non-assimilation of the Other, in her distinctiveness, any attempt to represent that difference is to draw it back into one's own understanding of it, which is a form of assimilation. In other words, representation or knowledge of the other 'at least in the sense of representation of exteriority, is always a violation of otherness'.[29] The dilemma is this: 'We cannot escape representational schemes. Yet, at the same time, we must recognize their inevitable infidelity to radical otherness.'[30]

Cornell also draws our attention to the danger 'inherent in the very effort to name or symbolize what difference is, particularly feminine difference.'[31] The danger is that of reinstating past and damaging understandings, because they are the only ones that we have. It is also the danger of declaring 'this is what woman is' which, yet again, fixes an idea of woman, and limits women once again.

Why these strategies are not trying to designate the ideal woman

I have already alluded to some of the philosophical and ethical problems of rethinking women, of imagining different female subjectivities. One is the problem of fixing women down, once again, to another ideal type, which is necessarily a stereotype that constrains and limits them. It is for this reason that Irigaray herself wishes to define neither clearly, nor determinately, this other woman whose being resists congruence with that of a man. Indeed, for Irigaray 'the female sex eludes the very requirements of representation' for woman is neither simply man's complement (what he projects onto her as congruent with his desires), nor is she his 'lack' (that which he is not, something only to be understood as his negative).[32]

Irigaray sees dangers in the very attempt at a precise definition of woman in her specificity, as this would serve only to confine and distort women's natures once again. It would repeat the violence of telling woman what she really is, what is appropriate for her.[33] To decide upon the 'true' site and manner of female articulation would be to rigidify the boundaries of womanhood. It would be to trap women, once again, in a single mode that is deemed the correct one. As Cornell explains:

> the appeal to the essence of Woman . . . is precisely this metaphorical transport of the so-called proper. Therefore, what one is really doing when one states the essence of woman is reinstating her in her proper place . . . the appeal to the essence of Woman, since it cannot be separated completely from the *prescription* of properties for her, reinforces the stereotypes that limit our possibilities . . .[34]

Any endeavour to say what a woman really is must, therefore, always be reductive. It returns us, once again, to a universal archetype, a crude simplification, an abstracted being bearing little relation to the particularity and infinite variability of real flesh-and-blood women. And, it repeats the exclusion of all those versions of being a woman that inevitably escape any singular definition. And, as Butler observes:

> Paradoxically, it may be that only through releasing the category of women from a fixed referent that something like 'agency' becomes possible. For if the term permits of a resignification, if its referent is not fixed, the possibilities for new configurations of the term become possible.[35]

This is not to suggest that the stereotypes applied to women have ever done their work fully. The fact of woman's irreducibility to these shallow impressions, of her being more than his measure, has always presented itself as a problem and as a source of constant irritation (much as this book is seeking to irritate the sexual conventions of criminology). Women have always felt the difference between themselves and the stereotypes, and spoken of it. Even when Romantics such as Byron wrote with such eloquent verve of the naturalness of women's subordination and surrender to man, they failed to convince completely. Certainly, they could not rely on nature alone (nor the beauty of their verse) to make it true. The incompleteness of the eclipse of female subjectivity, the woman who wriggled beneath the oppressive forms of social and sexual convention, the woman who spoke up, has always been both recognized and feared. Always, there were those women who 'as witches, *femmes seules*, marriage resisters, spinsters, autonomous widows, and/or lesbians' managed not to conform.[36]

To do justice to the other is to admit the impossibility of her full representation within our scheme of things, to admit the interval or distance between us. It is only by admitting our inability to have and know her that we admit of her separate and distinct subjectivity, with which she looks back at us. 'The Other is allowed to be in her distance precisely so that she can look back.'[37] We must, therefore, always concede the deficiencies of our schemes of representation to represent the Other, and to admit that the Other is also one who reduces us to her schemes. Rather than trying to grasp the Other, the respect for the Other lies in the admission of the limits of our understanding.

Cornell reminds us to 'care for difference', which is always a profoundly difficult but ultimately rewarding task. 'The care for difference needs a generosity that does not attempt to grasp what is other as one's own.' The ethical relation calls for 'the generous impulse to open oneself up to the Other, and to truly listen, to risk the chance that we might be wrong'.[38] Irigaray describes it in terms of a 'wonder which sees something as though always for the first time, and never seizes the Other as its object'.[39]

This idea of a separate subjective person, especially a separate subjective woman, another ego or self, looking back at the criminology of men and the men of criminology, making of them the objects of her understanding (making sense of them in relation to herself), is one that is alien to criminology in its current form. The universalising mode of criminology has eliminated the very thought of a separate female subjectivity that might indicate the limits of male criminology. Thus far, male criminology has conceived of women only in their relation to men, not in their specificity (while simultaneously failing to conceive of men in their relation to women). Man has occupied the full terrain of universality and, thus, his specific character has been blurred and distorted.

In criminology, a respect for Otherness may mean that we must relinquish the traditional scientific desire to document exhaustively, to know fully and, hence, to master the individual as scientific object of investigation. This may require the adoption of a position of greater modesty on the part of the inquiring criminologist. I am reminded here of Veena Oldenburg's study of the courtesans and her willingness to be taught by her subjects. We must recognize the expertise of our subjects, as indeed Pat Carlen did with the criminal co-authors of her volume, *Criminal Women*.

Criminological man needs also to recognize the expertise of women in relation to men, as well as in relation to themselves. He needs to recognize woman as subject of knowledge and of dialogue, woman as self-defining, and so not as a projection of man's ego, not what he thinks or imagines she is. This calls for an admission that he cannot know woman fully, that she is irreducible to his knowledge of her, as he must, to some extent, remain foreign to her. 'There will always remain a kind of outsideness or alienness of the experiences and lived reality of each sex for the other', according to Grosz. In her view:

> Men . . . can never, even with surgical intervention, feel or experience what it is like to be, to live, as women. . . . The problematic of sexual difference entails a certain failure of knowledge to bridge the gap, the interval, between the sexes. There remains something ungraspable, something outside, unpredictable, and uncontainable, about the other sex for each sex. This irreducible difference under the best conditions evokes awe and surprise; under less favourable conditions it evinces horror, fear, struggle, resistance. When respected, this difference implies distance, division, an interval: it involves each relating to the other without being engulfed or overwhelmed.[40]

This is not to suggest that men are incapable of doing valuable research on the social behaviour of women, research which is critical, reflective and aware of its limitations. Similarly, it is perfectly appropriate for women to study men, as this book has consistently argued. So, I am not saying that each sex is so utterly immersed in its own specific experience that it is incapable of reflecting on the nature of the other. In fact, such research across the sexes is likely to prove highly productive, especially when it is explicitly comparative (with each sex revealing to the other the limits of the other's experience). However, men must cease to regard themselves as the final authority on women, in the same way that women have not demanded to be the final authority on men.

We are reminded here of Dr Kay Scarpetta and her examination of female bodies that have been the objects of male violence. Her understanding of them is necessarily, irreducibly different from a man's understanding. She understands, with a specific personal appreciation of the female form, the significance of the intrusions, how they feel, what they mean, even though from woman to woman there will also be significant differences of understanding. A man can only imagine, speculate what such injury to women entails.

We might also say that Dr Scarpetta's understanding of violence done to man, especially sexual violence, will be limited by her own sex specificity, the fact that she is a woman and not a man. Necessarily, her understanding of injury done to man, especially sexual injury, will be formed at a distance and so, at some level, that injury will always remain a mystery to her. Her understanding cannot be the same as the understanding of a man who examines the violations done to his own form. In each case, she as forensic pathologist, we as criminologists, must learn to respect the insights of the other. 'Sexual difference entails the existence of a sexual ethics, an ethics of the ongoing negotiations between beings whose differences, whose alterities, are left intact but with whom some kind of exchange is nevertheless possible.'[41]

The final message of this story, then, is a simple one, though modern criminology has found it difficult to grasp. The most pressing intellectual and ethical obligation on those of us who wish to persist with the study of crime, its meaning and reasons, is to bring women (and other exiles) in from the cold. In order to know more about who we are as criminologists, about the very nature of our enterprise and whether it is worth pursuing at all, we need to open up the conventional borders of the discipline. We must let the exile bear witness.

Notes

—

Introduction

1 Mike Maguire, Rod Morgan and Robert Reiner (eds), *The Oxford Handbook of Criminology*.
2 Rod Morgan, Mike Maguire and Robert Reiner, 'Introduction', *The Oxford Handbook of Criminology*, eds M. Maguire, R. Morgan and R. Reiner, pp. 2–13.
3 Ibid., p. 11.
4 Frances Heidensohn, 'Gender and Crime', *The Oxford Handbook of Criminology*, eds M. Maguire, R. Morgan and R. Reiner, pp. 997–1040.
5 Frances Heidensohn, the author of this chapter, remarks apologetically about this fact but explains that the study of gender of crime has generally been translated as the study of women and crime – and so she is simply reflecting the nature of criminology.
6 Jonathon Culler, *On Deconstruction: Theory and Criticism After Structuralism*, p. 93.
7 Stephen E. Brown, Finn-Aage Esbensen and Gilbert Geis, eds. *Criminology: Explaining Crime and its Context*, p. 495.
8 Ibid., p. 495.
9 Lydia Voigt, William E. Thornton, Leo Barrile and Jerome M. Seaman, *Criminology and Justice*, p. 238
10 Ibid., p. 238.
11 Ibid., p. 249.
12 Elsewhere in the book, the 'socialist-feminism' of James Messerschmidt is allotted two paragraphs. There is no reference to feminism in the index to the book.
13 It is to be found in a variety of places: in specialist books; in journals from across the disciplines; and, as we will see in a later chapter, in fiction.

14 I am referring here especially to *Criminology*, the journal of the American Society of Criminology, and to the *British Journal of Criminology*. These journals are generally regarded as the top journals in their respective countries of origin. Ellen G. Cohn and David P. Farrington, 'Who Are the Most Influential Criminologists in the English-Speaking World?'*British Journal of Criminology*, 34 (1994), pp. 204–25.

15 For example, as Schwartz and Friedrichs observe, American criminology has been barely touched by postmodern theory. Martin D. Schwartz and David O. Friedrichs, 'Postmodern Thought and Criminological Discontent: New Metaphors for Understanding Violence', *Criminology*, 32 (1994), pp. 221–46.

16 Journal editors have it in their power to demand of their authors significant revisions, especially if they feel that the writer has ignored some pertinent literature. When the journal is prestigious, there is a considerable incentive to comply with such requests. Thus it is that the journals can shape the direction of criminological thought.

17 Ngaire Naffine, *Female Crime: The Construction of Women in Criminology*. In 1995, I published a related anthology of feminist writings in criminology entitled *Gender, Crime and Feminism*.

18 These are identfied by Cohn and Farrington, 'Who Are the Most Influential Criminologists?'.

19 Carol Smart, 'Feminist Approaches to Criminology or Postmodern Woman Meets Atavistic Man', *Feminist Perspectives in Criminology*, eds L. Gelsthorpe and A. Morris, pp. 70–84, esp. p. 84.

20 See Darrell Steffensmeier, 'Trends in Female Crime: It's Still a Man's World', *The Criminal Justice System and Women: Offenders, Victims, Workers*, eds B. Raffell Price and N.J. Sokoloff, pp. 89–104; Darrell Steffensmeier and Cathy Streifel, 'The Distribution of Crime by Age and Gender Across Three Historical Periods – 1935, 1960, and 1985', *Social Forces*, 69 (1991), pp. 869–94; Helen Boritch and John Hagan, 'A Century of Crime in Toronto: Gender, Class and Patterns of Social Control, 1859 to 1955', *Criminology*, 28 (1990), pp. 567–99; Kathleen Daly, 'Gender and Varieties of White-Collar Crime', *Criminology*, 27 (1989), pp. 769–94; and Mike Maguire, 'Crime Statistics, Patterns, and Trends: Changing Perceptions and their Implications', *The Oxford Handbook of Criminology*, eds M. Maguire, R. Morgan and R. Reiner, pp. 233–94.

21 In Australia and some jurisidictions of the United States, women can be charged as principal offenders; in England, rape is a crime which can only be committed by a man. For a comparison of two national approaches, see Ngaire Naffine, 'Possession: Erotic Love in the Law of Rape', *Modern Law Review*, 57 (1994), pp. 10–37.

22 See Michael Levi, 'Violent Crime', *The Oxford Handbook of Criminology*, eds M. Maguire, R. Morgan and R. Reiner, pp. 295–354.

23 For other breakdowns of the crime statistics by sex, see Darrell J. Steffensmeier and Renee Hoffman Steffensmeier, 'Trends in Female Delinquency: An Examination of Arrest, Juvenile Court, Self Report

and Field Data', *Criminology*, 18 (1980), pp. 62–85; Heidenson, 'Gender and Crime', p. 1001.

24 Maureen Cain, 'Towards Transgression: New Directions in Feminist Criminology', *International Journal of the Sociology of Law*, 1 (1990), pp. 1–18, esp. p. 11.

25 Anne R. Edwards, 'Sex/Gender, Sexism and Criminal Justice: Some Theoretical Considerations', *International Journal of the Sociology of Law*, 17 (1989), pp. 165–84, esp. pp. 165–6.

26 For example, one could well start with the meaning of crime itself rather than with the motives of the criminal; that is, one might start with the question of why a given society regards certain forms of behaviour as criminal and not others.

27 See Naffine, *Female Crime*.

28 On the negative stereotyping of women by the discipline, see Heidensohn, 'Gender and Crime', p. 1012.

29 Elizabeth Grosz, *Volatile Bodies: Toward a Corporeal Feminism*, p. 198.

30 Also on the disavowal of men in criminology, see Judith Allen, 'Men, Crime and Criminology: Recasting the Questions', *International Journal of the Sociology of Law*, 17 (1989), pp. 19–39.

31 For data on the 'most influential' American and British criminologists, who are predominantly male, see Cohn and Farrington, 'Who are the Most Influential Criminologists?'.

32 A similar point can be made of the legal academy. See Richard Collier, 'Masculinism, Law and Law Teaching', *International Journal of the Sociology of Law*, 19 (1991), pp. 427–51.

33 Edward Said, *Orientalism: Western Conceptions of the Orient*, p. 10.

Chapter 1   The Scientific Origins of Criminology

1 Bertrand Russell, *A History of Western Philosophy*, p. 525.

2 Ibid., p. 536.

3 Ibid., p. 528.

4 John Jackson, 'Hart and the Concept of Fact', *The Jurisprudence of Orthodoxy: Queen's University Essays on HLA Hart*, eds P. Leith and P. Ingram, pp. 61–84 esp. p. 70.

5 Ibid., p. 70.

6 Ibid., p. 70.

7 My indicator of influence within the American academy is the citation analysis of Ellen G. Cohn and David P. Farrington in 'Who are the Most Influential Criminologists in the English-speaking World?', *British Journal of Criminology*, 34 (1994), pp. 204–25.

8 Lydia Voigt, William E. Thornton, Leo Barrile and Jerome M. Seaman, *Criminology and Justice*, p. 147.

9 John Hagan, 'The Assumption of Natural Science Methods: Criminological Positivism', *Theoretical Methods in Criminology*, ed. R. Meier, pp. 75–92, esp. p. 82.

10 Cohn and Farrington, 'Who are the Most Influential Criminologists?', p. 213.

11 John Hagan, 'The Poverty of a Classless Criminology – The American Society of Criminology 1991 Presidential Address', *Criminology*, 30 (1992), pp. 1–19.

12 Joan Petersilia, 'Policy Relevance and the Future of Criminology – The American Society of Criminology 1990 Presidential Address', *Criminology*, 29 (1991), pp. 1–15, esp. p. 9.

13 Ibid., p. 9.

14 Ibid., p. 12.

15 Anthony Bottoms, 'Reflections on the Criminological Enterprise', *Cambridge Law Journal*, 46 (1987), pp. 240–63.

16 Ibid., p. 242.

17 For a discussion of nineteenth century empiricism in criminology by some of the angry young men of the seventies, see Ian Taylor, Paul Walton and Jock Young, *The New Criminology: For a Social Theory of Deviance*, chapters 1 and 2.

18 Bottoms, 'Reflections on the Criminological Enterprise', p. 240.

19 Caesar Lombroso and William Ferrero, *The Female Offender*. Some feminist work has in fact endeavoured to recover Lombroso and treat his work on women as more than an historical curiosity. See Beverley Brown, 'Women and Crime: The Dark Figures of Criminology', *Economy and Society*, 15: 3 (1986), pp. 355–402.

20 David Garland, 'The Development of British Criminology', *The Oxford Handbook of Criminology*, eds M. Maguire, R. Morgan and R. Reiner, pp. 17–68, esp. p. 37.

21 I examined the addresses of the Presidents of the Society contained in the 1990–5 issues of *Criminology* and each year the message was much the same.

22 For example, some American criminologists seem to favour the longitudinal study, which enables them to document criminal careers over a long period, while others prefer the static population (offender or victim) study using either official or self-report data. It should also be noted that American criminologists are even more wedded to quantitative research methods than are the British.

23 Paul Rock, 'The Present State of Criminology in Britain', *British Journal of Criminology*, 28: 2 (1988), pp. 188–99, esp. p. 193. See also Paul Rock, 'The Social Organization of British Criminology', *The Oxford Handbook of Criminology*, eds M. Maguire, R. Morgan and R. Reiner, pp. 125–48.

24 Rock, 'The Present State of Criminology in Britain', p. 192.

25 Ibid., p. 193.

26 Ibid., p. 198.

27 Ian Taylor, 'Left Realist Criminology and the Free Market Experiment in Britain', *Rethinking Criminology: The Realist Debate*, eds J. Young and R. Matthews, pp. 95–122, esp. p. 109.

28 Jerome H. Skolnick, 'What Not to Do About Crime – The American

Society of Criminology 1994 Presidential Address', *Criminology*, 33 (1995), pp. 1–15.

29 A.C. Grayling, *Wittgenstein*, p. 73.

30 Immanuel Kant, *Critique of Pure Reason*, p. 98.

31 For example, contributors to the leading American journals *Criminology* and *Crime and Delinquency* tend to assume this epistemological stance.

32 Participant observation was however employed by some criminologists much earlier in the piece. See chapter 2.

33 Dialogue with Hubert Dreyfus, 'Husserl, Heidegger and Modern Existentialism', in *The Great Philosophers*, ed. B. Magee, p. 258.

34 Hagan, 'The Assumption of Natural Science Methods: Criminological Positivism', p. 82.

35 See Joan W. Scott, 'How Did the Male Become the Normative Standard for Clinical Drug Trials?', *Food and Drug Law Journal*, 48 (1993), pp. 187–93.

36 Again, Mike Maguire, Rod Morgan and Robert Reiner (eds), *The Oxford Handbook of Criminology* is a prime example of such scientific criminology.

37 Skolnick, 'What Not to Do About Crime', p. 2.

38 Ibid., p. 2.

39 Ibid., p. 2.

40 David Farrington's own citation studies reveal that he is the second most-cited author in the American journal *Criminology* while John Hagan is the seventh most-cited author in the same journal. See Cohn and Farrington, 'Who are the Most Influential Criminologists?'.

41 Farrington and Cohn's study reveal Farrington to be the third most-cited author in the *British Journal of Criminology*.

42 Hagan, 'The Poverty of a Classless Criminology', p. 1.

43 Ibid., p. 8.

44 This study is also known as the Cambridge Study in Deliquent Development . It was developed by David Farrington and Donald West. See references in Daniel S. Nagin and David P. Farrington, 'The Onset and Persistence of Offending', *Criminology*, 30 (1992), pp. 501–23.

45 Hagan, 'The Poverty of a Classless Criminology', p. 7.

46 Ibid., p. 11.

47 Ibid., p. 12.

48 John Hagan, 'The Social Embeddedness of Crime and Unemployment', *Criminology*, 31 (1993), pp. 465–91.

49 Helen Boritch and John Hagan, 'A Century of Crime in Toronto: Gender, Class and Patterns of Social Control, 1859 to 1955', *Criminology*, 28 (1990), pp. 567–99, esp. p. 567.

50 Ibid., p. 593.

51 See for example, David Farrington, 'Criminal Career Research in the United Kingdom', *British Journal of Criminology*, 32 (1992), pp. 521–36; Nagin and Farrington, 'The Onset and Persistence of Offending', *Criminology*, 30 (1992), pp. 501–23.

52 See Rock, 'The Social Organisation of British Criminology'.

53 Ian Taylor, 'Left Realist Criminology and the Free Market Experiment in Britain', p. 109.

54 Ibid., p. 109.
55 Vincenzo Ruggiero, 'Realist Criminology: A Critique', *Rethinking Criminology: The Realist Debate*, eds J. Young and R. Matthews, pp. 123–40, esp. p. 124.
56 For a sustained critique of mainstream criminology for its failure to accord rationality to women, see Ngaire Naffine, *Female Crime*.
57 Sandra Harding, *The Science Question in Feminism*, p. 149.
58 Loraine Gelsthorpe and Allison Morris, 'Introduction: Transforming and Transgressing Criminology', *Feminist Perpectives in Criminology*, eds L. Gelsthorpe and A. Morris, pp. 1–5, esp. p. 3. I should add that a number of the writers referred to in this quotation are highly sensitive to the limitations of simple empirical methods and that, consequently, their work can not be slotted neatly into this tradition of research. Indeed, as I will state again later, none of these categories of feminism have clearly defined boundaries and we find feminists constantly transgressing them and crossing over from one approach to another.
59 See also the review of feminist literature in Sally Simpson, 'Feminist Theory, Crime and Justice', *Criminology*, 27 (1989), pp. 605–31.
60 Other feminist critiques of criminological theory are to be found in Eileen Leonard, *A Critique of Criminology Theory: Women, Crime and Society*; Frances Heidensohn, *Women and Crime*; Meda Chesney-Lind, 'Women and Crime: The Female Offender', *Signs*, 12: 1 (1986), pp. 78–96; Kathleen Daly and Meda Chesney-Lind, 'Feminism and Criminology', *Justice Quarterly*, 5: 4 (1988), pp. 498–538; Gelsthorpe and Morris (eds), *Feminist Perspectives in Criminology*.
61 In *Women, Crime and Criminology*, Carol Smart documents the tendency of criminology to reduce women's behaviour to their biology.
62 See discussion in Daly and Chesney-Lind, 'Feminism and Criminology'.
63 Freda Adler, *Sisters in Crime: The Rise of the New Female Criminal*.
64 For just one of the many rebuttals of the 'liberation thesis', see Naffine, *Female Crime*.
65 Heidensohn, *Women and Crime*, p. 167. On this theme of women and social control, see also Bridget Hutter and Gillian Williams (eds), *Controlling Women: The Normal and the Deviant*.
66 Heidensohn, 'Gender and Crime'. *The Oxford Handbook of Criminology*, eds M. Maguire, R. Morgan and R. Reiner.
67 See, for example, Elizabeth Stanko, *Intimate Intrusions*; Elizabeth Stanko, *Everyday Violence*; Carol Smart, *Feminism and the Power of Law*; Sandra Walklate, *Victimology*; and R. Emerson Dobash and Russell P. Dobash, *Women, Violence and Social Change*.
68 Chesney-Lind, 'Women and Crime', p. 95.
69 Mary Eaton, *Justice for Women? Family, Court and Social Control*.
70 Ibid., p. 74.
71 Pat Carlen, *Women's Imprisonment: A Study in Social Control*, p. 67.
72 Ibid., p. 67.
73 Candice Kruttschnitt, 'Women Crime and Dependancy: An Application of a Theory of Law', *Criminology*, 19 (1982), pp. 495–513.
74 Ibid., p. 510.

75 Kathleen Daly, 'Neither Conflict Nor Labelling Nor Paternalism Will Suffice: Intersections of Race, Ethnicity, Gender, and Family in Criminal Court Decisions', *Crime and Delinquency*, 35: 1 (1989), pp. 136–68, and 'Class-Race-Gender: Sloganeering in Search of Meaning', *Social Justice*, 20: 1–2 (1993), pp. 56–71.

76 Kerry Carrington, *Offending Girls: Sex, Youth and Justice*. In fact, Carrington is highly critical of the work of Chesney-Lind which she feels overlooks these other vital factors.

77 See Carlen, *Women's Imprisonment*; Pat Carlen (ed.), *Criminal Women: Autobiographical Accounts*, Diana Christina, Jenny Hicks, Josie O'Dwyer, Chris Tchaikovsky and Pat Carlen; and Pat Carlen, *Alternatives to Women's Imprisonment*.

78 Lucia Zedner, *Women, Crime and Custody in Victorian England*.

79 On this point see Edwards, 'Sex/Gender, Sexism and Criminal Justice: Some Theoretical Considerations', *International Journal of the Sociology of Law*, 17 (1989), pp. 165–84'; and Cathleen Burnett, 'Review Essay', *Criminology*, 24 (1986), pp. 203–11, esp. p. 204.

80 Although the subsequent discovery that supposedly universal theories of crime do not work with women has then led to a questioning of the generality of these theories, and thus feminist empiricists have laid important foundations for other feminists to develop more thorough-going criticisms of mainstream criminology.

81 This is the same conflation of humanity with masculinity described by Catharine MacKinnon when she says that law is most masculine, most biased, when it professes to be most neutral. MacKinnon's critique of the traditional idea of objectivity is to be found in her two landmark articles: 'Feminism, Marxism, Method, and the State: An Agenda for Theory', *Signs*, 7: 3 (1982), pp. 515–44; and 'Feminism, Marxism, Method, and the State: Towards a Feminist Jurisprudence', *Signs*, 8: 4 (1983), pp. 635–58.

82 Carol Smart, 'Feminist Approaches to Criminology or Postmodern Woman meets Atavistic Man', *Feminist Perspectives in Criminology*, eds L. Gelsthorpe and A. Morris, p. 79.

83 Ibid., p. 78.

84 Ibid., p. 78.

85 Gayatri Chakravorty Spivak, 'Displacement and the Discourse of the Woman', *Displacement: Derrida and After*, ed. M. Krupnick, pp. 169–95, esp. p. 186.

86 Allen, 'Men, Crime and Criminology: Recasting the Questions', *International Journal of the Sociology of Law*, 17 (1989), pp. 21–39, esp. p. 35.

Chapter 2   The Criminologist as Partisan

1 Henry Mayhew, *London Labour and the London Poor*.

2 Though the Chicago school of criminology, several decades earlier, had already adopted what has been described as an 'appreciative' stance

towards the offender. See Colin Sumner, *The Sociology of Deviance: An Obituary*, p. 42.

3 Frances Heidensohn, *Women and Crime*, p. 131.

4 Ibid., p. 132.

5 Ibid., p. 131.

6 Howard S. Becker, *Outsiders: Studies in the Sociology of Deviance*.

7 Howard S. Becker, 'Whose Side are We On?', *Social Problems*, 14 (1967), pp. 239–47.

8 Sumner, *The Sociology of Deviance*, p. 200.

9 Ibid., p. 231.

10 For a more extended criticism of Becker's *Outsiders*, see Ngaire Naffine, *Female Crime: The Construction of Women in Criminology*.

11 Becker, *Outsiders*, p. 118.

12 Ibid., p. 93.

13 Alvin Gouldner, *For Sociology*, p. 38.

14 Much of this new research was associated with the Birmingham Centre for Contemporary Cultural Studies. For a detailed account of the work of the Centre, see Steve Redhead, *Unpopular Culture: The Birth of Law and Popular Culture*.

15 I am borrowing this term from social history where there is a more powerful tradition of conducting history from the viewpoint of the oppressed or 'from below'.

16 Phil Scraton, 'Scientific Knowledges or Masculine Discourses? Challenging Patriarchy in Criminology', *Feminist Perspectives in Criminology*, eds L. Gelsthorpe and A. Morris, pp. 10–25, esp. p. 18.

17 See for example Phil Cohen, 'Subcultural Conflict and Working Class Community', *Working Papers in Cultural Studies*; Paul Corrigan, *Schooling the Smash Street Kids*; and Dick Hebdige, *Subculture: The Meaning of Style*.

18 Heidensohn, *Women and Crime*, p. 140.

19 This was a point made by Carole-Anne Sheade in discussion at the Critical Legal Conference, University of Warwick, September 1994.

20 Howard Parker, *View from the Boys*, p. 171.

21 Angela McRobbie, 'Working-Class Girls and the Culture of Femininity', *Women Take Issue*, eds Women's Studies Group, Centre for Contemporary Cultural Studies.

22 In the United States, the emergence of Marxist-influenced criminologies was associated with the rise of the civil rights movement. For a discussion of the early days of radical criminology in America, see Albert P. Cardarelli and Stephen C. Hicks, 'Radicalism in Law and Criminology: A Retrospective View of Critical Legal Studies and Radical Criminology', *Journal of Criminal Law and Criminology*, 84 (1993), pp. 502–53; Tony Platt, 'Prospects for a Radical Criminology in the US', *Critical Criminology*, eds I. Taylor, P. Walton and J. Young, pp. 95–109.

23 The 'new criminology' in Britain was strongly associated with the work of Ian Taylor, Paul Walton and Jock Young, and their book of this name: *The New Criminology: For a Social Theory of Deviance*.

24 This term referred to the social conflict which was thought, by a number of radical criminologists, to underpin American society, replacing the consensus model that was implied by the more positivist or scientific criminology. Not all conflict criminologists, however, regarded themselves as Marxists. For example, see Austin T. Turk, 'Analysing Official Deviance: For Nonpartisan Conflict Analyses in Criminology', *Criminology*, 16 (1979), pp. 459–76. See also the commentary on the sympathies of the American conflict criminologists contained in Cardarelli and Hicks, 'Radicalism in Law and Criminology'.

25 The term 'critical' criminology has proven the most enduring way of identifying radical criminology. It is, for example, the term employed in a recent American anthology of mainstream and radical criminology: Gregg Barak (ed.), *Varieties of Criminology: Readings from a Dynamic Discipline*.

26 Richard Quinney, 'The Production of Marxist Criminology', *Contemporary Crises*, 2 (1978), pp. 277–92, esp. p. 289.

27 Here, I am referring to the early Marxist work of Quinney. Of late, Quinney has combined Marxist criminology with a form of 'Gandhian humanism'. See discussion in Lydia Voigt, William E. Thornton, Leo Barrile and Jerome M. Seaman, *Criminology and Justice*, pp. 274–75. See also Harold Pepinsky and Richard Quinney, *Criminology as Peacemaking*.

28 Taylor, Walton and Young, *The New Criminology*, p. 147.

29 Russell Hogg, 'Taking Crime Seriously: Left Realism and Australian Criminology', *Understanding Crime and Criminal Justice*, eds M. Findlay and R. Hogg, pp. 24–51, esp. p. 26.

30 Sumner, *The Sociology of Deviance*, p. 281.

31 Vincenzo Ruggiero, 'Realist Criminology: A Critique', *Rethinking Criminology: The Realist Debate*, eds J. Young and R. Matthews, p. 126.

32 Sumner, *The Sociology of Deviance*, p. 286.

33 Pat Carlen, 'Introduction', *Criminal Women: Autobiographical Accounts, Diana Christina, Jenny Hicks, Josie O'Dwyer, Chris Tchaikovsky and Pat Carlen*, ed. P. Carlen, pp. 1–13, esp. p. 8.

34 Chris Tchaikovsky, 'Looking for Trouble', *Criminal Women*, ed. P. Carlen, pp. 14–58, esp. p. 14.

35 Helen E. Longino, 'Feminist Standpoint Theory and the Problems of Knowledge', *Signs*, 19: 1 (1993), pp. 201–12, esp. p. 201.

36 Ibid., p. 201.

37 Ibid., pp. 201–2.

38 Sandra Harding, *The Science Question in Feminism*, p. 149.

39 Blanche Hampton, *Prisons and Women*, p. xiv.

40 Ibid., p. xiv.

41 Ibid., p. viii.

42 Ibid., p. viii.

43 Ibid., pp. viii–ix.

44 Ibid., p. 42.

45 Martha Mahoney, 'Legal Images of Battered Women: Redefining the Issue of Separation', *Michigan Law Review*, 90 (1991), pp. 1–94; Martha Mahoney, 'Exit: Power and the Idea of Leaving in Love, Work, and the Confirmation Hearings', *Southern California Law Review*, 65 (1992), pp. 1283–1319.

46 Peggy Morgan, 'Living on the Edge', *Sex Work; Writings by Women in the Sex Industry*, eds F. Delacoste and P. Alexander, pp. 21–8.

47 Ibid., p. 25.

48 Christina Crosby, 'Dealing with Differences', *Feminists Theorize the Political*, eds J. Butler and J.W. Scott, pp. 130–43, esp. p. 133.

49 Carol Smart, 'Feminist Approaches to Criminology or Postmodern Woman meets Atavistic Man', *Feminist Perspectives in Criminology*, eds L. Gelsthorpe and A. Morris, p. 80.

50 Maureen Cain, 'Realist Philosophy and the Standpoint Epistemologies or Feminist Criminology as Successor Science', *Feminist Perspectives in Criminology*, eds L. Gelsthorpe and A. Morris, pp. 124–40, esp. p. 125.

51 Carlen, 'Introduction', p. 10.

52 Ibid., p. 10.

53 A. Brannigan, 'Closing Note', *International Journal of Law and Psychiatry*, 14 (1991), pp. 133–35.

54 Elizabeth Spelman, *Inessential Woman: Problems of Exclusion in Feminist Thought*, p. 4.

55 Marcia Rice, 'Challenging Orthodoxies in Feminist Theory: A Black Feminist Critique', *Feminist Perspectives in Criminology*, eds L. Gelsthorpe and A. Morris, pp. 57–69, esp. p. 57.

56 Ibid., p. 58.

57 Ibid., p. 68.

58 Kimberley Crenshaw, 'Demarginalizing the Intersection of Race and Sex', *Feminist Legal Theory*, eds K.T. Bartlett and R. Kennedy, pp. 57–80.

59 Kathy Ferguson, *The Man Question: Visions of Subjectivity in Feminist Theory*, p. 161.

60 Barbara Omolade, 'Black Women, Black Men, and Tawana Brawley – The Shared Condition', *Harvard Women's Law Journal*, 12 (1989), pp. 11–23, esp. p. 11.

61 Ibid., p. 19.

62 Elizabeth Spelman and Martha Minow, 'Outlaw Women: An Essay on "Thelma and Louise"', *New England Law Review*, 26 (1992), pp. 1281–96, esp. pp. 1287–8.

63 Ibid., p. 1288.

64 Crosby, 'Dealing with Differences', p. 136.

65 This also of course leads to a problem of infinite regress because 'there is no limit to the particularity of women' (Personal communication – Alison Young).

66 Crosby, 'Dealing with Differences', p. 137.

67 Cain, 'Realist Philosophy and Standpoint Epistemologies', p. 130.

68 This, of course, raises again the problem of infinite regress.

69 Cain, 'Realist Philosophy and Standpoint Epistemologies', p. 135.
70 Drucilla Cornell, *Transformations: Recollective Imagination and Sexual Difference*, p. 190.
71 I am, of course, speaking here of recent history. Shakespeare's *Othello* was somewhat earlier.
72 Kathy Ferguson, *The Man Question: Visions of Subjectivity in Feminist Theory*, p. 160.
73 Ibid., p. 160.
74 Tamar Pitch, 'From Oppressed to Victims: Collective Actors and the Symbolic Use of the Criminal Justice System', *Studies in Law, Politics and Society*, 10 (1990), pp. 103–17.
75 Ibid., p. 115.
76 Crosby, 'Dealing with Differences', p. 140.

Chapter 3   Examining our Frames of Reference: Realism to Derrida

1 As we will see, several realist criminologists attribute to feminism an important shift in their thinking about crime and its harms.
2 I am not saying that feminists were the only or even the major catalyst for the study of power and its relation to knowledge. As we will see, criminologists who displayed no overt feminist sympathies were nevertheless taking up the ideas of Michel Foucault and his theories of power/knowledge. Standpoint feminists participated in a general shift in the intellectual climate of the social sciences – away from conventional dispassionate science and towards a recognition of the effects of identity on the constitution of knowledge.
3 Carol Smart, 'Feminist Approaches to Criminology or Postmodern Woman Meets Atavistic Man', *Feminist Perspectives in Criminology*, eds L. Gelsthorpe and A. Morris', p. 72.
4 Jock Young, 'Radical Criminology in Britain', *British Journal of Criminology*, 28 (1988), pp. 159–313, esp. p. 171.
5 Sharyn L. Roach-Anleu, *Deviance, Conformity and Control*, p. 40.
6 Jock Young, 'Radical Criminology in Britain', p. 174.
7 For example, the Islington Crime Surveys: T. Jones, B. Maclean and Jock Young, *The Islington Crime Survey*; and A. Crawford, T. Jones and Jock Young, *The Second Islington Crime Survey*.
8 Stuart Henry and Dragan Milovanovic, for example, acknowledge the effects of left realism on their work. See below for a discussion of their 'constitutive criminology'.
9 See the discussion of the Presidential debates in chapter 1 for an illustration of the importance of policy.
10 Roger Matthews and Jock Young, 'Reflections on Realism', *Rethinking Criminology: The Realist Debate*, eds J. Young and R. Matthews, pp. 1–23, esp. p. 17.

11 Jock Young, 'Ten Points of Realism', *Rethinking Criminology: The Realist Debate*, eds J. Young and R. Matthews, pp. 24–68, esp. p. 56.

12 Ibid., p. 26.

13 John Lea, 'The Analysis of Crime', *Rethinking Criminology: The Realist Debate*, eds J. Young and R. Matthews, pp. 69–94, esp. p. 69.

14 Young, 'Ten Points of Realism', p. 57.

15 I take up the problem of men and the pleasures of sexual violence in chapter 5. As Alison Young has pointed out to me, the realists are simply wrong when they say that our society abhors violence against women.

16 See, for example, Lynne Henderson, 'Rape and Responsibility', *Law and Philosophy*, 11 (1992), pp. 127–78; Dorothy Roberts, 'Rape, Violence and Women's Autonomy', *Chicago-Kent Law Review*, 69 (1993), pp. 359–88; Robin West, 'Legitimating the Illegitimate: A Comment on "Beyond Rape"', *Columbia Law Review*, 93 (1993), pp. 1442–59.

17 This is the law in England and in most parts of Australia. In some American jurisdictions, rape is defined as forcible sex and there is no reference to the victim's lack of consent (or to the accused's appreciation of that lack of consent). However, 'Even when such statutes omit any reference to consent, they imply the requirement that the sex be attributable to the violence. Thus consent can still be raised as a defense, because consent either negates force or negates the causal connection between the force and the sex.' Donald A. Dripps, 'Beyond Rape: An Essay on the Difference Between the Presence of Force and the Absence of Consent', *Columbia Law Review*, 92 (1992), pp. 1780–1809, esp. p. 1784.

18 In the United States, it has been required that the accused receive clear and manifest signs of non-consent to the point of a physical struggle. See the discussion in John Dwight Ingram, 'Date Rape: It's Time for "No" to Really Mean "No"', *American Journal of Criminal Law*, 21 (1993), pp. 3–36, esp. p. 12. English and Australian courts do not formally require the woman to struggle in order to convey her lack of consent to the accused, although signs of physical resistance help to secure conviction.

19 Alison Young and Peter Rush, 'The Law of Victimage in Urbane Realism: Thinking Through Inscriptions of Violence', *The Futures of Criminology*, ed. D. Nelken, pp. 154–72, esp. p. 157.

20 Ibid., p. 157.

21 Culler, *On Deconstruction: Theory and Criticism After Structuralism*, p. 93.

22 Young and Rush, 'The Law of Victimage', p. 158.

23 See *Criminal Law Consolidation Act* 1935 (SA), s. 39.

24 Young and Rush, 'The Law of Victimage', p. 169.

25 This was an observation of Betty Stanko made to Kathy Laster and reported to me.

26 Lea, 'The Analysis of Crime', p. 74.

27 I am not saying that sexual violence is not experienced as sexy. Sexual

violence does give men orgasms and, as Catharine MacKinnon has argued, is quite possibly sexy because it is violent. My point is that feminists have long rejected the proposition that rape is a function of a man who has lost sexual control over himself because of his passions for a woman. On the feminist debate about whether rape is a crime of sex or violence or both, see Vikki Bell, 'Beyond the "Thorny Question": Feminism, Foucault and the Desexualisation of Rape', *International Journal of the Sociology of Law*, 19 (1991), pp. 83–100.

28 Martin D. Schwartz and Walter S. DeKeseredy, 'Left Realist Criminology: Strengths, Weaknesses and the Feminist Critique, *Crime, Law and Social Change*, 15 (1991), pp. 51–72, esp. p. 63. See also the feminist critique of realism in Sandra Walklate, 'Appreciating the Victim: Conventional, Realist or Critical Victimology?', *Issues in Realist Criminology*, eds R. Matthews and J. Young, pp. 102–18.

29 Alice Jardine, 'Men in Feminism', *Men in Feminism*, eds A. Jardine and P. Smith, p. 56, quoted in Richard Collier, 'Masculinism, Law and Law Teaching', *International Journal of the Sociology of Law*, 19 (1991), pp. 427–51, esp. p. 434.

30 Edward Said, *Orientalism: Western Conceptions of the Orient*, pp. 19–20.

31 See Ian Taylor, Paul Walton and Jock Young, *The New Criminology: For a Social Theory of Deviance*.

32 Michel Foucault, *The Order of Things: An Archeology of the Human Sciences*, p. xiv.

33 It should be added that Marxist theory has become more subtle and is now often combined with the work of Foucault, as in the writings of Colin Sumner.

34 Michel Foucault, *Power/Knowledge: Selected Interview and Other Writings 1972–1977*.

35 Stanley Cohen, *Visions of Social Control*, p. 25.

36 For one of the last statements made by Foucault on this subtle relation between power and knowledge see Michel Foucault, 'The Ethic of Care for the Self as a Practice of Freedom: An Interview', *The Final Foucault*, eds J. Bernauer and D. Rasmussen, pp. 1–20.

37 On the way the different professional disciplines order and constitute knowledge see Michel Foucault, *The Archeology of Knowledge*.

38 As Duncan Kennedy observed of legal education in particular, it is an excellent training for hierarchy.

39 This is not to say that such a hierarchy is necessarily a bad thing, as Foucault himself made clear. See Foucault, 'The Ethic of Care for the Self'.

40 Michel Foucault, 'Lecture Two: 14 January 1976', in *Power/Knowledge*, extracted in M. Davies, *Asking the Law Question*, p. 252.

41 Alec McHoul and Wendy Grace, *A Foucault Primer: Discourse, Power and the Subject*, pp. 3–4.

42 Foucault, *Power/Knowledge*, pp. 81–2, quoted in McHoul and Grace, *A Foucault Primer*, p. 16.

43 It may equally be regarded as a work of cultural criticism which explains the provenance and nature of the modern body politic: see David Garland, *Punishment and Modern Society*, p. 162.
44 Clifford Geertz has described it as a reverse Whig history: see Garland, *Punishment and Modern Society*, p. 161.
45 Cohen, *Visions of Social Control*, p. 38. See also Jeff Ferrell, 'A Critical Criminologist Looks at Critical Criminology: A Review of Stanley Cohen's "Against Criminology"', *Social Justice*, 17: 1 (1990), pp. 132–5, esp. p. 132; and Stanley Cohen, 'The Punitive City: Notes on the Dispersal of Social Control', *Contemporary Crises*, 3: 4 (1979), pp. 339–63; Stanley Cohen, 'Social-Control Talk: Telling Stories about Correctional Change', *The Power to Punish*, eds D. Garland and P. Young.
46 David Garland, *Punishment and Welfare: A History of Penal Strategies*, p. 170.
47 Garland, *Punishment and Modern Society*, p. 167.
48 David Garland, 'Criminological Knowledge and its Relation to Power', *British Journal of Criminology*, 32 (1992), pp. 403–23, esp. p. 405. See also Adrian Howe's discussion of Garland's intellectual development in *Punish and Critique: Towards a Feminist Analysis of Penality*.
49 Garland, 'Criminological Knowledge', p. 403.
50 Martin D. Schwartz and David O. Friedrichs, 'Postmodern Thought and Criminological Discontent: New Metaphors for Understanding Violence', *Criminology*, 32 (1994), pp. 221–46, esp. p. 221.
51 Stuart Henry and Dragan Milovanovic would probably identify themselves as both critical criminologists and critical legal scholars. A partial list of their publications in both areas is to be found in Stuart Henry and Dragan Milovanovic, 'The Constitution of Constitutive Criminology: A Postmodern Approach to Criminological Theory', *The Futures of Criminology*, ed. D. Nelken, pp. 110–33.
52 Ibid., p. 113.
53 Ibid., p. 115.
54 Ibid., p. 119.
55 Ibid., p. 113.
56 Ibid., p. 113.
57 See especially Colin Sumner (ed.), *Censure, Politics and Criminal Justice*.
58 For a discussion of the masculinism of Foucault in the context of penology see Howe, *Punish and Critique*.
59 Colin Sumner, 'Foucault, Gender and the Censure of Deviance', *Feminist Perspectives in Criminology*, eds L. Gelsthorpe and A. Morris, pp. 26–40, esp. pp. 35 and 33.
60 Ibid., p. 34.
61 Ibid., p. 36.
62 This is a slightly misleading way of putting the point as the conventional notion of the feminine may also of course be regarded as a positive effect of power/knowledge. That is, characteristics are positively assigned to the feminine and then regarded as inferior and

unsatisfactory – qualities which the masculine man must repress and erase.

63 This is a term borrowed from Robert Connell, *Gender and Power: Society, the Person and Sexual Politics.*

64 Sumner, 'Foucault, Gender and the Censure of Deviance', p. 36.

65 Carol Smart, 'Disruptive Bodies and Unruly Sex: The Regulation of Reproduction and Sexuality in the Nineteenth Century', *Regulating Womanhood: Historical Essays on Marriage, Motherhood and Sexuality*, pp. 7–32.

66 Ibid., p. 7.

67 Ibid., p. 31.

68 Ibid., p. 7.

69 Anne Worrall, *Offending Women: Female Lawbreakers and the Criminal Justice System*, p. 21.

70 Ibid., p. 85.

71 Ibid., p. 160.

72 She describes Chesney-Lind's work on the sexualisation of female delinquency in this way: see chapter 1.

73 Kerry Carrington, *Offending Girls: Sex, Youth and Justice*, p. 53.

74 Michel Foucault, 'The Use of Pleasure', Vol. 2 of *The History of Sexuality*, pp. 8–9.

75 Wittgenstein's *Philosophical Investigations* is also about the impossibility of ever getting free from the ordering conditions of language, which is essentially a public business. For Wittgenstein, there can never be a private language game, something personal to us.

76 Dialogue with John Searle, 'Wittgenstein', *Great Philosophers*, ed. B. Magee, pp. 320–47, esp. p. 331.

77 Ludwig Wittgenstein, *Philosophical Investigations*, par. 122.

78 Drucilla Cornell, *The Philosophy of the Limit*, p. 174.

79 Jacques Derrida, *Positions*, p. 26.

80 Ibid., p. 26.

81 Davies, *Asking the Law Question*, p. 233.

82 It is here that Derrida differs from the structuralist linguist, Ferdinand de Saussure, and why Derrida is often referred to as a post-structuralist.

83 Derrida, *Positions*, p. 26.

84 Ibid., pp. 41–2.

85 Wittgenstein, *Philosophical Investigations*, par. 140.

86 Derrida, *Positions*, pp. 41–2.

87 Ibid., pp. 41–2.

88 Ibid., pp. 41–2.

89 Davies, *Asking the Law Question*, p. 258.

90 Butler, 'Contingent Foundations: Feminism and the Question of "Postmodernism"', *Feminists Theorize the Political*, eds J. Butler and J. Scott, p. 17.

91 Ibid., p. 15.

92 Alison Young, *Femininity in Dissent*, p. 2.

93 Ibid., p. 152.

94 Davies, *Asking the Law Question*, p. 16.
95 Ibid., p. 18.
96 This is the way David Wood explains the purpose of deconstruction in *Philosophy at the Limit: Problems of Modern European Thought*.
97 Ibid., p. 41.
98 Richard Bernstein, *The New Constellation: The Ethical-Political Horizons of Modernity/Postmodernity*, p. 225.
99 Mike Maguire, Rod Morgan and Robert Reiner (eds), *The Oxford Handbook of Criminology*.

Chapter 4   Reinterpreting the Sexes (through the Crime of Rape)

1 Richard Bernstein, *The New Constellation: The Ethical Political Horizons of Modernity/Postmodernity*, p. 321.
2 Indeed the concept of the West, has been formed against what the West takes to mean the East. See Edward Said, *Orientalism: Western Conceptions of the Orient*.
3 Jacques Derrida, 'Structure, Sign and Play in the Discourse of the Human Sciences', *Writing and Difference*, p. 280, quoted in Bernstein, *The New Constellation*, p. 183.
4 Think of the first question asked upon the birth of a child.
5 Monique Wittig, *The Straight Mind*, p. 7.
6 Ibid., p. 5. As Katherine O'Donovan remarks, 'the law continues to classify human beings as if there were two clear divisions into which everyone falls on an either/or basis'. See Katherine O'Donovan, *Sexual Divisions in Law*, p. 64.
7 See Katherine O'Donovan, 'Transsexual Troubles: The Discrepancy Between Legal and Social Categories', *Gender, Sex and the Law*, ed. S. Edwards, pp. 9–27.
8 See for example Diana Scully, 'Rape is the Problem', *The Criminal Justice System and Women: Offenders, Victims, Workers*, eds B. Raffell Price and N.J. Sokoloff, pp. 197–215; Julia Schwendinger and Herman Schwendinger, *Rape and Inequality*; Susan Griffin, *Rape: The Power of Consciousness*; Lorenne Clark and Debra Lewis, *Rape: The Price of Coercive Sexuality*.
9 Although many jurisdictions have introduced gender-neutral rape laws, I will argue that this does not fundamentally alter the heterosexual paradigm which rape law still presupposes. For a fuller discussion of the effects of gender neutrality, see Ngaire Naffine, 'Possession: Erotic Love in the Law of Rape', *Modern Law Review*, 57 (1994), pp. 741–67.
10 Elizabeth Grosz, 'Contemporary Theories of Power and Subjectivity', *Feminist Knowledge: Critique and Construct*, ed. S. Gunew, pp. 59–120, esp. p. 109.
11 From James C. Scott, *Weapons of the Weak: Everyday Forms of Peasant Resistance*.

12 Susan Brownmiller, *Against Our Will: Men, Women and Rape*, p. 14.
13 Ibid., p. 13.
14 Mary E. Hawkesworth, 'Knowers, Knowing, Known: Feminist Theory and Claims of Truth', *Signs*, 14: 3 (1989), pp. 533–57, esp. p. 555.
15 Catherine MacKinnon, 'Feminism, Marxism, Method and the State: An Agenda for Theory', *Signs*, 8: 4 (1983), pp. 635–58, esp. p. 638.
16 Andrea Dworkin, *Intercourse*, pp. 76–7.
17 Ibid., p. 77.
18 Sharon Marcus, 'Fighting Bodies, Fighting Words: A Theory and Politics of Rape Prevention', *Feminists Theorize the Political*, eds J. Butler and J. Scott, p. 394.
19 Ibid., p. 394.
20 Ibid., p. 387.
21 Ibid., p. 391.
22 There is also considerable legal literature on rape law but my main concern here, as a criminologist, is with criminological writing on rape.
23 A clear example is Stephen Box, writing on rape in *Power, Crime and Mystification*.
24 The less a man's social power over women, the more he will resort to brutal force, according to John Lea, 'The Analysis of Crime', *Rethinking Criminology: The Realist Debate* eds J. Young and R. Matthews, p. 74.
25 Ibid., pp. 74–5.
26 Jock Young, 'Ten Points of Realism', *Rethinking Criminology: The Realist Debate*, eds J. Young and R. Matthews, p. 57.
27 Glanville Williams, 'The Problem of Domestic Rape', *New Law Journal*, 15 February 1991, pp. 205–7, esp. p. 206. See also Part 2 of this article, *New Law Journal*, 22 February 1991, pp. 246–7.
28 Ibid., p. 206.
29 Ibid., p. 206.
30 Ibid., p. 206.
31 Ibid., p. 206.
32 Freud also spoke of 'the riddle of the nature of femininity'. See Sigmund Freud, 'Femininity', *The New Introductory Lectures on Psychoanalysis*, pp. 112–35.
33 James H. Chadbourn (ed.), *Wigmore on Evidence*.
34 Brent Fisse, *Howard's Criminal Law*, p. 178.
35 Ibid., p. 178.
36 See, for example, Luce Irigaray, 'And the One Does Not Stir Without the Other', *Signs*, 7: 1 (1981), pp. 60–67, and Luce Irigaray, *This Sex Which is Not One*; Julia Kristeva, *Desire in Language*; Toril Moi, *Sexual/ Textual Politics: Feminist Literary Theory*; Drucilla Cornell, 'The Doubly-Prized World: Myth, Allegory and the Feminine', *Transformations: Recollective Imagination and Sexual Difference*, pp. 57–111; Margaret Whitford, *Luce Irigaray: Philosophy in the Feminine*.
37 As Lois Pineau remarks in her feminist analysis of sexuality and rape, 'the way to achieve sexual pleasure ... decidedly does not involve overriding the other person's express reservations and providing them

with just any kind of sexual stimulus.' See Lois Pineau, 'Date Rape: A Feminist Analysis', *Law and Philosophy*, 8 (1989), pp. 217–43, esp. p. 231.

38 Jennifer Temkin, *Rape and the Legal Process*, p. 37.

39 A more sustained analysis of the role of consent or agreement in English and Australian rape law is to be found in Naffine, 'Possession'. On consent in American rape law see Donald A. Dripps, 'Beyond Rape: An Essay on the Difference between the Presence of Force and the Absence of Consent', *Columbia Law Review*, 92 (1992), pp. 1780–1809. Even in those American jurisdictions which have removed the requirement of proving the victim's lack of consent and that rely only on the offender's use of force to achieve sex, the victim's consent can still be raised as a defence. Therefore, even in these jurisdictions, sex can still be characterised as a deal, and rape as the deal gone wrong. See Dripps, 'Beyond Rape', p. 1784.

40 Men remain the vast majority of known rapists, and women are usually their victims, and in our socio-legal culture, it is, of course, still men who are expected to take the initiative in consenting sex.

41 In those jurisdictions that have introduced gender-neutral language to their rape laws, the sexual form assumed remains much the same. See discussion in Naffine, 'Possession'.

42 It should be noted that some American and Australian jurisdictions have at last recognised the inadequacy of the traditional legal interpretation of 'consent' to sex described here. Legislation has, therefore, been enacted which endeavours to ensure that there is true volition in a woman's agreement to have sex. For example, Washington rape law requires 'words or conduct indicating freely given agreement to have sexual intercourse'. See John Dwight Ingram, 'Date Rape: It's Time for "No" to Really Mean "No"', *American Journal of Criminal Law*, 21 (1993), pp. 3–36, esp. p. 16. Similar legislation has been enacted in the Australian state of Victoria. See Ngaire Naffine, 'Windows on the Legal Mind: The Evocation of Rape in Legal Writing', *Melbourne University Law Review*, 18 (1992), pp. 741–67.

43 American rape statutes have traditionally required the prosecution to prove both the positive use of physical force by the accused and that the woman 'resisted to the utmost'. However, in a number of American states, this requirement of resistance has now been removed. For a description of American trends in rape law reform, see Ronet Bachman and Raymond Paternoster, 'A Contemporary Look at the Effects of Rape Law Reform: How Far Have We Really Come?', *Journal of Criminal Law and Criminology*, 84 (1993), pp. 554–74.

44 Stephen Schulhofer, 'Taking Sexual Autonomy Seriously', *Law and Philosophy*, 11 (1992), pp. 35–94, esp. p. 67.

45 *Egan* (1985) 15 A Crim R 20, esp. pp. 25–6.

46 For a critique of the American consent standard, see Schulhofer, 'Taking Sexual Autonomy Seriously'. For a critique of the Australian consent standard, see Vicki Waye, 'Rape and the Unconscionable Bargain', *Criminal Law Journal*, 16 (1992), pp. 94–105.

47 But note the (statutory) exceptions of those jurisdictions which now look for clear and positive agreement to sex. See n. 42 above.

48 As Lord Hailsham made clear in the landmark case of *DPP v Morgan* [1976] AC 182, 'It matters not why [the belief in lack of consent] is lacking if only it is not there, and in particular it matters not that the intention is lacking only because of a belief not based on reasonable grounds.'

49 See Alison Assiter, *Pornography, Feminism and the Individual*; and Stella Rozanski, *Obscenity*, for feminist readings of this literary genre.

50 Veena Oldenburg, 'Lifestyle as Resistance: The Case of the Courtesans of Lucknow, India' *Feminist Studies*, 16: 2 (1990), pp. 259–87, esp. p. 266.

51 Ibid., p. 266.

52 Ibid., p. 270.

53 Ibid., p. 270.

54 Ibid., p. 272.

55 Ibid., p. 275.

56 Interview with Gulbadan, November 1980, at her *kotha* in Lucknow, quoted in Oldenburg, 'Lifestyle as Resistance', p. 275.

57 Ibid., p. 275.

58 Butler, *Gender Trouble: Feminism and the Subversion of Identity*, p. 33.

59 Ibid., p. 115.

60 Luce Irigaray, *Marine Lover of Friedrich Nietzsche*, p. 82.

61 Ibid., p. 109.

62 Ibid., p. 118.

63 Butler, *Gender Trouble*, p. 137.

64 Ibid., p. 138.

65 See Margaret T. Gordon and Stephanie Riger, *The Female Fear*.

66 Elizabeth Stanko and Kathy Hobdell, 'Assault on Men: Masculinity and Male Victimization', *British Journal of Criminology*, 33 (1993), pp. 400–15, esp. p. 405.

67 See, for example, Gordon and Riger, *The Female Fear*.

68 The empirical work on men who have experienced criminal assault conducted by Elizabeth Stanko and Kathy Hobdell confirms that men are reluctant to discuss the injuries they have suffered through criminal violence. See Stanko and Hobdell, 'Assault on Men'.

69 Ibid., p. 407.

70 This is not to suggest that the sexually violent woman constitutes a significant social problem. All the evidence suggests that women are, in fact, the main victims of sexual assault, and in jurisdictions where the law of rape has been extended to cover the female offender, there have been very few prosecutions of women. My point is a cultural one. It is about how law colludes in the view of women as invariably the victim, never the predator.

71 See Family Violence Professional Education Taskforce, *Family Violence: Everybody's Business, Somebody's Life*.

72 See Richard Davenport-Hines, *Sex, Death and Punishment: Attitudes to Sex and Sexuality in Britain Since the Renaissance.*
73 See Butler, *Gender Trouble.*

Chapter 5   Relocating the Sexes (through Crime Fiction)

1 Cornell, *Transformations: Recollective Imagination and Sexual Difference*, p. 98.
2 Delys Bird and Brenda Walker, *Killing Women: Rewriting Detective Fiction.*
3 Ibid., p. 9.
4 Ibid., p. 9.
5 Ibid., p. 35.
6 Ibid., p. 38.
7 Butler, *Gender Trouble: Feminism and the Subversion of Identity*, p. vii.
8 Bird and Walker, *Killing Women*, p. 38.
9 Ibid., p. 10.
10 Ibid., p. 44.
11 John Williams, *Into the Badlands: Travels Through Urban America*, p. 154.
12 Quoted in Williams, *Into the Badlands*, p. 155.
13 Sue Turnbull, 'Bodies of Knowledge and Anxiety in the Detective Fiction of Patricia Cornwell', *Australian Journal of Law and Society*, 9 (1993), pp. 19–41.
14 John Cawelti, *Adventure, Mystery, and Romance.*
15 Turnbull, 'Bodies of Knowledge', p. 24.
16 My thanks to Toni Makkai for this observation.
17 Turnbull, 'Bodies of Knowledge', p. 27.
18 Patricia D. Cornwell, *Postmortem*, p. 91.
19 Turnbull, 'Bodies of Knowledge', p. 27.
20 Cornwell, *Postmortem*, p. 6.
21 Ibid., p. 5.
22 Ibid., p. 5.
23 Patricia D. Cornwell in an interview with Mary-Ann Metcalf for Sisters in Crime, September 1992, quoted by Turnbull, 'Bodies of Knowledge', p. 33.
24 Sharon Marcus, 'Fighting Bodies Fighting Words: A Theory and Politics of Rape Prevention', *Feminists Theorize the Political*, eds J. Butler and J.W. Scott, p. 400.
25 Helen Zahavi, *Dirty Weekend*, p. 8.
26 Ibid., p. 11.
27 Ibid., p. 20.
28 Ibid., p. 21.
29 Ibid., p. 47.
30 Ibid., p. 48.
31 Ibid., p. 48.

32 Ibid., p. 49.
33 Ibid., p. 56.
34 Ibid., p. 105.
35 Ibid., p. 106.
36 Ibid., p. 107.
37 Ibid., pp. 107–8.
38 Ibid., p. 108.
39 Ibid., p. 114.
40 The female revenge fantasy is in fact not uncommon in crime literature. See, for example, Mary Wings, 'Kill the Man for Me', in *A Woman's
Eye: New Stories by the Best Women Crime Writers*, ed. S. Paretsky, pp.
235–49, in which a group of women who have been beaten by a man
in domestic circumstances conspire to kill him, do so, and get away
with it; or Angela Carter, *The Passion of New Eve*.

Chapter 6   An Ethical Relation

1 John Jackson, 'Hart and the Concept of Fact', *The Jurisprudence of
Orthodoxy: Queen's University Essays on H.L.A. Hart*, eds P. Leith and
P. Ingram, p. 72.
2 Ibid., pp. 73–4.
3 Ludwig Wittgenstein, *Philosophical Investigations*, p. 132.
4 Monique Wittig, *The Straight Mind*, p. 7, provocatively calls our public
obligation to be women our 'yellow star'.
5 Silvia Vegetti Finzi, 'The Female Animal', *The Lonely Mirror: Italian
Perspectives on Feminist Theory*, eds S. Kemp and P. Bono, pp. 128–51,
esp. p. 130.
6 This would entail a recognition of the social, economic and political
realities of life as a woman and the constraints they place on our choices
and opportunities.
7 Elizabeth Grosz, 'Contemporary Theories of Power and Subjectivity',
Feminist Knowledge: Critique and Construct, ed. S. Gunew, p. 59.
8 Ibid., p. 59.
9 Margaret Whitford, *Luce Irigaray: Philosophy in the Feminine*, p. 19.
10 Carol Farley Kessler (ed.), *Daring to Dream: Utopian Stories by United
States Women: 1836–1919*, p. 7, quoted in Whitford, *Luce Irigaray*, p. 19.
11 The exception to this is, of course, a sex change, and even then one is
still a woman/man who was always a man/woman, and law and
society are reluctant to let the person who changes sex ever forget that
fact. And even then, one's new status always stands as a rejection of
the old, and therefore, as Derrida says, is still inscribed with the old
cloth.
12 Drucilla Cornell, *Transformations: Recollective Imagination and Sexual
Difference*, p. 5.
13 On the imposition and limitations of this sexual division, see Thomas
Lacquer, *Making Sex: Body and Gender from the Greeks to Freud*; and
Katherine O'Donovan, *Sexual Divisions in Law*.

14 Whitford, *Luce Irigaray*, p. 20.

15 Cornell, *Transformations*, p. 6.

16 Richard Bernstein, *The New Constellation: The Ethical-Political Horizons of Modernity/Postmodernity*, pp. 66–7.

17 Ibid., p. 181.

18 On legal attitudes towards the impotent and the homosexual man, see Richard Collier, ' "The Art of Living the Married Life": Representations of Male Heterosexuality in Law', *Social and Legal Studies*, 1 (1992), pp. 543–63.

19 The explicitly hysterical man ceases to be a real man and becomes the feminine or gay man.

20 On the cultural erasure of aggression in women, see Ann Campbell, *Out of Control: Men, Women and Violence*.

21 Similarly, the woman who is the object of female violence has received little attention because she falls outside of the conventional sexual framework – which may well have contributed to the neglect, until recently, of lesbian domestic violence. See Ruthann Robson, *Lesbian (Out)Law: Survival Under the Rule of Law*.

22 This argument has been developed further in Monique Plaza, 'Our Costs and their Benefits', *M/F: A Feminist Journal*, 5 (1980), p. 4. See also Vikki Bell, 'Beyond the 'Thorny Question' ": Feminism, Foucault and the Desexualisation of Rape', *International Journal of the Sociology of Law*, 19 (1991), pp. 83–100.

23 This cultural depiction has clear legal backing. See Ngaire Naffine, 'Possession: Erotic Love in the Law of Rape', *Modern Law Review*, 57 (1994), pp. 10–37.

24 Collier, ' "The Art of Living the Married Life" ', p. 556.

25 See Richard Collier, *Masculinity and Criminology*. See also, Robert Connell, *Gender and Power: Society, the Person and Sexual Politics*.

26 On the culture of gender resistance and 'drag', see Judith Butler, *Gender Trouble: Feminism and the Subversion of Identity*.

27 Consider, for example, gay bashing generally and male rape in prison.

28 Drucilla Cornell, *The Philosophy of the Limit*, p. 62.

29 Ibid., p. 68.

30 Ibid., p. 70.

31 Ibid, p. 89.

32 Butler, *Gender Trouble*, p. 10.

33 This concern is sometimes referred to as the 'totalising' or 'colonizing gesture', which seeks to assimilate the heterogeneous into a single idea, thus suffocating the differences between people.

34 Drucilla Cornell, 'The Doubly-Prized World; Myth, Allegory and the Feminine', *Transformations: Recollective Imagination and Sexual Difference* p. 69.

35 Judith Butler, 'Contingent Foundations: Feminism and the Question of "Postmodernism" ', *Feminists Theorize the Political*, eds J. Butler and J.W. Scott, p. 16.

36 Adrienne Rich, 'Compulsory Heterosexuality and Lesbian Existence', *Signs*, 5: 4 (1980), pp. 631–60, esp. p. 635.

37 Cornell, *The Philosophy of the Limit*, p. 77.
38 Ibid., p. 57.
39 Luce Irigaray, 'Sexual Difference', *French Feminist Thought: A Reader*, ed. T. Moi, pp. 118–30, esp. p. 124.
40 Elizabeth Grosz, *Volatile Bodies: Toward a Corporeal Feminism*, pp. 207–8.
41 Ibid., p. 192.

Bibliography

—

Adler, Freda, *Sisters in Crime: The Rise of the New Female Criminal*, McGraw-Hill, New York, 1975.

Allen, Judith, 'Men, Crime and Criminology: Recasting the Questions', *International Journal of the Sociology of Law*, 17 (1989), pp. 21–39.

Assiter, Alison, *Pornography, Feminism and the Individual*, Pluto Press, London, 1989.

Bachman, Ronet and Raymond Paternoster, 'A Contemporary Look at the Effects of Rape Law Reform: How Far Have We Really Come?', *Journal of Criminal Law and Criminology*, 84 (1993), pp. 554–74.

Barak, Gregg (ed.), *Varieties of Criminology: Readings from a Dynamic Discipline*, Praegar, Westport, Connecticut, 1994.

Becker, Howard S., 'Whose Side are We On?', *Social Problems*, 14 (1967), pp. 239–47.

——, *Outsiders: Studies in the Sociology of Deviance*, Free Press, New York, 1973.

Bell, Vikki, 'Beyond the "Thorny Question": Feminism, Foucault and the Desexualisation of Rape', *International Journal of the Sociology of Law*, 19 (1991), pp. 83–100.

Berns, Sandra, *Concise Jurisprudence*, Federation Press, Sydney, 1993.

Bernstein, Richard, *The New Constellation: The Ethical-Political Horizons of Modernity/Postmodernity*, Polity Press, Cambridge, 1991.

Bird, Delys and Brenda Walker, *Killing Women: Rewriting Detective Fiction*, Angus & Robertson, Pymble, New South Wales, 1993.

Boritch, Helen and John Hagan, 'A Century of Crime in Toronto: Gender, Class and Patterns of Social Control, 1859 to 1955', *Criminology*, 28 (1990), pp. 567–99.

Bottoms, Anthony, 'Reflections on the Criminological Enterprise', *Cambridge Law Journal*, 46 (1987), pp. 240–63.

Box, Stephen, *Power, Crime and Mystification*, Tavistock, London, 1983.

Brannigan, A., 'Closing Note', *International Journal of Law and Psychiatry*, 14 (1991), pp. 133–5.

Brown, Beverley, 'Women and Crime: The Dark Figures of Criminology', *Economy and Society*, 15: 3 (1986), pp. 355–402.

Brown, Stephen E., Esbensen Finn-Aage, and Gilbert Geis (eds), *Criminology: Explaining Crime and its Context*, Andersen Publishing Co., Cincinnati, Ohio, 1991.

Brownmiller, Susan, *Against Our Will: Men, Women and Rape*, Simon and Schuster, New York, 1975.

Burnett, Cathleen, 'Review Essay', *Criminology*, 24 (1986), pp. 203–11.

Butler, Judith, *Gender Trouble: Feminism and the Subversion of Identity*, Routledge, London, 1990.

——, 'Contingent Foundations: Feminism and the Question of "Postmodernism"', in *Feminists Theorize the Political*, eds Judith Butler and Joan W. Scott, Routledge, New York, 1992.

Butler, Judith and Joan W. Scott (eds), *Feminists Theorize the Political*, Routledge, New York, 1992.

Cain, Maureen, 'Realist Philosophy and the Standpoint Epistemologies or Feminist Criminology as Successor Science', in *Feminist Perspectives in Criminology*, eds Loraine Gelsthorpe and Allison Morris, Open University Press, Milton Keynes, 1990.

——, 'Towards Transgression: New Directions in Feminist Criminology', *International Journal of the Sociology of Law*, 1 (1990), pp. 1–18.

Campbell, Ann, *Out of Control: Men, Women and Violence*, Pandora, London, 1993.

Cardarelli, Albert P. and Stephen C. Hicks, 'Radicalism in Law and Criminology: A Retrospective View of Critical Legal Studies and Radical Criminology', *Journal of Criminal Law and Criminology*, 84 (1993), pp. 502–53.

Carlen, Pat, *Women's Imprisonment: A Study in Social Control*, Routledge & Kegan Paul, London, 1983.

——, *Alternatives to Women's Imprisonment*, Open University Press, Milton Keynes, 1990.

Carlen, Pat (ed.), *Criminal Women: Autobiographical Accounts, Diana Christina, Jenny Hicks, Josie O'Dwyer, Chris Tchaikousky and Pat Carlen*, Polity Press, Cambridge, 1985.

Carrington, Kerry, *Offending Girls: Sex, Youth and Justice*, Allen & Unwin, St. Leonards, New South Wales, 1993.

Carter, Angela, *The Passion of New Eve*, Virago, London, 1982.

Cawelti, John, *Adventure, Mystery, and Romance*, University of Chicago Press, Chicago, 1976.

Chadbourn, James H. (ed.), *Wigmore on Evidence*, Little Brown, Boston, 1970.

Chesney-Lind, Meda, 'Women and Crime: The Female Offender', *Signs*, 12: 1 (1986), pp. 78–96.

Clark, Lorenne and Debra Lewis, *Rape: The Price of Coercive Sexuality*, Women's Press, Toronto, 1977.

Cohen, Phil, 'Subcultural Conflict and Working Class Community', in *Working Papers in Cultural Studies*, University of Birmingham, Centre for Contemporary Cultural Studies, 1972.

Cohen, Stanley, 'The Punitive City: Notes on the Dispersal of Social Control', *Contemporary Crises*, 3: 4 (1979), pp. 339–63.

——, *Visions of Social Control*, Polity Press, Cambridge, 1985.

——, 'Social-Control Talk: Telling Stories about Correctional Change', in *The Power to Punish*, eds David Garland and Peter Young, Aldgate, Aldershot, 1992.

Cohn, Ellen G. and David P. Farrington, 'Who are the Most Influential Criminologists in the English-Speaking World?', *British Journal of Criminology*, 34 (1994), pp. 204–25.

Collier, Richard, 'Masculinism, Law and Law Teaching', *International Journal of the Sociology of Law*, 19 (1991), pp. 427–51.

——, ' "The Art of Living the Married Life": Representations of Male Heterosexuality in Law', *Social and Legal Studies*, 1 (1992), pp. 543–63.

——, *Masculinity and Criminology*, Routledge, London, 1996.

Connell, Robert, *Gender and Power: Society, the Person and Sexual Politics*, Polity Press, Cambridge, 1987.

Cornell, Drucilla, *The Philosophy of the Limit*, Routledge, New York, 1992.

——, *Transformations: Recollective Imagination and Sexual Difference*, Routledge, New York, 1993.

Cornwell, Patricia D., *Postmortem*, Warner Books, London, 1990.

Corrigan, Paul, *Schooling the Smash Street Kids*, Macmillan, London, 1979.

Crawford, A., T. Jones and Jock Young, *The Second Islington Crime Survey*, Middlesex Polytechnic, Centre for Criminology, 1990.

Crenshaw, Kimberley, 'Demarginalizing the Intersection of Race and Sex', in *Feminist Legal Theory*, eds Katherine T. Bartlett and Rosanne Kennedy, Westview Press, Boulder, Colorado, 1991.

Crosby, Christina, 'Dealing with Differences', in *Feminists Theorize the Political*, eds Judith Butler and Joan W. Scott, Routledge, New York, 1992.

Culler, Jonathon, *On Deconstruction: Theory and Criticism After Structuralism*, Cornell University Press, Ithaca, New York, 1982.

Daly, Kathleen, 'Gender and Varieties of White-Collar Crime', *Criminology*, 27 (1989), pp. 769–94.

——, 'Neither Conflict Nor Labeling Nor Paternalism Will Suffice: Intersections of Race, Ethnicity, Gender, and Family in Criminal Court Decisions', *Crime and Delinquency*, 35: 1 (1989), pp. 136–68.

——, 'Class-Race-Gender: Sloganeering in Search of Meaning', *Social Justice*, 20: 1–2 (1993), pp. 56–71.

Daly, Kathleen and Meda Chesney-Lind, 'Feminism and Criminology', *Justice Quarterly*, 5: 4 (1988), pp. 498–538.

Davenport-Hines, Richard, *Sex, Death and Punishment: Attitudes to Sex and Sexuality in Britain Since the Renaissance*, Collins, London, 1990.

Davies, Margaret, *Asking the Law Question*, Law Book Co., North Ryde, New South Wales, 1994.

de Beauvoir, Simone, *The Second Sex*, trans. and ed. H.M. Parshley, Pan Books, London, 1988.

Derrida, Jacques, 'Structure, Sign and Play in the Discourse of the Human Sciences,' in *Writing and Difference*, trans. Alan Bass, Chicago University Press, Chicago, 1978.

——, *Positions*, trans. and annot. Alan Bass, University of Chicago Press, Chicago, 1981.

Dobash, R. Emerson and Russell P. Dobash, *Women, Violence and Social Change*, Routledge, London, 1992.

Downes, David, 'The Sociology of Crime and Social Control in Britain, 1960–1987', *British Journal of Criminology*, 28, 2 (1988), pp. 175–87.

Dreyfus, Hubert (Dialogue with), 'Husserl, Heidegger and Modern Existentialism', in Bryan Magee, *The Great Philosophers*, Oxford University Press, Oxford, 1987.

Dripps, Donald A., 'Beyond Rape: An Essay on the Difference Between the Presence of Force and the Absence of Consent', *Columbia Law Review*, 92 (1992), pp. 1780–1809.

Dworkin, Andrea, *Intercourse*, Arrow Books, London, 1987.

Eaton, Mary, *Justice for Women? Family, Court and Social Control*, Open University Press, Milton Keynes, 1986.

Edwards, Anne R., 'Sex/Gender, Sexism and Criminal Justice: Some Theoretical Considerations', *International Journal of the Sociology of Law*, 17 (1989), pp. 165–84.

Estrich, Susan, *Real Rape*, Harvard University Press, Cambridge, Mass., 1987.

Family Violence Professional Education Taskforce, *Family Violence: Everybody's Business, Somebody's Life*, Federation Press, Sydney, 1991.

Farrington, David, 'Criminal Career Research in the United Kingdom', *British Journal of Criminology*, 32 (1992), pp. 521–36.

Ferguson, Kathy, *The Man Question: Visions of Subjectivity in Feminist Theory*, University of California Press, Berkeley, 1991.

Ferrell, Jeff, 'A Critical Criminologist Looks at Critical Criminology: A Review of Stanley Cohen's "Against Criminology"', *Social Justice*, 17: 1 (1990), pp. 132–5.

Finzi, Silvia Vegetti, 'The Female Animal', in *The Lonely Mirror: Italian Perspectives on Feminist Theory*, eds Sandra Kemp and Paola Bono, Routledge, London, 1993.

Fisse, Brent, *Howard's Criminal Law*, 5th edn, Law Book Co., North Ryde, New South Wales, 1990.

Foucault, Michel, *The Order of Things: An Archeology of the Human Sciences*, Tavistock, London, 1970.

——, *The Archeology of Knowledge*, Tavistock, London, 1972.

——, *Discipline and Punish: The Birth of the Prison*, trans. Alan Sheridan, Allen Lane, London, 1977.

——, 'The Use of Pleasure', Vol. 2 of *The History of Sexuality*, Viking, Harmondsworth, 1979.

——, *Power/Knowledge: Selected Interview and Other Writings 1972–1977*, Harvester Press, London, 1980.

——, 'The Ethic of Care for the Self as a Practice of Freedom: An Interview', in *The Final Foucault*, eds James Bernauer and David Rasmussen, MIT Press, Cambridge, Mass., 1988.

Freud, Sigmund, 'Femininity', in *The New Introductory Lectures on Psychoanalysis*, trans. James Strachey, Norton, New York, 1964.

Garland, David, *Punishment and Welfare: A History of Penal Strategies*, Gower, Aldershot, 1985.

——, *Punishment and Modern Society*, Clarendon Press, Oxford, 1990.

——, 'Criminological Knowledge and its Relation to Power', *British Journal of Criminology*, 32 (1992), pp. 403–23.

——, 'The Development of British Criminology', in *The Oxford Handbook of Criminology*, eds Mike Maguire, Rod Morgan and Robert Reiner, Clarendon, Press, Oxford, 1994.

Garland, David and Peter Young (eds), *The Power to Punish*, Aldgate, Aldershot, 1992.

Gelsthorpe, Loraine, and Allison Morris (eds), *Feminist Perspectives in Criminology*, Open University, Milton Keynes, 1990.

——, 'Introduction: Transforming and Transgressing Criminology', in *Feminist Perspectives in Criminology*, eds Loraine Gelsthorpe and Allison Morris, Open University Press, Milton Keynes, 1990.

Gordon, Margaret T. and Stephanie Riger, *The Female Fear*, Free Press, New York, 1988.

Gouldner, Alvin, *For Sociology*, Pelican, Harmondsworth, 1975.

Grayling, A.C., *Wittgenstein*, Oxford University Press, Oxford, 1988.

Griffin, Susan, *Rape: The Power of Consciousness*, Harper and Row, New York, 1979.

Grosz, Elizabeth, 'Contemporary Theories of Power and Subjectivity', in *Feminist Knowledge: Critique and Construct*, ed. Sneja Gunew, Routledge, London, 1990.

——, *Volatile Bodies: Toward a Corporeal Feminism*, Allen & Unwin, St. Leonards, New South Wales, 1994.

Hagan, John, 'The Assumption of Natural Science Methods: Criminological Positivism', in *Theoretical Methods in Criminology*, ed. R. Meier, Sage, Beverley Hills, California, 1985.

——, 'The Poverty of a Classless Criminology – The American Society of Criminology 1991 Presidential Address', *Criminology*, 30 (1992), pp. 1–19.

——, 'The Social Embeddedness of Crime and Unemployment', *Criminology*, 31 (1993), pp. 465–91.

Hampton, Blanche, *Prisons and Women*, New South Wales University Press, Kensington, New South Wales, 1993.

Harding, Sandra, *The Science Question in Feminism*, Open University Press, Milton Keynes, 1986.

Hawkesworth, Mary E., 'Knowers, Knowing, Known: Feminist Theory and Claims of Truth', *Signs*, 14: 3 (1989), pp. 533–57.

Hebdige, Dick, *Subculture: The Meaning of Style*, Methuen, London, 1979.

Heidensohn, Frances, *Women and Crime*, Macmillan, London, 1985.

——, 'Gender and Crime', in *The Oxford Handbook of Criminology*, eds Mike Maguire, Rod Morgan and Robert Reiner, Clarendon, Press, Oxford, 1994.

Henderson, Lynne, 'Rape and Responsibility', *Law and Philosophy*, 11 (1992), pp. 127–78.

Henry, Stuart and Dragan Milovanovic, 'The Constitution of Constitutive Criminology: A Postmodern Approach to Criminological Theory', in *The Futures of Criminology*, ed. David Nelken, Sage, London, 1994.

Hogg, Russell, 'Taking Crime Seriously: Left Realism and Australian Criminology', in *Understanding Crime and Criminal Justice*, eds Mark Findlay and Russell Hogg, Law Book Co., North Ryde, New South Wales, 1988, pp. 24–51.

Howe, Adrian, *Punish and Critique: Towards a Feminist Analysis of Penality*, Routledge, London, 1994.

Hutter, Bridget and Gillian Williams (eds), *Controlling Women: The Normal and the Deviant*, Croom Helm, London, 1981.

Ingram, John Dwight, 'Date Rape: It's Time for "No" to Really Mean "No"', *American Journal of Criminal Law*, 21 (1993), pp. 3–36.

Irigaray, Luce, 'And the One Does Not Stir Without the Other', *Signs*, 7:1 (1981), pp. 60–7.

——, *This Sex Which is Not One*, Cornell University Press, Ithaca, New York, 1985.

——, 'Sexual Difference', in *French Feminist Thought: A Reader*, ed. Toril Moi, Basil Blackwell, New York and Oxford, 1987.

——, *Marine Lover of Friedrich Nietzsche*, trans. Gillian C. Gill, Columbia University Press, New York, 1991.

Jackson, John, 'Hart and the Concept of Fact', in *The Jurisprudence of Orthodoxy: Queen's University Essays on H.L.A Hart*, eds Philip Leith and Peter Ingram, Routledge, London, 1988.

Jardine, Alice, 'Men in Feminism', in *Men in Feminism*, eds Alice Jardine and Paul Smith, Methuen, London, 1987.

Jones, T.B. Maclean, and Jock Young, *The Islington Crime Survey*, Gower, Aldershot, 1986.

Kant, Immanuel, *Critique of Pure Reason*, trans. J.M.D. Meiklejohn, Everyman's Library, London, 1934.

Kessler, Carol Farley (ed.), *Daring to Dream: Utopian Stories by United States Women: 1836–1919*, Pandora, London, 1984.

Kristeva, Julia, *Desire in Language*, Columbia University Press, New York, 1982.

Kruttschnitt, Candice, 'Women Crime and Dependancy: An Application of a Theory of Law', *Criminology*, 19 (1982), pp. 495–513.

Laquer, Thomas, *Making Sex: Body and Gender from the Greeks to Freud*, Harvard University Press, Cambridge, Mass., 1990.

Lea, John, 'The Analysis of Crime', in *Rethinking Criminology: The Realist Debate*, eds Jock Young and Roger Matthews, Sage, London, 1992.

Leith, Philip and Peter Ingram (eds), *The Jurisprudence of Orthodoxy: Queen's University Essays on H.L.A Hart*, Routledge, London, 1988.

Leonard, Eileen, *A Critique of Criminology Theory: Women, Crime and Society*, Longman, New York and London, 1982.

Levi, Michael, 'Violent Crime', in *The Oxford Handbook of Criminology*, eds Mike Maguire, Rod Morgan and Robert Reiner, Clarendon Press, Oxford, 1994.

Lombroso, Caesar, *L'Uomo Delinquente*, Hepli, Milan, 1876.

Lombroso, Caesar and William Ferrero, *The Female Offender*, Fisher Unwin, London, 1895.

Longino, Helen E., 'Feminist Standpoint Theory and the Problems of Knowledge', *Signs*, 19: 1 (1993), pp. 201–12.

MacKinnon, Catharine, 'Feminism, Marxism, Method, and the State: An Agenda for Theory', *Signs*, 8: 4 (1983), pp. 635–58.

——, 'Feminism, Marxism, Method, and the State: Towards a Feminist Jurisprudence', *Signs*, 8: 4 (1983), pp. 635–58.

Magee, Bryan (ed.), *The Great Philosophers*, Oxford University Press, Oxford, 1987.

Maguire, Mike, 'Crime Statistics, Patterns, and Trends: Changing Perceptions and their Implications', in *The Oxford Handbook of Criminology*, eds Mike Maguire, Rod Morgan and Robert Reiner, Clarendon Press, Oxford, 1994.

Maguire, Mike, Rod Morgan and Robert Reiner (eds), *The Oxford Handbook of Criminology*, Clarendon Press, Oxford, 1994.

Mahoney, Martha, 'Legal Images of Battered Women: Redefining the Issue of Separation', *Michigan Law Review*, 90 (1991), pp. 1–94.

——, 'Exit: Power and the Idea of Leaving in Love, Work, and the Confirmation Hearings', *Southern California Law Review*, 65 (1992), pp. 1283–1319.

Marcus, Sharon, 'Fighting Bodies, Fighting Words: A Theory and Politics of Rape Prevention', in *Feminists Theorize the Political*, eds Judith Butler and Joan W. Scott, Routledge, New York, 1992.

Matthews, Roger and Jock Young, 'Reflections on Realism', in *Rethinking Criminology: The Realist Debate*, eds Jock Young and Roger Matthews, Sage, London, 1992.

Mayhew, Henry, *London Labour and the London Poor*, 4 vols, Griffin, London, 1851–61.

McHoul, Alec and Wendy Grace, *A Foucault Primer: Discourse, Power and the Subject*, Melbourne University Press, Carlton, Victoria, 1993.

McRobbie, Angela, 'Working-Class Girls and the Culture of Femininity', in *Women Take Issue*, eds Women's Studies Group, Centre for Contemporary Cultural Studies, Hutchinson, London, 1978.

Moi, Toril, *Sexual/Textual Politics: Feminist Literary Theory*, New York Methuen, 1985.

Morgan, Peggy, 'Living on the Edge', in *Sex Work; Writings By Women in the Sex Industry*, eds Frédérique Delacoste and Priscilla Alexander, Virago, London, 1988.

Morgan, Rod, Mike Maguire and Robert Reiner, 'Introduction', in *The Oxford Handbook of Criminology*, eds Mike Maguire, Rod Morgan and Robert Reiner, Clarendon Press, Oxford, 1994.

Naffine, Ngaire, *Female Crime: The Construction of Women in Criminology*, Allen & Unwin, Sydney, 1987.

——, 'Windows on the Legal Mind: The Evocation of Rape in Legal Writing', *Melbourne University Law Review*, 18 (1992), pp. 741–67.

——, 'Possession: Erotic Love in the Law of Rape', *Modern Law Review*, 57 (1994), pp. 10–37.

Naffine, Ngaire (ed.), *Gender, Crime and Feminism*, Dartmouth, Aldershot, 1995.

Nagin, Daniel S. and David P. Farrington, 'The Onset and Persistence of Offending', *Criminology*, 30 (1992), pp. 501–23.

O'Donovan, Katherine, 'Transsexual Troubles: The Discrepancy Between Legal and Social Categories', in *Gender, Sex and the Law*, ed. Susan Edwards, Croom Helm, London, 1980.

——, *Sexual Divisions in Law*, Weidenfeld and Nicolson, London, 1985.

Oldenburg, Veena, 'Lifestyle as Resistance: The Case of the Courtesans of Lucknow, India' *Feminist Studies*, 16: 2 (1990), pp. 259–87.

Omolade, Barbara, 'Black Women, Black Men, and Tawana Brawley – The Shared Condition', *Harvard Women's Law Journal*, 12 (1989), pp. 11–23.

Parker, Howard, *View From the Boys*, David and Charles, Newton Abbott, 1974.

Pepinsky, Harold and Richard Quinney, *Criminology as Peacemaking*, Indiana University Press, Bloomington, 1991.

Petersilia, Joan, 'Policy Relevance and the Future of Criminology – The American Society of Criminology 1990 Presidential Address', *Criminology*, 29 (1991), pp. 1–15.

Pineau, Lois, 'Date Rape: A Feminist Analysis', *Law and Philosophy*, 8 (1989), pp. 217–43.

Pitch, Tamar, 'From Oppressed to Victims: Collective Actors and the Symbolic Use of the Criminal Justice System', *Studies in Law, Politics and Society*, 10 (1990), pp. 103–17.

Platt, Tony, 'Prospects for a Radical Criminology in the US', in *Critical Criminology*, eds Ian Taylor, Paul Walton and Jock Young, Routledge & Kegan Paul, London, 1975.

Plaza, Monique, 'Our Costs and their Benefits', *M/F: A Feminist Journal*, 5 (1980), p. 4.

Price, Barbara Raffell and Natalie J. Sokoloff (eds), *The Criminal Justice System and Women: Offenders, Victims, Workers*, 2nd edn, McGraw-Hill, New York, 1995.

Quinney, Richard, 'The Production of Marxist Criminology', *Contemporary Crises*, 2 (1978), pp. 277–92.

Redhead, Steve, *Unpopular Culture: The Birth of Law and Popular Culture*, Manchester University Press, Manchester, 1995.

Rice, Marcia, 'Challenging Orthodoxies in Feminist Theory: A Black Feminist Critique', in *Feminist Perspectives in Criminology*, eds Loraine Gelsthorpe and Allison Morris, Open University Press, Milton Keynes, 1990.

Rich, Adrienne, 'Compulsory Heterosexuality and Lesbian Existence', *Signs*, 5: 4 (1980), pp. 631–60.

Roach-Anleu, Sharyn L., *Deviance, Conformity and Control*, Longman Cheshire, Melbourne, 1991.

Roberts, Dorothy, 'Rape, Violence and Women's Autonomy', *Chicago-Kent Law Review*, 69 (1993), pp. 359–88.

Robson, Ruthann, *Lesbian (Out)Law: Survival under the Rule of Law*, Firebrand Books, Ithaca, New York, 1992.

Rock, Paul, 'The Present State of Criminology in Britain', *British Journal of Criminology*, 28 (1988), pp. 188–99.

——, 'The Social Organization of British Criminology', in *The Oxford Handbook of Criminology*, eds Mike Maguire, Rod Morgan and Robert Reiner, Clarendon Press, Oxford, 1994.

Rozanski, Stella, *Obscenity*, Unpublished Honours Thesis, University of Adelaide, 1991.

Ruggiero, Vincenzo, 'Realist Criminology: A Critique', in *Rethinking Criminology: The Realist Debate*, eds Jock Young and Roger Matthews, Sage, London, 1992.

Russell, Bertrand, *A History of Western Philosophy*, Simon and Schuster, New York, 1972.

Said, Edward, *Orientalism: Western Conceptions of the Orient*, Penguin, London, 1991.

Schulhofer, Stephen, 'Taking Sexual Autonomy Seriously', *Law and Philosophy*, 11 (1992), pp. 35–94.

Schwendinger, Julia and Herman Schwendinger, *Rape and Inequality*, Sage, Beverley Hills, California, 1983.

Schwartz, Martin D. and Walter S. DeKeseredy, 'Left Realist Criminology: Strengths, Weaknesses and the Feminist Critique', *Crime, Law and Social Change*, 15 (1991), pp. 51–72.

Schwartz, Martin D. and David O. Friedrichs, 'Postmodern Thought and Criminological Discontent: New Metaphors for Understanding Violence', *Criminology*, 32 (1994), pp. 221–46.

Scott, James C., *Weapons of the Weak: Everyday Forms of Peasant Resistance*, Yale University Press, New Haven and London, 1985.

Scott, Joan W., 'How Did the Male Become the Normative Standard for Clinical Drug Trials?', *Food and Drug Law Journal*, 48 (1993), pp. 187–93.

Scraton, Phil, 'Scientific Knowledges or Masculine Discourses? Challenging Patriarchy in Criminology', in *Feminist Perspectives in Criminology*, eds Loraine Gelsthorpe and Allison Morris, Open University Press, Milton Keynes, 1990.

Scully, Diana, 'Rape is the Problem', in *The Criminal Justice System and Women: Offenders, Victims, Workers*, eds Barbara Raffell Price and Natalie J. Sokoloff, 2nd edn, McGraw-Hill, New York, 1995.

Searle, John (Dialogue with), 'Wittgenstein', in Bryan Magee, *The Great Philosophers*, Oxford University Press, Oxford, 1987.

Simpson, Sally, 'Feminist Theory, Crime and Justice', *Criminology*, 27 (1989), pp. 605–31.

Skolnick, Jerome H., 'What Not to Do About Crime – The American

Society of Criminology 1994 Presidential Address', *Criminology*, 33 (1995), pp. 1–15.

Smart, Carol, *Women, Crime and Criminology: A Feminist Critique*, Routledge & Kegan Paul, London, 1977.

——, *Feminism and the Power of Law*, Routledge, London, 1989.

——, 'Feminist Approaches to Criminology or Postmodern Woman Meets Atavistic Man', in *Feminist Perspectives in Criminology*, eds Loraine Gelsthorpe and Allison Morris, Open University Press, Milton Keynes, 1990.

——, 'Disruptive Bodies and Unruly Sex: The Regulation of Reproduction and Sexuality in the Nineteenth Century', in *Regulating Womanhood: Historical Essays on Marriage, Motherhood and Sexuality*, Routledge, London, 1992.

Spelman, Elizabeth, *Inessential Woman: Problems of Exclusion in Feminist Thought*, Beacon Press, Boston, 1988.

Spelman, Elizabeth, and Martha Minow, 'Outlaw Women: An Essay on "Thelma and Louise"', *New England Law Review*, 26 (1992), pp. 1281–96.

Spivak, Gayatri Chakravorty, 'Displacement and the Discourse of the Woman', in *Displacement, Derrida and After*, ed. Mark Krupnick, Indiana University Press, Bloomington, 1983.

Stanko, Elizabeth, *Intimate Intrusions*, Routledge & Kegan Paul, London, 1984.

——, *Everyday Violence*, Pandora, London, 1990.

Stanko, Elizabeth and Kathy Hobdell, 'Assault on Men: Masculinity and Male Victimization', *British Journal of Criminology*, 33 (1993), pp. 400–15.

Steffensmeier, Darrell, 'Trends in Female Crime: It's Still a Man's World', in *The Criminal Justice System and Women: Offenders, Victims, Workers*, eds Barbara Raffell Price and Natalie J. Sokoloff, 2nd edn, McGraw-Hill, New York, 1995.

Steffensmeier, Darrell J. and Renee Hoffman Steffensmeier, 'Trends in Female Delinquency: An Examination of Arrest, Juvenile Court, Self Report and Field Data', *Criminology*, 18 (1980), pp. 62–85.

Steffensmeier, Darrell and Cathy Streifel, 'The Distribution of Crime by Age and Gender Across Three Historical Periods – 1935, 1960, and 1985', *Social Forces*, 69 (1991), pp. 869–94.

Sumner, Colin, 'Foucault, Gender and the Censure of Deviance', in *Feminist Perspectives on Criminology*, eds Loraine Gelsthorpe and Allison Morris, Open University Press, Milton Keynes, 1990.

——, *The Sociology of Deviance: An Obituary*, Open University Press, Milton Keynes, 1994.

Sumner, Colin (ed.), *Censure, Politics and Criminal Justice*, Open University Press, Milton Keynes, 1990.

Taylor, Ian, 'Left Realist Criminology and the Free Market Experiment in Britain', in *Rethinking Criminology: The Realist Debate*, eds Jock Young and Roger Matthews, Sage, London, 1992.

Taylor, Ian, Paul Walton and Jock Young, *The New Criminology: For a Social Theory of Deviance*, Routledge & Kegan Paul, London, 1972.

Tchaikovsky, Chris, 'Looking for Trouble', in *Criminal Women: Autobiographical Accounts, Diana Christina, Jenny Hicks, Josie O'Dwyer, Chris Tchaikovsky and Pat Carlen*, ed. Pat Carlen, Polity Press, Cambridge, 1985.

Temkin, Jennifer, *Rape and the Legal Process*, Sweet and Maxwell, London, 1987.

Turk, Austin T., 'Analysing Official Deviance: For Nonpartisan Conflict Analyses in Criminology', *Criminology*, 16 (1979), pp. 459–76.

Turnbull, Sue, 'Bodies of Knowledge and Anxiety in the Detective Fiction of Patricia Cornwell', *Australian Journal of Law and Society*, 9 (1993), pp. 19–41.

Voigt, Lydia, William E. Thornton, Leo Barrile and Jerome M. Seaman, *Criminology and Justice*, McGraw-Hill, New York, 1994.

Walklate, Sandra, *Victimology*, Unwin Hyman, London, 1989.

——, 'Appreciating the Victim: Conventional, Realist or Critical Victimology?', in *Issues in Realist Criminology*, eds Roger Matthews and Jock Young, Sage, London, 1992.

Waye, Vicki, 'Rape and the Unconscionable Bargain', *Criminal Law Journal*, 16 (1992), pp. 94–105.

West, Robin, 'Legitimating the Illegitimate: A Comment on "Beyond Rape"', *Columbia Law Review*, 93 (1993), pp. 1442–59.

Whitford, Margaret, *Luce Irigaray: Philosophy in the Feminine*, Routledge, London, 1991.

Whyte, W.F., *Street Corner Society*, 2nd edn, University of Chicago Press, Chicago, 1955.

Williams, Glanville, 'The Problem of Domestic Rape Part 1', *New Law Journal*, 15 February 1991, pp. 205–7.

——, 'The Problem of Domestic Rape Part 2', *New Law Journal*, 22 February 1991, pp. 246–7.

Williams, John, *Into the Badlands: Travels Through Urban America*, Flamingo, London, 1991.

Williams, Patricia, *The Alchemy of Race and Rights*, Harvard University Press, Cambridge, Mass., 1991.

Wings, Mary, 'Kill the Man for Me', in *A Woman's Eye: New Stories by the Best Women Crime Writers*, ed. Sara Paretsky, Virago, London, 1992.

Wittgenstein, Ludwig, *Philosophical Investigations*, Basil Blackwell, Oxford, 1958.

Wittig, Monique, *The Straight Mind*, Beacon Press, Boston, 1992.

Wood, David, *Philosophy at the Limit: Problems of Modern European Thought*, Unwin Hyman, London, 1990.

Worrall, Anne, *Offending Women: Female Lawbreakers and the Criminal Justice System*, Routledge, London, 1990.

Young, Alison, *Femininity in Dissent*, Routledge, London, 1990.

Young, Alison and Peter Rush, 'The Law of Victimage in Urban Realism: Thinking Through Inscriptions of Violence', in *The Futures of Criminology*, ed. David Nelken, Sage, London, 1994.

Young, Jock, 'Radical Criminology in Britain', *British Journal of Criminology*, 28 (1988), pp. 159–313.

——, 'Ten Points of Realism', in *Rethinking Criminology: The Realist Debate*, eds Jock Young and Roger Matthews, Sage, London, 1992.

Young, Jock and Roger Matthews (eds), *Rethinking Criminology: The Realist Debate*, Sage, London, 1992.

Zahavi, Helen, *Dirty Weekend*, Flamingo, London, 1991.

Zedner, Lucia, *Women, Crime and Custody in Victorian England*, Oxford University Press, Oxford, 1991.

Index

—